CONTINUITY NOTES

Roger Singleton-Turner

in association with

Gill Partridge

BBC *Television Training Manuals*

Already published:

SHOOTING ON LOCATION
EDITING FILM AND VIDEOTAPE
STAND BY STUDIO!
FROM SCRIPT TO SCREEN: DOCUMENTARIES
AFTER TEA WE'LL DO THE FIGHT: FILMING ACTION
DIRECTING SITUATION COMEDY

First published in 1988 by
BBC Television Training
BBC Elstree Centre
Clarendon Road
Borehamwood
Hertfordshire

ISBN 0 948694 30 0

Throughout this booklet it is assumed that the producer and director are the same person. The pronoun 'he' should also be taken to refer to 'she' throughout. 'Programme' means any material gathered for transmission or showing from the simplest short item to be included into a longer programme to a major documentary.

General Editor: Gordon Croton

Design and production: Shirley Greenfield

Graphics: Peter Kendall

Printed by BBC Print Unit, Evesham, England

Contents

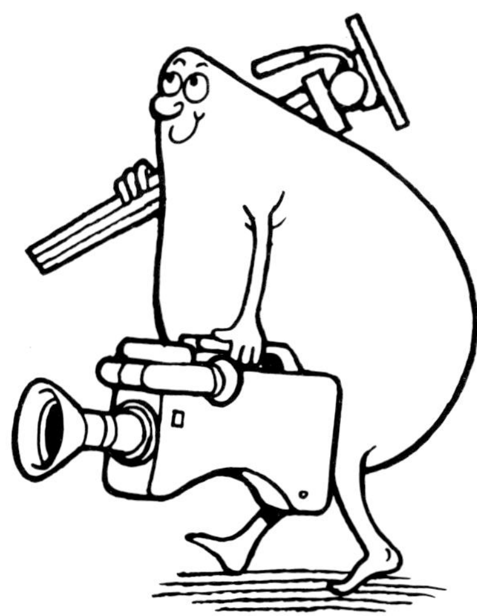

What is Continuity?

INTRODUCTION

The threads of continuity tie into almost every aspect of programme making. No definition is going to cover every instance, every pitfall that you may encounter from a production of *Blue Peter* to *Superman 43*.

Any film or videotape shot with a single camera needs far more shooting time than the finished article takes to show. Shots that will appear consecutively on the screen, giving an appearance of a few moments of real time, must be shot over a period of hours, if not days, weeks, or in some cases, months. Continuity, therefore, is the quality in a film or tape which gives the illusion that each sequence, as it is viewed, is taking place in real time, that there is no need for retakes, that jets do not fly over nineteenth century England, that actors do not forget lines, and that hairs do not get into gates — in fact, that what the audience sees is a record of reality.

Who needs continuity?

If you are a film or TV director, a film or videotape editor, a production assistant, or continuity assistant, then the answer to the question is YOU — especially if you are working with a single camera. If you are an actor, presenter, cameraman, sound recordist, set, make-up or costume designer, AFM, production manager, production operative or set dresser, you have the power to create or destroy continuity.

So how is it achieved?

This question is the subject of the rest of this book. The text is based on the experience of the authors, as well as production assistants within the BBC, film editors, videotape editors, cameramen, and anyone else who seemed to have something relevant to say. Continuity depends on good memory, observation and notes. However many people on a unit have an interest in the subject, the continuity assistant (or PA) is the only person making a record of everything — action, dialogue, props, set, costume, make-up, lighting and sound. She (for there are still very few men even training for this kind of job) is the central reference point for all matters of continuity. It is for this reason that the book focusses on her and looks at continuity primarily from her point of view.

If there is a bias towards television in general and BBC practices and vocabulary in particular, we apologise, but the principles are the same everywhere.

Where to Begin

Continuity happens on location. There is no point in worrying about it before you get there. All you can do is make sure you have a few vital items with you: your copy of the script (and a few spares), **Continuity Pads, Shot Lists, Shooting Script** (if any), **Shooting Schedule** (and a few spares), a good pen and pencil (and a few spares), a rubber or twelve, a stopwatch and plenty of notepads. If you choose to type notes as you go along, then you will also need a portable typewriter, a folding table and a stool. Also, do not forget wet and cold weather gear, and boots, copies of Make-up and Costume Plots, Running (or Story) Orders, and copies of letters pertaining to hotels, location, and cast — especially children's licences (if any). A list of personnel involved in the production will also be useful if it includes contact addresses and telephone numbers.

There is one other item you will need — a **Polaroid camera** and plenty of film.

In feature films the script supervisor has to think only about the script and items concerned with her notes. If you are a PA, you will have been working on the show for some time, sorting out paperwork, hotel arrangements and so on. From now on, where necessary, we shall use the term continuity assistant to cover the title script supervisor and the continuity aspects of the PA's job. You turn up on location — what next?

LOCATIONS

The director will call together the cameraman (and lighting director, if this is an Outside Broadcast), and possibly the sound recordist. The director will be familiar with the location — he will have been on a recce. If you are in your home country, the cameraman, too, may have seen the location, on a well-run drama production, indeed, this is almost certain to be the case.

The director may have written a **Shooting Script**, sufficiently far ahead for copies to be prepared for all concerned, or (s)he may have notes or a shot list.

When the cameraman and director meet, they will talk about the day's shoot, what needs to be achieved, what order they should work in, and what, if anything, depends on specific weather (or sunlighting) conditions. They will probably move on to discuss the first sequence to be shot — its content, its mood, its component shots, and the order in which they may best be achieved.

Ideas may occur that have not been previously discussed. Perhaps a building site has suddenly begun operations fifty yards away. Perhaps an almond blossom tree is in bloom (and the scene is supposed to be set in September). Both sorts of event can cause a change in plan. It has even been necessary to move a scene from one site, under a tree, to another, after shooting had started, because of the excessive noise of bees collecting honey from the blossom of the first tree. But this is the beauty of single camera shooting — its flexibility.

It is this very flexibility that causes continuity problems. You should stick to the director like jam to a toddler at times like this.

It is your first chance to get an idea of how the sequence should look.

CAUTIONARY TALES

Gliding

A production assistant was with a unit filming gliders at Lasham airfield. On the first day, they filmed the flying sequences, with the featured pilot. On the second day, the interview with the same pilot was filmed. The PA was concerned about the fact that the pilot had not brought along the same jacket. The cameraman asked if they had been given the same glider. The PA had not noted that — it was too obvious.

Any nagging doubts were resolved at rushes. On day one, an orange glider had been used, and on day two, a white one. This necessitated a re-shoot.

Dancing

On a major project, filmed over three years, there was one particular dance sequence featuring Dame Margot Fonteyn. There was a gap of several months in the filming, during which time there were several changes of PA. No notes in either written or photographic form could be found, so the new PA could only guess at the continuity.

When the sequence came to be cut together, the continuity was very wrong — the jewels appeared and disappeared as the dance progressed. Most unfortunate — especially as re-shoots were out of the question. Had it been possible, a look in the cutting room at the earlier shots would have helped.

The briefcase

In a documentary, a man approached camera, carrying a briefcase. The director decided to do a reverse (i.e. the camera was moved 180° round behind the man to see him moving away). The question arose as to which hand had held the briefcase.

Simple enough — but the PA had allowed herself to become sidetracked — she was concerned that the crew were about to ask her about the arrangements for lunch. She did not have a ready answer for that question, either.

As one of the PA's concerned said, 'Continuity doesn't apply just to drama, it applies to everything'.

Having made that point, it should be said that in many current affairs/documentary locations, there is a large element of unpredictability, and it will be impossible to replicate action from one shot to another. You can hardly ask a visiting Head of State to do her Grand Entrance again, nor ask a racehorse to throw its rider so you can get a closeup, nor even ask for Concorde '... just to do that take-off again.'

A good system of note-taking, however, will help everyone to know what has been shot, what needs to be shot to cover the

Where to begin

action ideally, and what is likely to cut with what, if the ideal shots are not available.

FILM/VIDEOTAPE — THE DIFFERENCE

Film negative is a plastic strip coated in silver oxide (and a few other things). Videotape is a plastic strip coated in an iron or chromium oxide. It also directly records the sound. That is about as much detail as this book needs. There is no difference in continuity between the two media, but there can be differences in the approach to it and to keeping notes.

On film

You can almost always stay very close to the camera, so your view of the action is at least on the same line as the camera's.

You will be noting the slate number and take — these are the main references for logging the film and accuracy is vital. If a mistake *does* slip through, make sure the editor has a clear note — this applies to a missed slate number or wrongly identified take. The editor lives and breathes take and slate numbers. Also note if the take is synchronous (with sound running) or not — it is usually worth recording sync sound as it can be useful (see *Lumière et Son*). A mute board is held the right way up, but with the clapper stationary. A board at the end of a take is held upside down and a mute end board is held upside down, with the clapper held open. A board may go on the end for a number of reasons. If the cameraman has to set up the start of the shot in a very cramped area, showing the board first, then readjusting the camera carefully would waste film — the end board, though, can be added quickly.

You must also note the film roll number (a roll of 16mm colour film is likely to be four hundred feet or approximately ten minutes long) and the sound reel number (the standard reel holds twenty minutes of recording).

After each accepted take, the gate on the camera will need checking for debris — emulsion off the negative, usually called a hair. The assistant cameraman will also check for evidence of

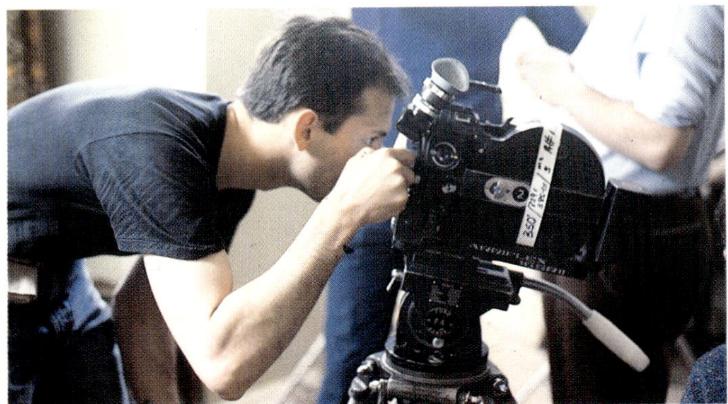

The assistant checks for hairs in the gate...

any scratching of the film. This period is clearly useful for keeping notes up to date.

You can ask the assistant for lens details — the type of lens, the exposure, focussing distance and what filters, if any, are being used. Since the rushes reports from producer, laboratory, production services manager (a BBC term for an office based crew co-ordinator), and whoever else, will not be available until the day after the shoot at the earliest, and since accidents can happen to film in the camera, in transit or in the developing bath, reshoots may be necessary at a later date, even on the best regulated programmes. This being so, the PA's notes may make the difference between the matching of a remounted shot (or shots) with original shots — and disaster. Such notes are not kept by the camera crew.

On videotape

You may be with a single camera unit or a two camera unit — anything bigger, and you are almost certain to be shooting 'multicamera', in which case continuity becomes less of a problem. It is quite possible, too, to use both cameras of a two-camera unit to record a complete scene in one operation.

Video-cameras almost always use one zoom lens. The tape will be spot checked at the end of each accepted take. There is the possibility of reviewing a whole shot, and even the possibility to check an 'old' shot with continuity to a current one. But this is time consuming and can use up battery power, so do not expect to do either often. Video recorders are changing all the time: at the moment most systems will record at least twenty minutes of sound and vision before any tape change is necessary.

In essence, you need to note shot and take numbers as for film, and the use of a clapperboard is sometimes advised. The keys to VT editing, though, are the spool and time code numbers.

Learn the difference between mute and sync, and front and end boards

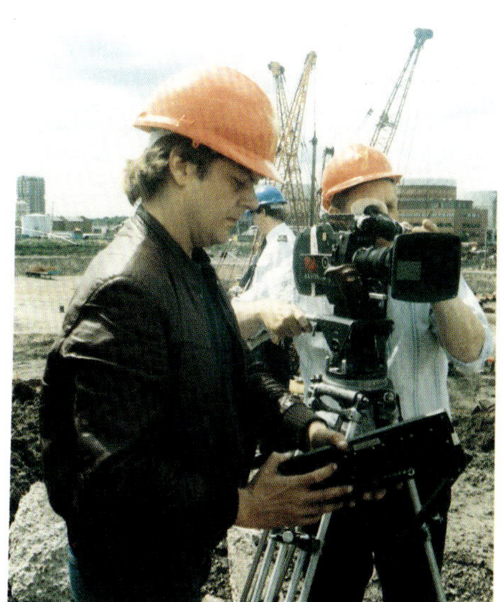

Always check with the recording engineers, before shooting starts, on any special system you want to identify the tapes. Agree, too, about which scenes should be recorded on which tapes (keeping scenes from one episode on one tape is generally helpful).

If you are with a two-camera unit, your place is probably in the scanner (control vehicle). Here you have a small control gallery with colour monitors and visible time code, for ease of logging. In practice it is common to use one camera at a time, perhaps setting the other up in a different area for another sequence. The advantage is that you can see exactly what the camera sees, as it happens. The disadvantage is that you may be some distance from the scene, thus remote from the actors, or presenters, and any costume, make-up and prop staff. This means all messages about continuity have to be relayed through a **production** or **stage manager.**

Finally: at the editing stage, videotape needs a complex piece of electrical equipment to analyse its magnetic patterns, whereas you can look at two pieces of film and see if they are roughly right. On the other hand, the easiest place to see for yourself why a shot will or will not cut to another is at a videotape edit, where you can see both frames on each side of a possible cut simultaneously. The principles and criteria are identical for both videotape and film, but, unless you are a film editor or an assistant, you are unlikely to have both pictures side-by-side in a film cutting room.

ACTION!

The first shot is lined up — a close-shot, let us say, of the presenter, seated. She rises, and moves to look at a statue. The second shot might be a wide angle, a long shot, to bridge the move. Suppose the presenter speaks, and moves like this on slate 1, take 1 (the close-up), which is accepted:

PRESENTER
... and the second Duke imported a number of ancient Greek statues. (RISES) Statues like this — but you will see they are clearly contemporary copies.

On slate 2, the wide angle, on take 1:

PRESENTER
... and the second Duke imported a number (RISES) of ancient Greek statues. Statues like this — but you will see they are clearly contemporary copies.

You point out the discrepancy, so on slate 2 take 2:

PRESENTER
... and the second Duke imported a number of ancient Greek statues. Statues like this (RISES) but you will see they are clearly contemporary copies.

Again, you point out the error, and slate 2 take 3 is perfect — except for the passing aeroplane. Take 4 is fine — Presenter rises correctly between saying '...statues.' and 'Statues...'

And so you can move on to the next shot. But. ...

Why all the fuss?

Watch any good film or taped programme. A change of shot happens when it is right — that is when it is motivated by a move, by the pace of the sequence or by the rhythm (dramatic or musical) of the sequence. The editor will want to cut from slate 1, the close shot, as the presenter starts to rise, and before her head leaves frame. He will cut to slate 2, the wide angle, at the same point in the action. If you try this cutting from slate 1, take 1, to slate 2, take 1, you will get a form of double action, repeated dialogue:

PRESENTER
...and the second Duke imported a

number of ancient Greek statues.(RISE BEGINS) (EDIT) (RISE COMPLETED) ...of ancient Greek statues. Statues like this — but you will see they are clearly contemporary copies.

Or, the presenter can appear to say the right words, but she will jump from the half-risen position to walking — this would be a jump cut. Or, the cut will come after the word 'number', and will look awkwardly framed. Using take 2 will not help. This time, cutting on the action gives:

PRESENTER
...and the second Duke imported a number of ancient Greek statues. (RISE BEGINS) (EDIT) (RISE ENDS)... like this — but you will see they are clearly contemporary copies.

This might work, but the intonation leading to a full stop will probably not fit with '...like this...', which is halfway through a sentence.

Or, using all the words :

PRESENTER
...and the second Duke imported a number of ancient Greek statues. (RISES) (EDIT) Statues (RISES AGAIN) like this — but you will see they are clearly contemporary copies.

This would be another version with double action.

Again, by cutting early, the editor could cure the worst of the problem, but the best solution is to use take 4, where words and actions fit and make sense. The cut could come anywhere without losing or gaining words or action. The precise moment can be chosen for aesthetic reasons, and not just to avoid a problem.

This example would have been from a documentary but the principle applies equally to a drama. It might have related to a person speaking and, halfway through a speech, starting to walk; or to bend and tie a shoelace; or to reach in a pocket and pull out a gun — anything where words and actions are inter-linked. We have examined the first example in detail. The principle is that many continuity errors can be disguised or mitigated at the edit. To achieve this the editor will have to make compromises, to cut the piece in a way that the director did not plan. Good continuity allows the editor the freedom to edit in the most artistically pleasing way. It is true that there are errors, some of which you may lose sleep over, which may not be noticed until the fourth repeat — if ever. Others, which seem insignificant on location, may prove quite embarrassing, and may even involve letters to the producer from 'Observant' of Eccles.

A Word on Words

If you are working to a script, it is usually fairly easy to note if the performer has deviated from it. Sometimes it will be necessary to amend dialogue slightly — perhaps because your location does not exactly match that described in the script. (There is no point, for instance, in a character commenting on a rose bush, if he is having to make the speech next to a peony.)

In general terms, on a drama, script alterations should be agreed with the author or script editor. As indicated elsewhere, though, minor changes do creep in, and a director may well accept a fine performance rather than do a retake because the leading man has said 'someone' instead of 'somebody'. The continuity aspects of dialogue become important if there is going to be a change of shot in the middle of, for instance, a list. The witness says:

> First, I went to the newsagents, then I got some drink. After that, I went to buy some new jeans, then I had to go down to the launderette for my washing. It was after that I threw the brick through the jeweller's window.

Clearly, the order of events up to that last statement could be vital to the plot. Equally it could be irrelevant and a transposition might be acceptable. However, if a complementary shot is organised, the transposition must then be retained. The same would apply if a second actor had to pick up, or remark on the precise words used by the witness. If the order on this speech is wrong, it would be simplest to retake this rather than force an actor to re-learn the speech.

In the case of a demonstration, the order in which items are spoken of, and pointed at, must also be noted. The cutaway shots of a hand pointing to switches and moving to dials, must show things in the same order as the master shot. The alternative — for the hand to move in the opposite direction to the one suggested by the commentary would be laughable.

In documentaries, things are different. In general, questions in interviews need to be accurately noted, as the shot of the interviewer asking the question will often be shot after the main interview is over, with little reference to the answer, a clear note of which must also be kept for the editor.

If you are out of doors, it is easy to mis-hear what is said by actor, presenter or 'subject'. There are occasions when it is wise to order a second and third pair of headphones (see also *Lumière et Son*).

On a drama, do make sure you note who says what, and that nothing vital has actually been left out. The definition of vital will be decided by the director. At a later stage, this accuracy will be helpful when the executive producer is convinced he can hear a different four-letter word from the one scripted. It is also needed when the film is sold to Japan and a dubbing script in Japanese is prepared.

Really, continuity is something that has to be considered as a whole, in each shot. Breaking the subject up into headings is therefore only a device, to make the principles easier to absorb.

Clothes

All of this subject can be divided, unlike Gaul, into two parts: **Costume**, and **Non-costume**. Costume means anything provided by a costume designer, whether hired or specially made.

If there is one, the **costume designer** and his or her staff should be informed which scene is about to be shot. This information should be given on the schedule, or on the amendments, or, in case of sudden, unavoidable changes of plan, by word of mouth. They should then ensure that each artist is in the correct costume, with correct hats, handbags, umbrellas, and non-prop accoutrements. Continuity dirt and sweat will also be supplied.

What they cannot necessarily tell you is how the costume should be worn: how many jacket buttons were done up, whether the scarf was outside the coat collar or round the neck, and so on. These are points that are likely to change during the course of action and the continuity assistant should be noting this.

It is quite usual for the **continuity assistant** to take a **Polaroid** picture of each artist, perhaps front, rear *and* close-up views, after the end of each accepted master shot — if there has been material change — so that all subsequent shots can be made to match. The pictures are probably taken at the end, because there is likely to be a picture from a preceding scene to match the top of the scene. All other shots — close-ups, cutaways, etc., will refer to this master.

If in doubt, take a picture

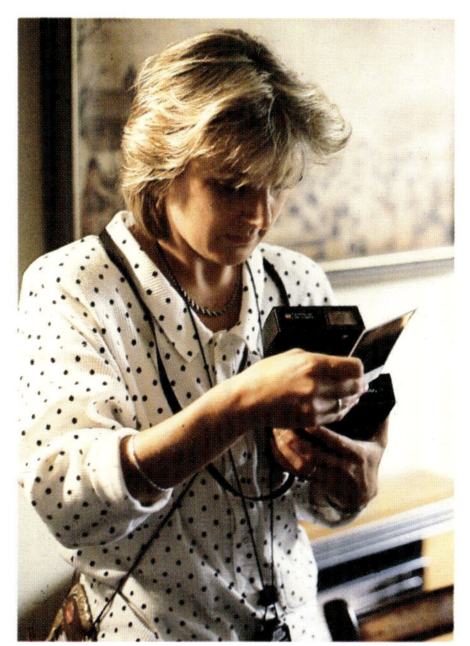

With new characters or costumes, a good time to take the photographs and make notes will be in the rehearsal period.

If the clothes are non-costume, it is most likely that the artist, presenter or guest is wearing his or her own clothes, or clothes bought for the series. If this is the case, decisions must be made about the degree to which it matters that the clothes are the same from one sequence to another, and thought must be given to laundry, 'spare' items, and so on.

Wherever the clothes come from, they require concentration. If an item is removed, or put on, it can present editing problems. Take the action of putting on a coat:

You may need to note if the subject is carrying anything, e.g. a handbag. If so:

Was it put down?
How?
Where?
Where was the coat to start with?
How was it folded/arranged?
Which hand picks the coat up?
Which arm goes into which sleeve first?

Down to Business

Are there gloves or a scarf?
Are they put on?
Which order?
How?
Is the collar adjusted?
Up or down?
Is the carried object to be picked up again?
Which hand?
Does the subject turn (away from the coat-hook/chair etc.)?
Which way?
How fast does he/she move off?
What sort of expression does he/she have?
Finally, how does the dialogue fit with each stage of these movements?

Clearly, not all of these questions will be relevant every time you have someone donning a coat. Equally clearly, there will be occasions when there will be lots of other factors to consider, too.

Even in this example, there are points that overlap with later 'Headings'. This is typical — the threads of continuity really do reach into almost all areas of programme making.

There are other, more specific points to watch: the general continuity of costume from one scene to another, that is which items should be worn with which, which items are to be carried, as well as how clean/dusty/wet/bloody they should be.

Next, there is the 'state' of the clothes. This includes the way coats and jackets are buttoned, how ties are tied and how jewellery is positioned.

Period costume has its own problems

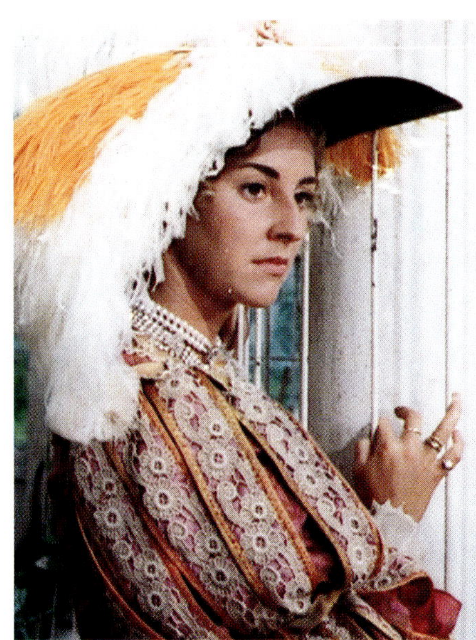

If you ever become involved in filming with small boys, watch out! They are particularly bad about losing items, leaving school bags in ridiculous places, having fights in the coffee break, and thus changing the level of continuity dirt, finding new ways of wearing their ties (thus starting a craze which sweeps through the junior cast in the lunch hour), and of exposing their shirt-tails. This can get very tedious, when after ten weeks you still find yourself saying several times a day, 'Tom, (Dick and Harry), tuck your shirt in.'

Period drama presents its own hazards. There may be, in the extreme, an item or items of clothing with which you, the actor, and the director are unfamiliar. It is quite easy in these cases to get an actor to do something wrong. One example might concern a gentleman disposing of his top hat on an afternoon visit in Paris, early this century. That is something that could easily slip by unnoticed, except by 'M. Proust, of Paris'.

Problems do crop up with all sorts of **specialized costume**. This may not be purely a matter of continuity. For example, take a courtroom scene. There are specific costumes for different types of judge, there is correct dress for junior barristers (like Rumpole) and a different style for Queen's Counsel. There are further differences between Ushers, Clerks of Court, etc. In any given scene, some of these are likely to be non-speaking artists. It has been known for a costume designer to go to a lot of trouble to get non-speaking artists for one sequence dressed to fill the appropriate roles, and for the director then to ignore this, and just scatter the legally costumed people at random. This is very irritating to 'Barrister, Inner Temple'. The functionaries mentioned have a specific place to occupy in Court. If each one is in the right place, continuity of people is simplified: if order is removed, chaos may enter.

These examples cannot be comprehensive. None of these sections can give you all possible cases. What we intend is that you should be put on your guard about the sorts of things you may meet.

Most costume designers are conscientious, and will be helpful to you. They do need to be kept thoroughly up to date over changes to the schedule, if the unit is not to waste time. There does need to be a good liaison system between the continuity assistant and the costume department. If there is time a thorough **Costume Plot** is helpful. This is something drawn up by the production office, between the director and the costume designer, and which at least serves as a statement of intent — a reference point that can be changed.

It is worth noting that some odd things are regarded as **costume** and some as **props** (especially in the BBC). Handbags, umbrellas, glasses and jewels are costume; briefcases and walking sticks are props. Snakes, like Medusa's, in the hair are make-up, unless they move, when they are visual effects. Hats, veils and many items that go in the hair are costume, except for the ones that belong to make-up. In other words there is quite an overlap, and it is dangerous to assume one department is responsible for another's item.

Make-up

The involvement of make-up in a production can vary enormously, not only with the subject matter, but also from day-to-day depending on the numbers of artists, speaking and non-speaking, required. It is clearly going to take more make-up effort to get fifty crowd extras and six actors ready for a scene from *Becket*, than it would to prepare Billie Whitelaw for a monologue by Beckett. One, after all, is period, the other, fairly modern. The sheer bulk of hairstyles, ageing, 'dirtying-up' and so on, in the first example, means more problems than for the preparation of a single actor for a modern piece.

This is not the whole story: the fifty extras in *Becket* will probably not be seen in any great detail — it is as a group that they will make their mark. It will be on the principles that you will have to concentrate. Mind you, the one thing that will stand out clearly in any group shot will be that tall, dark-haired extra's new watch.

It could well be that the principal actors have grown their own hair long and grown their own beards. This will save some problems for make-up, and create others. Wigs do not grow, so an actor with one wig has hair of a constant length — this helps

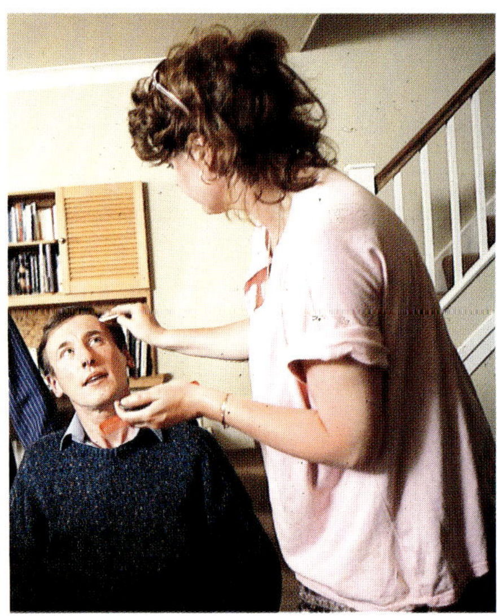

Make-up designer maintaining a constant state'

maintain continuity. On the other hand, natural hair does not keep coming unstuck, and it can be quicker to wash and dry.

Programmes like *The Singing Detective* did have nice simple scenes with little make-up, but that production was famous for one particular body make-up — showing the effect of psoriasis over the whole of actor, Michael Gambon. This took about four hours to prepare. It would actually take less time to prepare the fifty extras etc., since there is more scope for bringing in extra effort. An individual make-up can take anything from five minutes upwards. In BBC terms it is the **make-up designer**'s job to stay behind the camera closely watching that make-up is correct and stays correct. It is easy for wigs, beards, moustaches, hair-pieces and so on, to come adrift, especially in windy and wet conditions. The designer should ensure that this does not happen — at least in vision. She should also keep careful continuity notes and pictures, especially for such developments as ageing, or progressive diseases, etc.

In the BBC, make-up designers would certainly appreciate notes from PA's about, for instance, the degree to which hair has been disturbed by the weather, and if the artist is looking hotter (sweatier) than a previous occasion. They would not expect much more detail than that — unless of course there had been a disaster over a set of notes. The make-up is something carefully and individually created, over what may be a considerable period of time, and comments on such a matter need a tactful approach.

In the world of film, the **continuity assistant** is the final arbiter on continuity in this area as in most others. In *all* cases the continuity assistant will be the only person on the set holding notes about this area *plus all the others*.

The basic points to watch for are:

- Consistency — is the artist's appearance the same as in preceding shots?
- Should it be the same? Or should the character be older/iller/-younger or whatever?
- Should the character look hot/sweaty or not? Remember that costume sweat is quite often sprayed-on water, while make-up sweat may well be a liquid that will not evaporate quickly.
- Has the hair been disturbed by the weather, i.e. wind and rain?

It is worth noting that one possible reason why Hollywood Stars always look perfect, even when they are supposed to have been cast away on a desert island for weeks, is that it is much easier to maintain a 'steady state' than to be consistent about a changing one, shot over a period of weeks, out of sequence. Often, it is appropriate to take the 'steady state' course: on a series like *Grange Hill* (set in a London Comprehensive school, and with a cast of about thirty major characters, mostly children under sixteen), the only way to keep hair length right, over a nine-month shoot, and with a nine-week serial transmission, is to keep it constant.

Set Design

The **designer**'s job is to organise the design and the building of scenery. This may be a complete set, to be placed on a sound stage (that is a film studio); it may be a complete set to be built outside, like Albert Square, in *Eastenders* (a BBC soap opera); it could be two treated flats and a pillar to convert the hall of a small-scale Stately home to a period Fleet Steet newspaper office reception area. It could be something to disguise a row of modern parking meters for a 'Fifties play. In short, it could be almost anything you or the designer (or the director), could imagine.

The designer will also provide props including furniture and drapes to furnish the set, which might even be a real house, rented for the production. It might be necessary to re-paper the walls of one or more rooms to provide the right 'feel', to give what both designer and director want. It might also ultimately be necessary to reinstate the house to something like its original state when shooting is completed!

The **designer, assistant designer**, and appropriate crew will be responsible for making sure that each scene is set up according to the director's wishes. In the BBC, the crew would include the **assistant floor manager** and **production operatives**.

As a scene progresses, the camera will be moved around the set. This will probably mean moving furniture that will be temporarily out of vision, out of the way. If everything is functioning properly, no item that should, in logic, be visible will be removed. When necessary, the same group of people will put the items back and the **designer** or **AFM** will almost certainly take reference pictures (probably Polaroids).

Once again, the **continuity assistant** will be the final arbiter as to what is or is not in shot.

The main problem under this heading is with background props:

An actor sits with his back to a bookcase. There is a prominent copy of *Catwatching* clearly visible over his left shoulder. Over lunch someone picks this up and takes it outside to read. They forget to put it back. You have a problem. (Actually, there are two problems — you need copyright clearance to show the book-cover, but that is another story.) The fact is people do thoughtlessly move continuity items, eat unauthorized food and generally make life difficult. The designer can sometimes help put things back into some semblance of order, but often it will be the continuity assistant's responsibility.

Once again, the key to continuity in this area is consistency and liaison. It is always helpful to know what the designer is planning, or if there are problems with setting and striking any given item.

One point, in particular, to remember is that any change of plan — skipping a scene, moving early (or late) to a new location, can have serious repercussions for a designer, who may well have effort planned to a fine tolerance. If a location is not ready when you arrive, but rehearsals commence, it is possible that the director will want to begin filming almost before the designer is ready. The designer may then be adding items after certain things have been established, which is most confusing for all concerned! (This should not happen, but lots of things do happen that should not, on locations, in the heat of the moment and the cold of the night.)

As soon as you get on the set or location, look at it. You can begin taking notes:

- Is it in its final state?
- What does it look like? A Polaroid picture probably gives the quickest answer.

  (A WORD OF CAUTION: Polaroid cameras have been known to break down and the quality of the pictures will vary with lighting and temperature conditions. The prints can also get lost. Remember, too, that the most beautiful prints in the world are useless unless you can identify them: they need marking up as soon as possible after they are taken.)

- Are there problem points? E.g. is there a clock — what time should it register, should it be stopped? (In a drama, the answer is probably 'Yes', then the hands can be advanced little by little, manually, as the scene progresses.)
- Is there a window? What can you see through it? Are there any cars, (especially with BBC markings)? Are they likely to move?
- Is there brilliant sunshine?
- Is it raining and, if it is, are the spots visible on the glass?
- Are there curtains? Open or shut? If open, how far?
- Are there practical lights? On or off?
- Is there a fire? Is it on or burning? If the answer to this is 'Yes', keep an eye on it when it is in shot — the changes can be dramatic.
- Are there practical candles? Are they lit? If they are, be very careful. In the extreme, you and the AFM (or the equivalent) may have to measure each one at the start and end of each take. On a short scene, this is simple enough, but for a long one or where the length of the candles is featured to indicate passage of time, the trouble is worth taking.

It is helpful, perhaps, to suggest starting with very slightly used candles. The difference between a brand new one, newly lit, and one that has burnt for (say) five minutes, is much greater than between one that has burnt for five, and one that has burnt for ten minutes. Thus the second case makes the continuity easier to deal with — especially as such matters, whilst disturbing if wrong, are usually peripheral to the main action. Remember, too, that you can meet candle problems both in the making of the fourteenth version of *Dracula*, and in a series such as *Timewatch* or even in Handel's *Messiah* from King's College, Cambridge. Candles are props, and everything pertaining to props can be complicated for a continuity assistant. Most of the matters arising concern people other than the designer.

Props

All props are divided into two sorts — Action and Dressing.

All **Action Props** are divided into three sorts: **Non-practical, Practical** and **Fully Practical**. Thus a non-practical gas stove would be one which *looked* fine, and on which you could put a saucepan, but the oven door might not open. A Practical stove would have all doors, knobs and flaps operational, but would not be connected to a gas supply. Fully Practical, on the other hand, means just that, it would be connected to a gas supply, and you could cook on it. If cooking were to take place, it would be an Action Prop (although selected by the designer), if it were not to be used (except perhaps as a parking place for a saucepan), it would probably be a Dressing prop — there for its visual impact, and any 'design statement' about the set, or the scene, but not there as an essential bit of hardware handled by the actor or presenter.

On the whole, **Dressing Props** are not moved around much, unless they have to make room for the camera, lights, sound equipment, or off screen personnel (like the director). They do occasionally disappear, and people who should know better do move things, to examine them, read them, or eat them. (It has been known for cakes that have been sprayed with hair colour, and protected by a note saying that spraying had taken place, to disappear. It has also been known for BBC Catering roast potatoes to be removed!).

You do have to note the state of dressing — preferably by taking a picture. In the film world, the continuity assistant has the final responsibility for keeping these records up to date. Within the BBC, the designer will have his own photographs and notes, and the AFM should also have something useful to contribute.

The AFM will set up **Action Props** and maintain them in the right state. She might be keeping cigarettes at the right length, glasses filled to the right level, or piles of ironing at the right height. Clearly these are all items that could well change as action progresses. It is the continuity assistant's job to note on paper, if not on Polaroid, the state of such items at each stage of the scene — especially if the director is planning an edit at a certain point. The AFM will also be noting such points, but her position is not necessarily by the camera, and she may easily miss a crucial moment.

- Are there many action props? Where do they start the scene? Where do they end? Were they involved in an earlier sequence? Will they be needed later? Is there any difference or change between the earlier and/or the later scene?

  This is very much the province, in the BBC, of the AFM. Outside, responsibilities and job titles vary.

Set Design

- If there is a desk involved in the action, there will probably be papers and all sorts of odds and ends. Has the AFM (or equivalent) marked the positions of vital items? It may be worth anchoring the flimsier pieces in place with a removable gum.

- Is there food? Does it have a very characteristic look to start with (e.g. whole roast turkey)? Have the props people provided a spare for carving?

- Is there running water? How full are sinks filled? How much foam can you see?

Always, with such items, look and think as soon as you arrive on the set: What could change? Remember, anything that can change or move can cause a continuity problem.

There are as many examples of prop continuity and discontinuity as there are filming locations. Each occasion needs to be looked at afresh. Apart from the examples already mentioned or hinted at, there are some general points to remember:

- If it is brightly coloured, or shiny, it will show up in every conceivable shot, and several inconceivable ones.

- If it is mentioned in the script, everybody's eyes will be drawn to it.

- If it moves, or if it is moved, both previous points apply twice over.

If you get it right, the shot will not be used. If you get it wrong, they use the shot in the new season's Presentation Promo tape!

As with the example in Costume, you may find it helpful to go through a form of questionnaire:

- Which hand picks it up? Which way round was it and which way round was it as it was picked up? (Think, perhaps, of a pencil on a table.)

- If it is a bag, or Dick Whittington's stick and bundle, which shoulder did it go on?

- If it is a telephone handset, how is it held? Near the mouthpiece, on the shaft, near the top?

- If it is a glass, how full was it at the start of the action? And at the end? Where was the swizzle stick? Which glass was it? What colour was the drink, earlier? On which line did the character take sips? Eat the cherry? Spill the contents?

- If there is food, what did it look like at the start and end of the action? In practice, unless there is a very clear shape inherent in the food item (e.g. an ice cream cone), it may not be very obvious how much has been consumed in the 'in-between' state. At what point in the dialogue is it eaten?

Most games feature props heavily. If you have a game — good luck. Cards are fairly controllable — they can be stacked, so each person always ends up with the right cards in a deal, and they will be in constant order. If much play is made of the cards, as in a poker game, discussion beforehand with the director, combined with close attention to rehearsals, should reduce problems.

With luck, the scriptwriter will know the subject, and give clear indications about the state of play (see p.22) — but do not bank on accuracy here.

If you have a ball game like snooker, pray that your director is planning lots of close-ups on the actors. And do not be afraid to rush in after a take and take a Polaroid picture of how the balls have actually ended up. The AFM will probably be able to help.

Action or contact games, like football and rugger are best shot with planning — careful planning, and preferably with a **Storyboard**. The more frustrating way is to take lots of shots of general ball-kicking/carrying, in wide angle and close-up, and hope that the editor can make something work. This is very wasteful of stock, and editor's time and the crew's goodwill.

The same comments can be applied to games like tennis.

With any prop item — is it old/new/clean/dirty enough? There was a suitcase in *Tenko*, that went from 'Nearly new', via shipwreck, from location (film), to studio (video) through the whole of the Pacific war and out the other side. Needless to say, its first appearance on location was nearly-new, its second, shipwrecked, and so on, back to the studio where it was seen nearly new again, about to be carried out in direct continuity with the first sequence. All this took planning — and close liaison between the PA and the design team.

If it can change ...

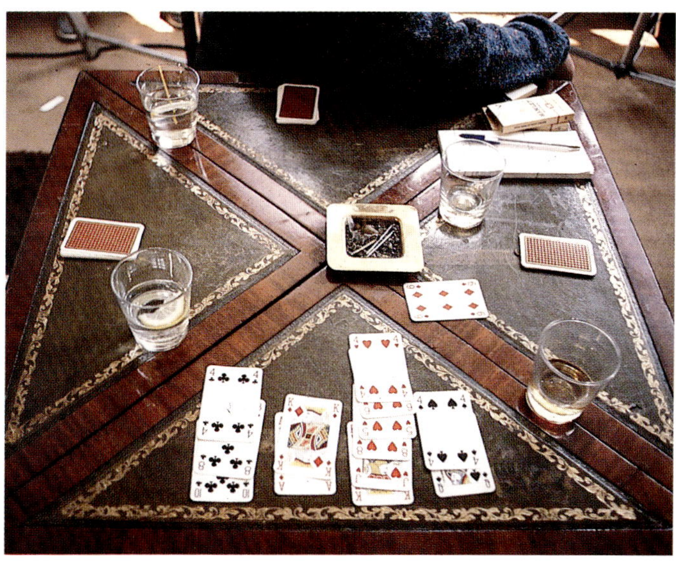

Specimen: Stage Directions

(Scene 5 cont.)

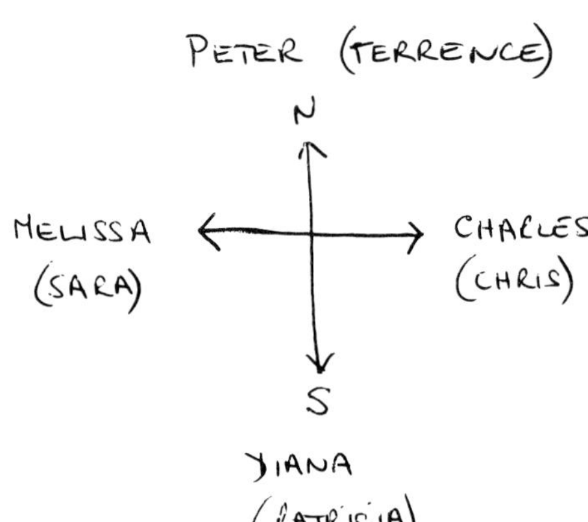

(DIANA, SITTING SOUTH, TAKES CARDS AND DEALS. MELISSA ON HER LEFT IS WEST, PETER OPPOSITE IS NORTH, CHARLES, PLAYING WITH MELISSA, IS EAST. DIANA DEALS, STARTING WITH MELISSA, AND DEALING CLOCKWISE. IN ORDER TO ACHIEVE THE CORRECT END RESULT, THE SUGGESTED ORDER OF CARDS IS:

W01:JC.>	N01:AS.>	E01:3H.	>S01:8H.
2:5S.	2:10D.	2:3C.	2:KH.
3:2D.	3:QH.	3:9S.	3:KD.
4:10H.	4:7C.	4:3D.	4:4H.
5:5C.	5:7S.	5:JD.	5:6H.
6:3S.	6:KC.	6:9D.	6:10C.
7:5D.	7:JS.	7:2H.	7:QS.
8:7H.	8:AC.	8:KS.	8:8C.
9:2S.	9:7D.	9:6S.	9:4C.
10:6C.	10:8S.	10:8D.	10:5H.
11:9C.	11:9H.	11:10S.	11:AD.
12:2C.	12:AH.	12:6D.	12.JH.
13:QD.	13:4D.	13:QC.	13.4C.

IT IS IMPROPER TO PICK UP THE CARDS UNTIL THE DEAL IS COMPLETE. WHEN THEY PICK UP THE CARDS, THEY SORT THEM INTO THE STANDARD FAN. AS THE PLAYER LOOKS AT THE CARDS, WHEN SORTED, THEY ARE ARRANGED WITH SPADES ON THE LEFT, THEN HEARTS, DIAMONDS, AND CLUBS ON THE RIGHT. EACH SUIT IS SORTED SO THE HIGHEST CARD IS ON THE LEFT, AND THE LOWEST ON THE RIGHT. i.e. MELISSA'S HAND, AS SHE SEES IT SORTED, WOULD READ, LEFT TO RIGHT:
5S,3S,2S; 10H,7H; QD,5D,2D; JC,9C, 6C,5C,2C.
PETER'S:
AS,JS,8S,7S; AH,QH,9H; 10D,7D,4D; AC,KC,7C.
CHARLES':
KS,10S,9S,6S; 3H,2H; JD,9D,8D, 6D,3D; QC,3C.
DIANA'S:
QS,4S; KH,JH,8H,6H,5H,4H; AD,KD; 10C,8C,4C.

LIGHTING

In the absence of light, visible or otherwise, no video or film camera will produce a picture. (For the purist, this excludes those special cameras used to record sub-atomic events, and the like.) Light is therefore needed for illumination. The **lighting cameraman** or **lighting director** will use lights, other than ambient light, also to even out excessively high contrast ratios, to give an acceptable picture.

The main function of lighting, on film or video, after these two criteria have been fulfilled, is to create a mood. This might mean anything from reproducing the effect of a Neopolitan sunset to making credible the stealthy figure on the stair, bearing a single candle. It also includes solving such problems as lighting where no light should be in reality, and creating, for example, moonlight at midday in Epping Forest.

Most lighting directors and lighting cameramen are pretty good about continuity of lighting, but the continuity assistant or PA should be aware of lighting factors at all times.

Exteriors

The most obvious points arise with exterior shooting. It is quite common to begin filming at 08.30, with a thick cloud cover, and a dubious weather forecast. As the morning progresses, the cloud thins and blue sky shows through. After coffee, the cameraman starts to look anxiously at the sky. Then halfway through a take, the sun suddenly bursts through. This means the exposure on that take will be ruined and a retake is necessary.

If you have almost completed the sequence, there may be no problem, just wait for a patch of cloud and do the retake. If, however, you are in the middle of a long sequence, you, as a unit, could be in trouble. The cloud is now rapidly thinning and periods of brilliant sunshine are increasing. By the time lunch is over, not a cloud remains on the horizon.

There are two consequent problems:

- Early shots will not match later shots.
- Each 'sunlit' set-up will require, probably, more time for fine lighting to balance brilliant sunlight, than bright-cloudy conditions.

Keep an eye on the lighting ...

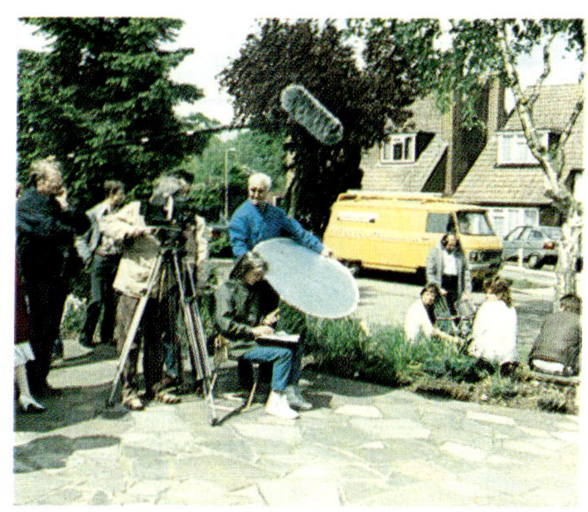

At the worst, you can be in the situation of having shot all the wide-angles and close-ups for a whole sequence from one direction, into the cloud, and all the shots in the other direction, into bright sun. When these are intercut, the effect is ludicrous. The solution must fit the case. If the scene has been shot more or less in story order, then it might be possible for the sun to appear to come out within the scene — that is a matter for the director to decide with Lighting. It is also possible to cheat close-ups; an actor can be shaded to disguise the worst effects of the sun, and, again for close-ups the effect of bright sunlight can be achieved

Lumière et Son

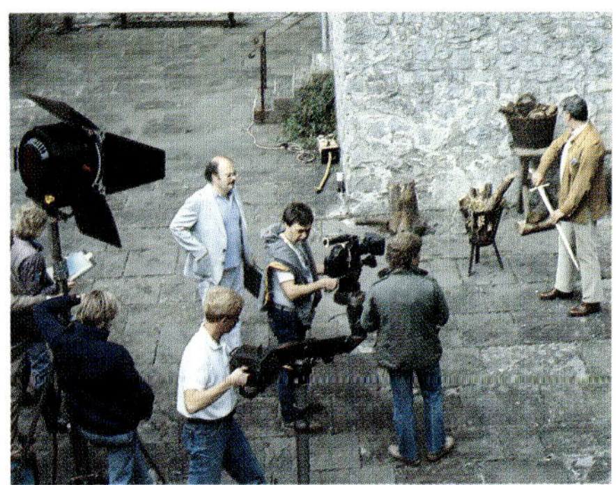

Lights can *be needed out-of-doors too*

even in poor conditions. The problems are greatest on wide angles with lots of background disappearing off into the distance.

The other solution, if your production has the budget, is to wait for the right weather conditions. It has been known for a film unit to hang around for weeks, just to catch a particular mood of the weather.

The continuity assistant's concern should be to note the conditions, cloudy/cloudy-bright/sunny, for each slate. Remember, the next scene in the story may be only minutes later, but may not be shot for weeks.

Another major problem with the sun is that it moves. (Again, for the purist, it appears to move.)

If you have a long scene, shot over the whole day, it is quite possible to find that a character's shadow which was falling to your left in the morning, is falling to your right in the afternoon. This will look odd when different shots are juxtaposed. It is a tribute to the skill of the best lighting experts that such faults so rarely become obvious on the screen.

If you are supposed to be shooting in cloudy conditions, you could find yourself working in the shade of a large building. This is a practical solution to a real problem, but the effect is ruined if the sun moves and floodlights your acting area.

The fact that the sun moves and sets presents problems in the winter too, simply with rapidly changing light levels. The worst problems occur when you are filming in November a scene set in June. The sun will not be high enough in the sky, there will be few — if any — leaves on the trees, and the cast will be gently turning blue, breathing steamily and complaining (in the script) about 'flaming June'.

It follows, of course, that the Christmas Eve sequence can only be shot on June 24 which, naturally, presents the complementary set of problems.

Interiors

With interior shots, and in the context of television, the PA does not have much to worry about over lighting. The main source of light, simulating a window or sunlight or a candelabra, is known as the **key-light** or simply, **the key**. It is as well to be aware from which direction a scene is keyed. It is possible to imagine a situation in which wrong lights are moved between shots, thus giving hard shadows from the other direction on the close-up. Outside the BBC, the continuity assistant would be well advised to pay closer attention to keeping notes of such matters.

If the production is taking place in a studio or film stage, lighting is relatively easy to control whether the scene is nominally indoors or out. If you are on a real location, the probability is that there will be real windows, with real light pouring in. If the windows are blocked off in some way, possibly with 'paper' or 'scrim', and possibly with large lights, there need not be any problem. If, however, there are shots incorporating the window, there may be a potential hazard — especially in a south-facing room. As the sun moves round, goes in, or comes out, there may be all sorts of changes in lighting for the cameraman, or lighting director to disguise. Beware if anybody masks a shaft of sunlight by the simple and obvious expedient of adjusting a curtain or two. It may not make any difference, but one of the things to avoid in the background of a succession of shots, is a curtain that appears to open and close of its own accord.

Another interior problem that can arise concerns smoke. Take a card game — it is quite likely that one or more of the characters will begin to smoke. This will make the atmosphere smoky, and there may well come a point when the smoke is visible as haze, on camera. A heavy drag and exhalation of smoke is quite likely to be visible. If a change of shot is planned, this may become relevant. If the cut is to a close-up, it might take a disproportionate amount of smoke to match the wide angle. (This is because the camera is likely to be moved closer to the subject for a close-up — there will be less air, therefore less smoke between the lens and the subject.) A less obvious example involves smoke from a smoke-gun which may well be used to diffuse light for an effect, such as shafts of light shining through stained glass windows, slanting romantically down to hit the dusty floor.

Candles were mentioned earlier. They should be watched and noted, if they are real. They burn down as scenes progress — and at a very high rate as shooting progresses. In extreme cases, it may be necessary to measure all burning candles at the start and finish of each take. Candles in the background of shot shooting up and down on successive edits can be most distracting.

SOUND

For all practical purposes, the sound recordist looks after **sound continuity**, but it may be helpful to look at some of the things he will do.

The sound recordist can hear all the dialogue. (If not, he is in the wrong job.) He is wearing cans (headphones), and is concentrating on what the microphone(s) is(are) picking up. He is therefore in a position to be helpful in picking up any deviations from the script — any changes from the rehearsed version. Sometimes such changes will not be felt to be important, just minor changes, where the recorded dialogue makes perfect sense. Sometimes though, he may pick up something missed by the continuity assistant. If camera, director and assistant are some distance from the action, and there is a fairly high ambient noise level, as from traffic, a waterfall, etc., the recordist may be the only one who can hear anything at all relevant. It is possible, by prior arrangement, for the director and continuity assistant to listen in on a second and third set of cans. Of course, in an OB van the situation is different; the director may be outside, and it may be the PA who can hear, not the director.

Lumière et Son

It is possible for a sound recordist to play a take back, in the case of any doubt or dispute, but as with video, this takes time and battery power. It should not be a ploy used by the continuity assistant, except as a last resort.

The recordist will quite often stop a take if there is a sudden change in background noise levels. A common reason for doing this is because an aircraft is approaching, but road vehicles, the release of school-children at break, and, as mentioned earlier, bees can also cause problems. Problems are made worse in any project that is trying to suggest times past — you might be able to accept a passing Bentley in *Bergerac*, but not even the hint of an electric drill in *Dombey & Son*.

It is also worth saying that the same sorts of problem can make difficult the recording of an interview in a standard documentary.

If the recordists were not so scrupulous, editing and sound dubbing would become a nightmare: the sound of the 'plane might jump in and out on each of several cuts; vital lines might be lost or drowned out. For consistency, extra appropriate noise might have to be added, which would make even the 'clean' sound totally unacceptable. This, of course, applies to organisations like the BBC which do not have the time and resources to regard post-syncing as normal.

The sound recordist will help the dubbing mixer in another way, by recording **wild track**. Unless conditions are exceptionally difficult and time is at the utmost premium, he should record at least two minutes, preferably more, of ambient sound for each and every location. This is sound without the noise of the crew clearing up and without actors chattering, just the natural local noise of that location's silence. This might include birdsong and the roar of the M25, four miles away, and the quarry lorries' bleepers as they back round the local quarry, three miles away. It can include the constant whirr of air conditioning plant or a word processor, and perhaps the ticking of the grandfather clock, which the recordist insisted was stopped before shooting began. These sounds will be used at the dub (whether on film or videotape) to fill in any holes in the soundtrack produced in the editing processes. Listen yourself to the silence around you, now.

The recordist will also advise on the necessity or otherwise of **filming/taping** certain shots without dialogue. For example, in one of the companion tapes to this book, there was a sequence with dialogue over cards being dealt. The director chose to film a close-up of hands dealing cards. The recordist suggested that dialogue was not recorded. There was no lip-sync, and the sound of the cards falling could be used to bridge gaps — as with a wildtrack. The same recordist also helped in a later sequence, a fight. As the fight progressed, he felt the actors should have started to show stress — to breathe harder — and this was accepted.

Any sound recordist worth his salt will make sure that the actual quality of recorded sound is the best available — and that it is consistent. For the continuity assistant, the main sound problem is dialogue, which is dealt with on pages 9-12.

Personalities

Performers

Presenters, actors, and actresses are in the television and film world front line. Very often it is they who draw the audience, and it is certainly their performance that validates any project from the local news to *Ben-Hur*. Without a thoroughly competent and appropriate delivery, no show can be successful. This comment applies even for 'non-professional' presenters, people who are expert in their own fields or who are simply interesting in themselves as the subject of a documentary.

An actor says of acting that it is showing to millions the emotions you would normally display to your nearest and dearest: it is rather like stripping naked in public. Presenters and performers, therefore, do deserve help and sympathy from all on the unit. Some do exploit this, go over the top and create difficulties, but in the last analysis it is the performer who is going to look a fool if the continuity goes wrong, not the continuity assistant. It is well to remember this.

Actors in particular do find it reassuring to have an observant continuity assistant around. You can save them — and the unit — a lot of trouble by a judicious reminder about the order of events on a take: whether the hand went into the handbag on this line or that, whether she ran her hand through his hair before or after he turned away from the window, and so on.

On the other hand, watch out for the actor who 'knows' about continuity, and who decides that his cigar should start off at this or that particular length on this or that particular shot. To achieve this, he pinches off the end of the cigar and then finds that the slate is starting earlier in the action, and the cigar is now too short.

It is all a matter of tact and understanding, knowing how much to say and when to say it. (A bad time to go into great detail with an actor is just when there has been a flaming row with the director, except where a quiet, calming word of routine might actually help to cool things down. Yes, you do need a lot of tact and sensitivity.)

Directors

Talking of sensitivity, what about directors? They come in all shapes, sexes and sizes. Some know down to the last frame what they are going to shoot and how it will look. Of these, some actually do know, and some are only hoping. Another group make things up as they go along, changing the script and interpretations with the weather. Some are easy going and come in on budget, on time and with a fine production, some rant and rave, overspend, and consider themselves brilliant. (Some actually are.) All thoroughly understand continuity, crossing the line, and the film or tape making process. (At least, they think they do.) Unfortunately, these characteristics can occur in any combination, and at times all may be displayed by one individual.

Dealing with directors again takes a lot of tact. Do trust your notes and your pictures. The director may over-ride you and may deliberately change action for legitimate reasons, thus changing continuity. It is your job, though, to make it clear to the director what the continuity should be in a sequence. If he does over-ride you, you can then make a note that the continuity has deliberately been changed.

You must never be afraid of stepping in and making your point. It is far better to do this than to have to stage a remount because you were to afraid to speak up.

Another thing to remember is that if you are wrong, be definitively wrong. The director and crew, and especially the actors must have confidence in you. If they do not, much time will be wasted in spurious argument, and more time, as well as stock, could be wasted in 'doing it both ways, just to make sure.'

If an actor does ask about the one point you had not actually noted, it will be more worrying to him if you do not know, than if you give the logical but wrong answer. At least, for all subsequent takes and shots, that action will be consistent.

Editors

As the continuity assistant, you could regard your work as being for the editor. He will be the one actually sorting out any mistakes before he can start cutting. He will be reading your notes and making sense of them. It is both useful and desirable that you should talk to the editor before shooting starts to sort out any problems involved with a particular shoot, e.g. children, animals, awkward locations, and to see if either of you have any special quirks, fancies or fads over the way editing information is presented.

Keeping it simple — one at a time

Watching even one presenter, one actor, one contributor, can have its problems. To make these more manageable, break them down. You could not possibly make proper continuity notes, if the only time you saw the contributor was on the take, actually speaking, and doing something more or less complicated. In practice, there is usually some time available before a take starts. Depending on the type of project, there may even be a rehearsal or three.

Nil desperandum

So far, the picture may seem terrifying — and we have not even discussed, in any detail, the handling of more than one performer. The first time you actually go out and try and make continuity notes, you will, unless you are most unusual, be very nervous. You will also, unless you are most fortunate, get something wrong.

As already indicated in Cautionary Tales, mistakes do happen, and the continuity assistants do survive. While this book, and the tapes can open your eyes to the range of problems, there is no substitute for experience. If and when you do make a mistake — learn from it, and be a better continuity assistant. Once you get past the first tentative steps, you will probably find you love the job.

There are some more matters to consider on exterior shoots.

Weather

What is the weather like now? What should it be like? If it begins to rain, does it matter?

Often, rain does not show on camera and it is surprising how dry-looking performers can appear. However, rain can still make nonsense of continuity:

There was a tennis game, once, in which shooting began under lowering cloud. The rain began, but shooting continued. Everything would have been fine if the water had not begun to form itself, most inconsiderately, into puddles on the clay court. Those players would not have played in those conditions.

The best that could be done was to shoot the wide angles first, and close-ups last. Even then there was a problem — not all the puddles could be kept out of shot.

The scene, fortunately, was one that could be split, and the conversation ended in a new scene shot at a later date, in cloud, as the characters returned home. This was clearly a directorial decision and the script lent itself to this sort of lateral thinking — but not all scripts are this flexible.

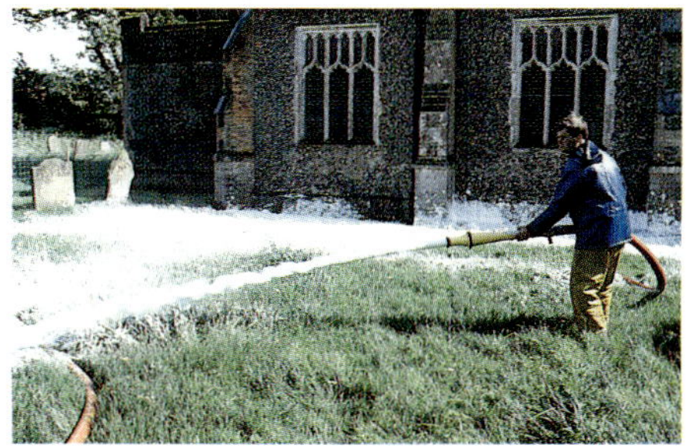

Turning summer into winter ...

These days, such matters are rather more fluid. In a recent children's drama, *The Children of Green Knowe*, the boy hero arrived in midsummer at the railway station, in brilliant sunshine. The local fire brigade provided convincing rain at one end of the platform and the boy sat in an area of natural shade, against the bright blue sky. This was changed in post-production, by paintbox, to a cloudy sky. The same equipment allowed the fields that the boy could see to be flooded (seemingly) with water. In a later episode it also turned the view from his bedroom window into a snow scene — only a small area needed to be covered by artificial snow.

This is a slight digression from the main point, which is that one of the biggest continuity problems concerning rain is the degree to which wetness is actually visible on any surface.

Whilst on the subject of wetness, there is another cautionary tale. A lady had her coat splashed in the course of the action, and a plot point was made about the incident. During a subsequent shot, water was sprayed on to the coat prior to each take. Unfortunately, the material was such that it did not show up at all well. There were quite a few comments at the editing stage and later, because of this apparent lack of continuity. In this instance, it was not so much the PA's fault, as the costume designer's — who could perhaps have found something wetter than water!

Gentle zephyrs

Outside, you will find one other factor that can make life difficult on any occasion — wind. It blows hair all over the place, and decreases the quality of actuality sound (although new furry microphone socks have helped enormously). Once again there is nothing much you can do — except to be aware of the hazard.

The Great Outdoors

Does it move?

Meanwhile, back on location:

- What else is moveable?

- If it is a modern piece, what cars are visible? Are they all plastered with BBC (or whatever) badges? Are they newly-registered vehicles? Will this look odd, for example, in a school playground, where teachers would normally park their older vehicles?

- Is the herd of cows in the next field about to be removed for milking? If not, are they the right cows for the period? (Freisians were not common in England before the First World War and you would not expect Charolais or Charolais crosses, much before the mid-'Seventies.)

- Has anyone thought to check the break and meal times at the 1200-strong Comprehensive across the road? The difference in noise levels will be astonishing. So will the level of lookers-on and passers-by.

Beside the seaside — beside the sea

If you are shooting by the sea, will it matter that the tide falls at about three feet an hour, and the boat you are filming could end up sitting on the mud? There is nothing you can do about this, and not much even the most forceful director can add, as Canute proved to his courtiers.

Filming at the seaside can become very complicated ...

The **director** and the **production manager** (or **first assistant** director) should have taken matters like this into account before

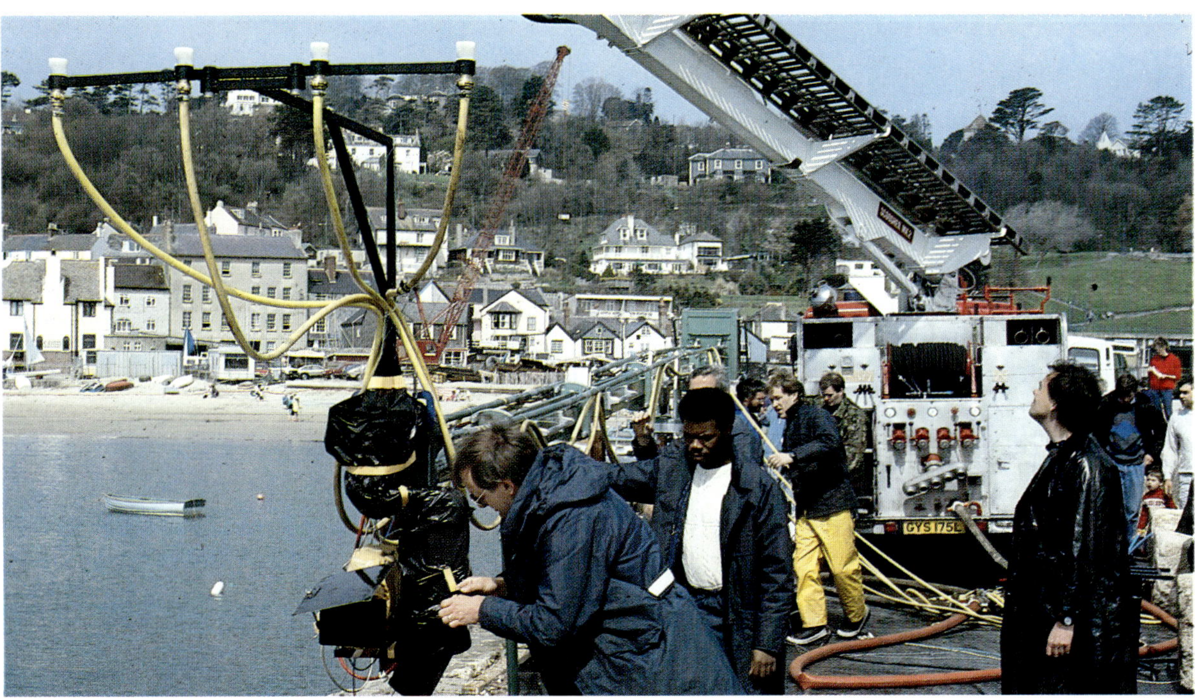

shooting started. If you want high water, start an hour or so before high-tide. This should give a fairly steady state for a couple of hours: that is, the rise and fall will be about equal, and you will not get a continuous drop in that time of about six feet.

If you are on a beach, filming as the tide recedes is probably safest — that way, the amount of space increases, and you do not have to keep on moving just to stay dry. It is probably a good idea to begin by looking towards the sea, and then to do the shots looking towards the land, when the receding tide will no longer be needed in shot. Again, this all comes into the scheduling. The continuity assistant, though, may be the one to pick up the pieces. There are directors who do not listen to people telling them about tide tables.

Putting it another way

There are so many variables that space prevents the retailing of all the possible anecdotes. Just remember, if it moves, it might be relevant.

Choosing locations

If you are lucky, the **recces** will have been done on working days, so that someone will have taken into account the market (noise and no parking), the low flying jets (NOISE, NOISE, NOISE), the carwash that does not open on Sunday (intermittent noise), early closing day (not enough passers-by), and the fact that the bit of land on which you and the rest of the crew are standing, is owned by someone other than the owner of the bit you are filming (you do not want an irate landowner to move you on halfway through a take).

If your project is a drama, or has drama elements, there will probably be a production manager, and possibly a location manager as well as the assistant floor manager(s) or their equivalents. In the film world, there will be first, second and third assistant directors, and maybe a runner.

In some areas of television, especially where the use of actors and drama sequences are unusual, some or all of these staff may be missing. In such cases the production assistant is likely to have been closely involved in setting up — and even finding — locations. Factors like those mentioned in the last paragraph do interfere with filming, and anything that does that makes keeping of good continuity notes more difficult. The more frequently you have to stop a take because you are under the airport flightpath, the longer it will take to complete a given sequence. Concentration is disturbed, tempers fray, time runs out and mistakes creep in.

On location...

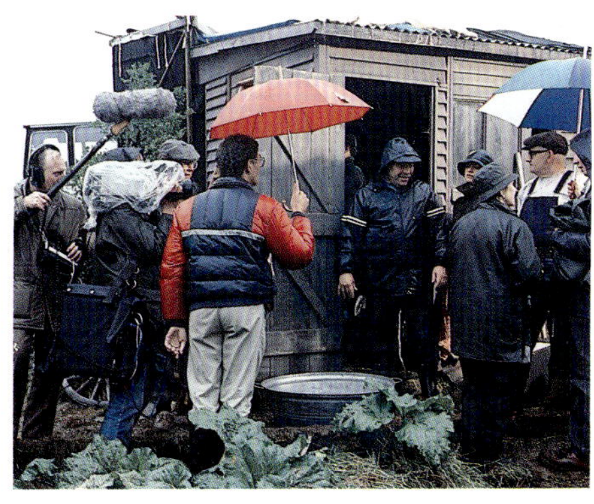

If, as a PA, you do end up in a position where you have influence over the choice of location, then ask one question before all others: what will be, or may be, *different* on the day? (There is no point in selecting a tatty house, with a ragged lawn, if the occupier is going to have fit of conscience the day before you arrive, and redecorate whilst bringing in the landscape gardeners.)

Any further advice on location finding becomes a treatise in its own right and would be outside the scope of this book.

The Paperwork

Story Orders

If you are doing more than a couple of short scenes, it is going to be useful to have a Story or Running Order. This is a table that shows the order of scenes and other information in the intended order that they will be shown in the final story (see p.33).

Episode, scene number, original script page number, the list of characters (and background artists), an indication of whether the scene is day or night, and a space for notes are the minimum requirements.

It is almost essential to include a very brief resume of the contents of each scene, and the '**Story Day**'. This is simply an index showing the change of day: the gap implied between '**Story Day One**' and '**Story Day Two**' may only be one day, but it could be a week or a hundred years.

The information is helpful to the costume designer, and others, to help determine whether a change of costume is likely to be necessary between two adjacent scenes. It is also helpful if there are flashbacks, to prevent confusion (at least among the production unit).

Because it provides quite a large proportion of the story in an 'at-a-glance' form, it is useful in helping to make notes. If you shoot scenes out of order (and you usually do) it helps 'continuity in reverse':

If a character in scene 8 is carrying travel catalogues into his office, he will need them in the lift sequence, in scene 7. If you shoot scene 8 first, where the catalogues are perhaps not mentioned, it is easy to forget you need them. This will be embarrassing when you come to shoot scene 7, where the character makes much play with them, in a conversation in the lift.

How these **Story Orders** are laid out will vary with production requirements.

They are also useful as the basis of recording orders, and filming schedules — especially if the information can be stored on a word processor, and called up in any chosen order.

Direct and indirect continuity

Once you have your Story Order, the concept of these two levels of continuity becomes plain.

If scene 1 takes place on the doorstep, ends with the front door opening, and continues as scene 2 in the hallway, the continuity between scene 1 and scene 2 is direct.

If we leave scene 1 just as the door opens, and go to another character buying a newspaper in scene 2, then go to the hallway as scene 3, then the continuity is indirect. Thus you would expect costume and props in scenes 1 and 3 to have continuity.

If scene 2 is actually quite long, there still has to be continuity between scenes 1 and 3, but you would not expect, say, your

Specimen: Story Order

DUMMY RUN

STORY ORDER

Page	Scene & Description	Time	Characters	Notes
1	DIANA'S OFFICE INT. Diana waits for 'phone call - answers phone incl. all her conversation	Day 6.00pm	DIANA	Drink, clock, bag, coat, actual work (pencils etc.) Prac. 'phone
2	CANTEEN LOBBY - PHONE BOOTH Peter 'phones Diana incl. all his conversation Exit with briefcase in correct, and incorrect, hands	Day 6.00pm	PETER	Briefcase (Phone - prac. + coins)
3	LOBBY INT. Diana waits for Peter He arrives. She puts on coat He takes her bag. Note: Dialogue on approach to vary with action	Day 6.45pm	PETER DIANA	Coats Briefcase (his) Bag (hers)
4	HOUSE EXT. OR CAR PARK T.B.A Arrival of car Peter and Diana get out, arguing, with gift. Exit frame	Evening 7.30pm	PETER DIANA	Car Flowers or wine
6	HOUSE INT. Peter and Diana greeted by Charles and Melissa Coats taken	Evening 7.30pm	PETER DIANA MELISSA CHARLES	Coats, drinks, snacks, cards out on table? score pads (bridge shop in Harrow) Clock, Tray, glasses, plate
7-9	HOUSE INT. They sit at table. The deal begins, with dialogue followed by bidding and lead to Dummy. Sequence ends on Diana's move	Evening 8.30pm	PETER DIANA MELISSA CHARLES	1st Cam.

leading lady to keep her raincoat on, and it might be quite logical to suppose she had had time to comb her hair.

This concept can be very important if you have a lot of short scenes and this possibility of minor changes between one scene and another could get you, and the rest of the production, out of trouble.

Keeping track

While there is no definitive way of taking notes, there are some guidelines we can offer, but remember that the best system of keeping notes is the one that works for you. There is a range of stationery available, at least within the BBC, to help the process.

The **Shot List** (see p.35) is usually used on documentaries, and allows space for basic information to be recorded where there is a degree of unpredictability in the shooting. In scripted sequences, it would be more usual to use a **Continuity Pad** (see p.36).

Let us assume that you are shooting a drama sequence with one or more actors:

Clearly, as soon as there is more than one actor, the taking of notes can become very complex. These notes fall into two broad sections: **Action** and **Shot Details**.

Shot details

These are the notes that go in the boxes on the Continuity Pads.

Some PA's find it convenient to clip a supply of the sheets inside their script folders, others use a clip-board, with just the relevant scenes for the day on the front, and the Continuity Pad held on the back with a bulldog clip and a rubber band. A slightly more complex approach is to interleave the full pages of script with half sheets of lined paper, covering the left-hand half of the script.

The method shown in the companion videotape to this manual is to have a spiral bound reporters note-book alongside the complete script.

Whichever method is used, these notes will include the shot or slate number, the take number, the scene number, the film roll number and the sound reel number, (if you are working on a single camera video set up, some sort of reference to the videotape spool number will be used instead for both of these).

On film it is useful, if not vital, to include details of the set-up, that is the lens, aperture, focussing distance, and filters or other effects — slow-motion and the like). It is also necessary to note if the sequence is day or night, or if it is shot in daylight, but exposed to give a night-time feel, that is 'day-for-night'. If this is not included, the laboratories and the film editor may get very confused (see p.8).

The duration of the take, and any faults must also be noted. **N/G** is not usually an adequate comment.

Specimen: Shooting Order Shot List

Strand/Series Title		**SHOOTING ORDER SHOT LIST**		
Programme Title	"CONTINUITY & THE SINGLE CAMERA"	Distribution	Denotes Recipient ✓	No of Cop
Episode/ Sub. Title		To:-	Room No. and Building	
Costing Number	Prod. Costing Wk(s) / Channel	Film Editor:	*	1
Programme Identificat'n Number	Studio	Snr. Asst. Enquiries Film Library		1
Production date(s)	Week(s)			
Filming/O.B. date(s)	Week(s)			
Producer Director Designer	Room No. / Building · Tel. Extn. · Department	File Copy		1
		Date	*	

To assist Film Library, please give full details of Location for each camera roll No.

Camera Roll No.	Slate No.	Take	Description	Sound	Tape No.	Duration
	605	1	Gill walks round table (WS) to tell Chris about his cigar. Actors check what they should be doing at the beginning of the scene	S		46"
	606	1 EB	CU Pat asking Colin if she should be dealing the cards Pan to Colin walking round to check Chris's cigar (Sound NG here, so new take)	S		40"
	607	1	MS Colin/Chris for above discussion	S		40"
	608	1	CU Pat's hands fiddling with cards	M		10"
	609	1	2-S Colin/Gill re. discussion of action in relation to dialogue, poss. problem with Chris. Colin says there isn't a problem, as the shots will be ... and ...	S		51"
	610	1	L/A 3-S of Colin/Tony/Gill at cam. for action 39/1A Gill watches, takes notes. Colin says "Cut". Chat between Colin/Tony, moves cam. to different angle. CU Gill writing.	S		2'30"
	611	1	MLS Colin, Gill walks in LoF, says "It's a bit long"	S		1'05"
	612	1	CU stopwatch. Gill starts it for rehearsal, stops it and notes times on script	S		40"
	613	1	CU table lamp next to BBC one	M		10"
	614	1	CU curtain. Hand enters R. and pulls it back	S		10"
12B	615	1	WS actors + crew around table. Discussion as to when Chris should drag and drink in rel. to dialogue. Reh. of action, Colin identifies cutting point. CU's Colin/Gill	S		5'00"
	616	1	CU Tony listening	M		20"
	617	1	(false start to 15") WS as Colin says "Cut - I'd like to go again straightaway" Don moves in to change mag. Gill checks "Roll 9, OK?" 2-S Don/Tony at cam.	S		1'04"

Specimen: Continuity Notes

BBC TV FILM CONTINUITY NOTES Date: 11.6.86

Programme: DUMMY RUN
Costing no.:
Episode no. or sub title:
Slate no.: 31

Set-up/location:
INT. CHARLES & MELISSA'S PLACE
EARLY EVENING
1615

Int. (circled) / Ext. — Day (circled) / Night — Sync. (circled) / ~~Silent~~ / Guidetrack with camera

Sequence no.:
Shot no.:
Script page no.:
Shot list page no.:

Costume/make-up/prop notes:
9.5mm/6'/T 2.8½/no filter

Sound Roll No.	3							
Film Roll No.	5A							
circle TAKES printed	1	2	3	4	5 (circled)	6	7	8
End board								
TIMING	46"	11"	48"	47"	49"			
FOOTAGE								
REASON for use or n/g	One more for Diana's pos	NG - boom in	Diana's hands went to cards before cue line	NG for dealing	OK			

SHOT DESCRIPTION

W/A - GROUP by drinks cabinet - CARD TABLE f/g - the move away from shelf to sit at table - PETER f/g R (MELISSA puts 'nibbles' on top of stereo on shelving unit before ~~mex~~ moving R to sit last) - CHARLES check the scoring pad & DIANA*the packof cards, she shuffles & deals the cards - they start to collect up their cards at ~~teh~~the end of the dealing.

* Picks up

DIALOGUE

CHARLES:
Here we are. Now, down to business.
Let battle commence!! ...

TO

DIANA
Can't afford to,my love. ~~Sux~~
Simply can't afford to.

ANY WILD TRACK/S RECORDED AFTER THIS SLATE

The Paperwork

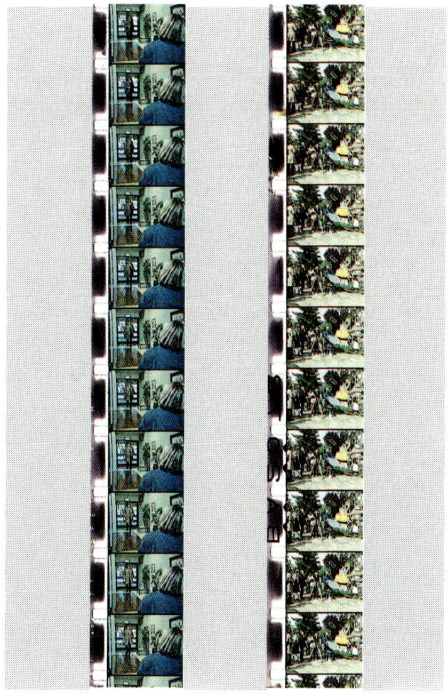

Slate 15 T1 15" W/F in cam.
Slate 15 T2 12" Man in b/g.
Slate 15 T3 16" OK.

If the duration of a good take is, say, thirty seconds, and if it actually transpires that it cannot all be used because it does not match a complementary shot, then a take that is supposedly N/G may help out, even if the director thought it would be useless. Examples include H(air) I(n the) G(ate), where the hair often turns out to be invisible until the end of the shot, or **Wrong Words** where part of the take may still provide a reaction.

On the other hand, the note **Wrong Filter** would tell the editor not even to bother looking at the take — it would almost certainly be impossible to match with other shots in the same sequence.

The duration indicates what proportion of the slate is likely to be available, and therefore worth looking at. It also provides a double check for the assistant cameraman, while he keeps track of film left on the roll. A take of five seconds, here, is unlikely to be helpful, but one of twenty seconds might be.

Notes like **F/S (False Start)**, **Lorry**, etc. showing the nature of a problem help by showing if the soundtrack is usable or not, without going to the trouble of finding the actual piece of mag. track.

The possible combinations are numerous and circumstances alter cases — there is much room for discretion here.

These details will all be noted in some way that is clear to you at the time of shooting. Common practice would then be to write or type up the relevant details, with the action notes, at some convenient pause in the shooting or back in the hotel room once shooting is over for the day.

Action notes

This heading merely differentiates the content from Shot Notes. Costume and prop details, as well as dialogue all come into this section.

There is usually plenty of space on a television or film script when the continuity assistant first gets it. This is not likely to be the case at the end of shooting.

The area at the top of the scene can be used for your own abbreviated notes about the set, costume of the characters involved, and props — the things that are broadly speaking not likely to change much in the action (see p.39).

Part of the larger blank area, usually on the left in a television script, can be used to describe the action. Writing down key descriptive words close to the relevant piece of dialogue, or stage direction, may be helpful. You might want to add a blank page for your own use opposite the start of each scene — or even opposite each page (see p.38).

If there is a movement, like a turn, or a wave, the picking up of a pen, etc., this should be noted in a way you will be able to interpret days later, if necessary.

Specimen: Additional Continuity Notes

37
9.5mm / 5'
T2.8½
no filter

Wide 2-shot P. ([illegible]) facing to R.o.f. / Clarke – facing cam – glass looks to R.o.f. to D. & closer to cam. to M.
C. drinks from [illegible] & picks cards up & see out, & starts bidding – C. lays 6D outside

P – JJ

T.2 – drags after "[illegible]" rather than after "afford to."

38
25mm / 4½'
T1.8½
no filter

CU Charles looks to R.o.f. to D. & closer to cam. to M. & L.o.f. to P.

P-JJ

T.1 up to CC

(dialog probs) @ beg.

39
37mm / min focus
T2.8½

CS P.'s cards on table –
[illegible] [illegible] from
up as C.'s glass comes back
down at table & cigarette [illegible] –
[illegible] see C.'s cards picked up –
see [illegible] P.'s being [illegible] out & goes with R.

(no dialogue)

T.2 cam. move o/s P.

41
7.5mm / 5'
T4
no filter

Wide 2 shot D./M. sitting @ table –
M. [illegible] R.o.f. – puts glass down @ beg.
as D. finishes dealing – picks cards up
& sorts them bidding – look to L.o.f.
to C. & eyeline closer to cam. for R. – D. lays out @ end & takes drink – R. [illegible] – rises & [illegible] R.o.f. – leaving @ P.
(cam. [illegible] R. back)

P – JJ

42
CU Diana – looks to L.o.f.

Specimen: Script with Continuity Notes

Scene 5 cont.)

AS THE DEAL PROGRESSES, THERE IS A LITTLE DESULTORY CHAT.

PETER
When are you two going down to Brighton?

MELISSA
We're driving down on Friday afternoon, aren't we, Charles?

CHARLES
Right, and play begins at 10 o'clock on Saturday morning. Wonderful - a whole weekend ~~playing~~ of Bridge.

DIANA
Wonderful...such a shame I can't go too. I know Peter wouldn't miss the Tournament for worlds, but I've got this wretched client wo insists on holding her ~~Grand~~ Opening on a Saturday afternoon. Such a bore.

MELISSA
Can't you give it a miss?

DIANA
Can't afford to, my love. Simply can't afford to.

CHARLES (AS PETER FINISHES DEAL, AND THEY ALL BEGIN SORTING THE CARDS). Yes, it's rotten when work interferes with pleasure. By the way, Mel, did I tell you Schliemann phoned today? Said he might be coming over to tie up some loose ends on the Champness Park project.

PETER
What, not this week-end?

CHARLES
'Fraid so. You know what he's like. Bound to need sheperding around.

The Paperwork

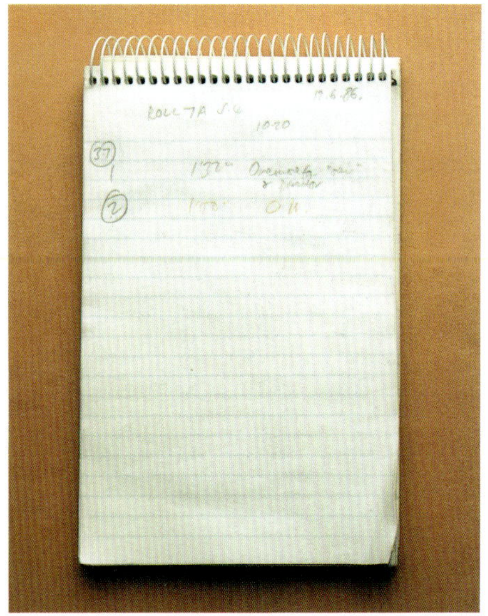

Shot details of slate 37 from 'Dummy Run'

The exact point that the action occurs on the chosen take can be marked with a tick on the appropriate word. If this point then varies on a subsequent shot, it can be pointed out, or the director can accept it as unlikely to cause an editing problem. It is sometimes expedient deliberately to change continuity between shots. This must be done with great care, and with the director knowing exactly what he is doing!

If you point out a discrepancy, and the director accepts it, any subsequent problems become his responsibility. It is surprising the number of times you will hear the phrase, 'Oh, we can sort that out at the edit'. (It is surprising how often this proves difficult!)

Sometimes it will be helpful to use matchstick drawings to show hand positions or, perhaps, how someone has fallen in action. Sometimes, it might be helpful to use different coloured pens/pencils to differentiate information about different takes — or even different characters.

The other use of colours is to differentiate between slates. This is usually done in any case on the copy of the script sent to the editor, but can also be useful on location.

The examples show the sort of thing that were produced during the filming of *Dummy Run*. In the tapes Gill Partridge is shown actually doing the job, and it was her notes that the editor used in cutting together the drama sequences (see p.35).

An example of her typed notes is also shown. You will notice that clarity is paramount, not exquisite 'Board of Directors' typing. There are some continuity assistants who write their notes straight on to self-carbonned sheets, and send these off to the editor, untyped. For this, you need very firm, clear writing. You should also get the editor's agreement first. With this method of working it is also a good idea to arrange not to have to work in the wind and rain.

There is only one rule — you must be able to interpret your own hieroglyphs quickly and accurately every time.

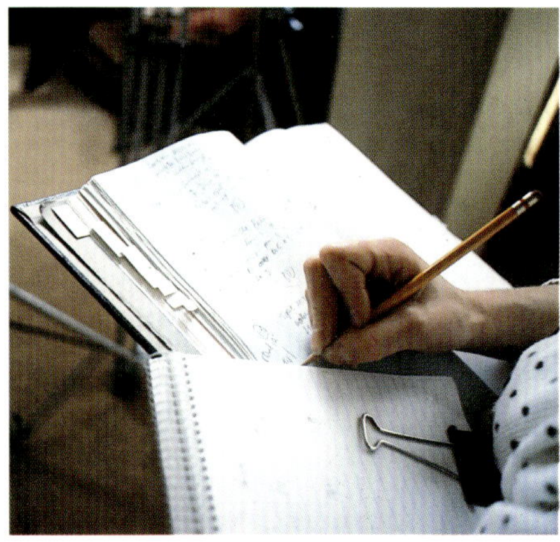

Keep thorough notes of action and *camera details*

WHAT THE EDITOR NEEDS

The editor needs the **shot details**, and a resumé of what is going on in each slate, as well as the start and finish points of the dialogue. If the continuity is wrong on the chosen take of a particular slate, he will need to know that, especially if there has been a conscious decision to accept the error. He will be quick enough to point out any unexpected mistakes!

He does not need a run-down of all the details you made in your notes. The examples show what is useful. Details of moves by the artists and the camera are helpful, as cutting points are usually associated with the former, and cannot usually be made during the latter.

The Paperwork

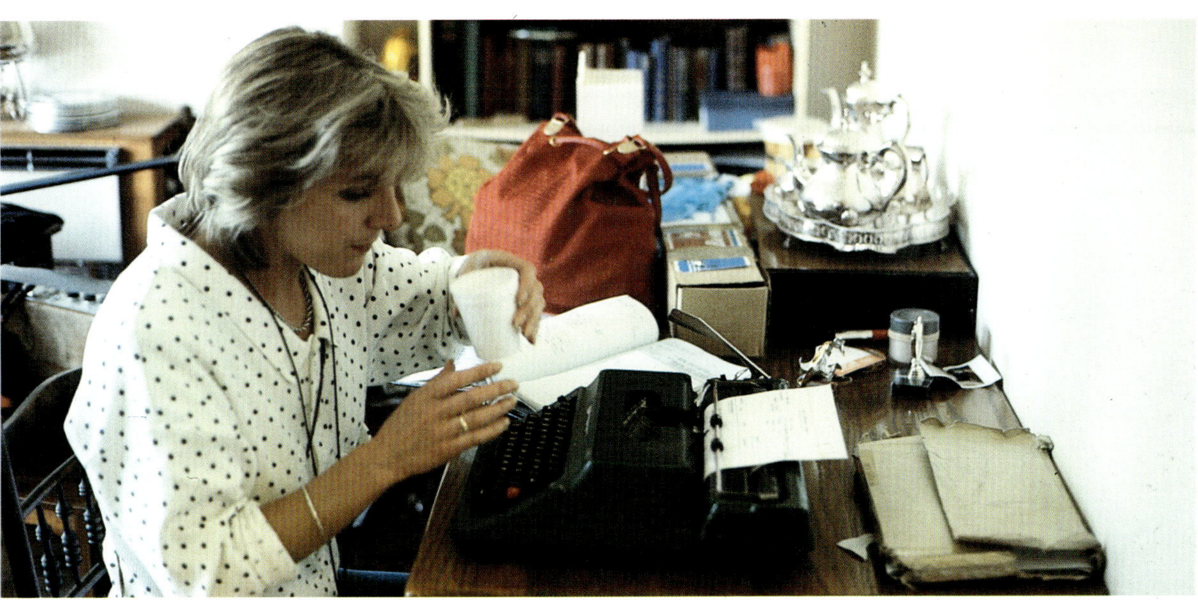

Keeping notes up-to-date — but not everyone uses a typewriter

The editor will need a **copy of the script**, which ultimately builds up into story order, with a summary of the shot details, i.e. slate number, number of takes, and the start and end point of each slate or take.

This marked-up document is sometimes referred to as the **Tramline Script** (see p.42). The example shows why. The lines show roughly where each slate begins and ends, and how many takes are available, and which slate overlaps with which. There is usually a different colour for each slate of each scene, or part of a scene.

The other item that might be useful is a suggested **Cutting Order**. This shows how the director was planning the shots should go together, at the moment of shooting. This is, of course, not always absolutely clear, especially in an action sequence.

It has been said that a film has a life of its own, and that the film itself will 'demand' the next shot, so the director's intentions can be altered by circumstances. This is all part of the creative process of editing.

It is because decisions made on location can be changed at this stage, that it is important not to take absolutely literally any statement by the director that one shot will be used to a specific point and another from that point onwards. By all means, be especially careful about the continuity around proposed editing points, but treat the proposal as you would a political manifesto.

On a **documentary** the editor would need the Shot List, and the Cutting Order. Clearly, many of the continuity problems involved in drama do not occur or, if they do occur, they cannot be re-shot. Other solutions need to be found, such as the insertion of cutaways, to disguise the effect of what would appear to be bad continuity.

Specimen: Tramline Script

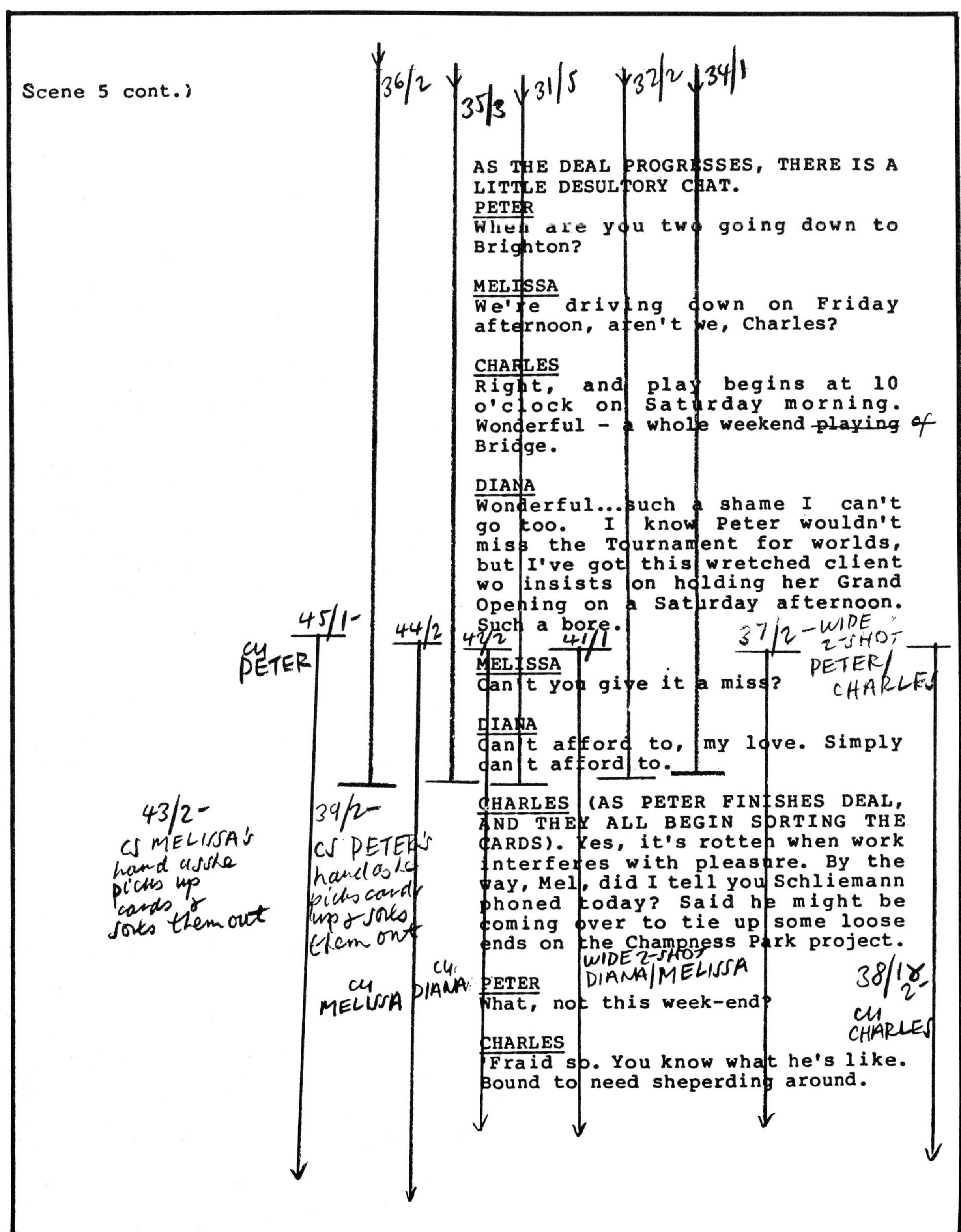

Scene 5 cont.)

AS THE DEAL PROGRESSES, THERE IS A LITTLE DESULTORY CHAT.

PETER
When are you two going down to Brighton?

MELISSA
We're driving down on Friday afternoon, aren't we, Charles?

CHARLES
Right, and play begins at 10 o'clock on Saturday morning. Wonderful - a whole weekend ~~playing~~ of Bridge.

DIANA
Wonderful... such a shame I can't go too. I know Peter wouldn't miss the Tournament for worlds, but I've got this wretched client wo insists on holding her Grand Opening on a Saturday afternoon. Such a bore.

MELISSA
Can't you give it a miss?

DIANA
Can't afford to, my love. Simply can't afford to.

CHARLES (AS PETER FINISHES DEAL, AND THEY ALL BEGIN SORTING THE CARDS). Yes, it's rotten when work interferes with pleasure. By the way, Mel, did I tell you Schliemann phoned today? Said he might be coming over to tie up some loose ends on the Champness Park project.

PETER
What, not this week-end?

CHARLES
'Fraid so. You know what he's like. Bound to need sheperding around.

VIDEO EDITING

This is a big subject. That which is possible is changing all the time.

At the time of writing, digital recording is on the horizon. Once it is here, the problems that occur when tape is copied from one generation to the next will disappear. Editing will become more fluid, and one of the major differences between film and tape editing will be eroded. This is the ease with which scenes in the middle of a film can be shortened, lengthened or otherwise amended, without causing a total re-edit. At present, the equivalent process on tape involves dropping a generation or a massive manual or electronic re-edit.

It is possibly for this reason that it is normal for the director to be present throughout a video edit, rather than allowing the editor to assemble sequences as often happens, on film. This being the case, the videotape editor does not usually need any documents, except a **copy of the script** to read before the editing starts. The director will usually need a **log of the recording** in a form he will understand. It can be helpful if details for each new scene start on a new page. After that, scene, shot and take numbers, duration of each take and the time code for the start of each take are necessary. Brief details of the contents of the shot (or shots, if using two cameras), and reasons for retakes should also be included. The only other information needed is the spool number and the VHS viewing copy cassette number, with any particular codes you and the recording engineer have agreed upon.

How the director then makes use of this information will depend on what viewing facilities there are, and whether or not off-line editing is possible. Of course, the continuity information you keep on your script will be much the same as you would keep from a film shoot.

TIME CODE

Time code is a display of hours, minutes, seconds and frames (e.g. 11.03.22.00—11.03.24.24 which is a duration of 1 frame less than 3 seconds). As recordings are made, it is currently common to make a VHS copy. You should request that this has built-in visible time codes with or without frames If the director is going to do an off-line edit, ask specifically for the frames to be shown. The time code is actually a read-out of the control track and can take one of two forms, time of day or arbitrary, where it will be continuous from 10.00.00.00 to 11.30.00.00. The former would jump from 21.40.20.24 to 10.30.26.05 if it was started one evening and used again the next morning. Make sure you request in advance the better system for your programme.

Complications may well arise if your show goes into a video effects workshop where several shots are combined to form one. Each of these cases will need to be treated on its merits!

Specimen: VT Editing Notes

SPOOL	SCENE	TAKE	SHOTS	TIMECODE	DUR	COMMENTS
H74543 74424	1208 (3)	1	345-364	175254	1'06	OK but more voice from Zammo
		2	345-366	175521	1'07	N/G Zammo's pos.
		P/UP 1	365-370	175647	0'37	Banks said 'colusions' instead of 'conclusions'
		2	367-370	175825	0'18	N/G corpsing
		3	"	175900	0'09	"
		4	"	175927	0'14	OK
H67535 67694	1209 (3)	1	321-327	161513	0'38	Boom in
		2	321-327	161710	0'35	"
		P/UP 1	325-327	161901	0'26	OK
H74543 74424	1210 (3)	1	371-376	185340	0'29	Miscut
		2	371-	185443	0'11	Shadow (boom?)
		3	371-376	185607	0'29	OK but P/UP
		P/UP 1	374-376	185714	0'14	OK
H61294 61842	1211 (2)	1	153-163	163004	1'17	Again
		2	"	163307	1'22	Banks better in this take but BOOM SHADOW - take from both.
		1	165-166	164637	0'14	N/G Janet fluffed
		2	165-166	164746	0'28	N/G " "
		3	"	165155	0'09	N/G Janet's pos. Roly out of shot

More Words on Actors

As soon as you have two or more actors to deal with, you have two (or more) sets of actions to watch, and two (or more) sets of lines to listen to. On the other hand, the more complex the scene, the longer, in all probability, you will have to make your notes.

As the number of actors increases, so the possibility of error increases. Actors vary enormously in their consistency. That is, some will always enter and hit their marks on the same word, on all takes and slates. Some will vary slightly each time, and some will be all over the place. Children can be very variable — they can also put some adults to shame on their accuracy over dialogue.

Take the example of a character entering the room and greeting another character already present. If, on a two-shot, the first enters, begins to speak, stops speaking, then sits, and then the second begins to speak, the point at which the editor will want to cut the film will be different from the same action, timed differently.

Suppose, on a mid-shot, the first character enters, begins to speak, sits, then stops speaking, and the second begins to speak, the editor will have problems in cutting the two shots together at a natural point, perhaps in the middle of the sit. This may be all right if the mid-shot is of the first character, but suppose the mid-shot is of the second character and includes the first's shoulder — then the timing of the second's speech will be wrong, or the editor will have to make a compromise.

In any given sequence, there will be key moments — turns, gestures, actions such as door-shutting, which relate to dialogue, or to the moves of other characters in the shot. Part of the purpose of the rehearsal is to make words and actions appear natural, and to show everybody, cameraman and boom-swinger included, what will happen, and the precise sequence of events. It is up to the continuity assistant to use tact and discretion to remind actors of this precise sequence when necessary — after the master and before a close-up, perhaps. Although it may sometimes be expedient to pass such notes through the director at other times, it can be positively reassuring for the actor to know that someone is paying close attention to his performance, which will be obvious if the note is given directly.

If the timing goes out, even by a little, the editor can be presented with quite a big problem. Perhaps a checklist will be helpful here:

- Have all the actors said the right words? If not, did the words make sense? Is the director, who has almost certainly been watching the actors rather than the script, aware of the discrepancy?

- Have the actors made the rehearsed moves? Have they made them at the rehearsed points?

This is fine on the takes, but for rehearsals, there are more questions to ask:

- Who starts sitting? Who is standing?

More Words on Actors

- Does anybody enter? Via which door? Which hand opens the door, which closes it?
- Which way is the body turned for the action?
- At what speed is a movement made? (It looks very odd if a character walks out of a room at one pace and into the next faster, or slower.)
- Which direction, to camera left or to camera right, has been taken?
- What sort of mood are the characters showing? Should they be laughing, smiling frowning, etc.?
- Which hand is used for picking up/putting down objects? For carrying accessories?
- Are heads inclined, forwards, or backwards, or to the side? If, on a wide angle, the head of one character is inclined one way or the other, a closer shot on that character will show up any discrepancy.
- Do the actors meet, touch, shake hands, kiss or kill each other? Where? On which line?

And so on.The list is endless, but it may help to remember one PA's experience — when she began, she concentrated on getting heads and hands right. These, the direction of turns and the timing of rises and sits, are good places to begin. The rest comes with practice.

THE BROADER CANVAS

Once you have a very large number of people on screen, involved with large-scale action, things can, in practice, become, not hideously complicated, but simpler. If there are large numbers of extras/walk-ons/ background artists, the detail on any individual is lessened. In the extreme, think of the funeral scene in *Gandhi*. What becomes significant is the overall impression.

Watch any movie action sequence. Quite often, there will be a very large number of brief shots, and you, as audience, will be left with an impression of something happening — the quickness of the shots will deceive your eyes.

Quite often, too, the rules of film making can be broken. The director can **cross the line**, or make the action change direction, without upsetting the audience. It is the flow of action, rhythm and pace that take over from normal continuity. This does not mean you can go to sleep. If the rules are to be broken, this should be done by the director's choice, not simply out of necessity.

In *Dummy Run* (the drama sequence from the training tapes *Continuity and the Single Camera*), there was a fight. This was all carefully choreographed with the fight arranger. The director, the cameraman and the fight arranger worked out, not only the shape of the action, but also how the fight would be shot: a punch here, a fall there, a kick next, and so on.

In this case none of the fourteen shots lasted longer than fifteen seconds, and most were between five and ten seconds long. In other words, the complicated action was broken down into easily manageable sections. One major reason for this, of course, is the safety of the actors — doing it step-by-step reduces the risks to a minimum.

This technique makes it possible, for instance, to shoot a long sequence in a mediaeval castle, with lots of sword fights, soldiers falling off stairs and down battlements, and so on, with only one stunt arranger*.

What works in situations like this is careful planning. If everyone knows what should happen, it is easier to cope with the unexpected. There are far more potential hazards for the continuity assistant shooting something like a card game than large-scale action, where an adequate number of **cutaways** will cover a multitude of sins, and where no one pair of eyes can be expected to recall everything — and where action in several places is being followed, thus breaking up continuity problems.

The particular problems with something like a card game are twofold: the first concerns the props, the fifty-two easily identifiable significant cards, plus their likely companions, cigar(ette)s and alcohol, and the second concerns eye-lines (q.v.).

There should be enough in this book to help you come to terms with the prop aspect of card games — just remember that cigars and cigarettes burn down, like candles, and the length at any given moment in the action might be significant. In *Dummy Run,* Christopher Timothy's character smokes throughout the card game. In fact, as cut together, you would not be aware whether the continuity of his cigar is right or wrong — that is just chance, though. The other general point to watch for is the ashtray that mysteriously empties and refills itself.

Rehearsing the fight

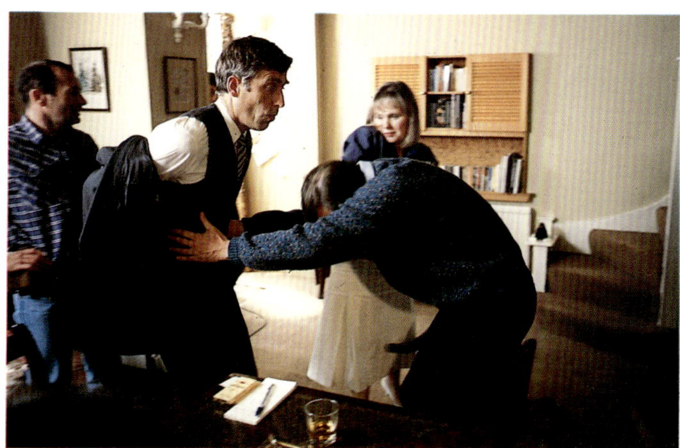

*See BBC Television Training manual *After Tea We'll do the Fight*

Eyelines

The subject of eyelines is complicated. Cameramen and directors, and editors and directors have nearly come to blows on the subject.

Basic principles

If you are sitting, listening to two other seated people talking and you are between them, you will look from one to the other. As you perceive them, the one on your left will be looking to your right, and the one on your right will be looking to your left.

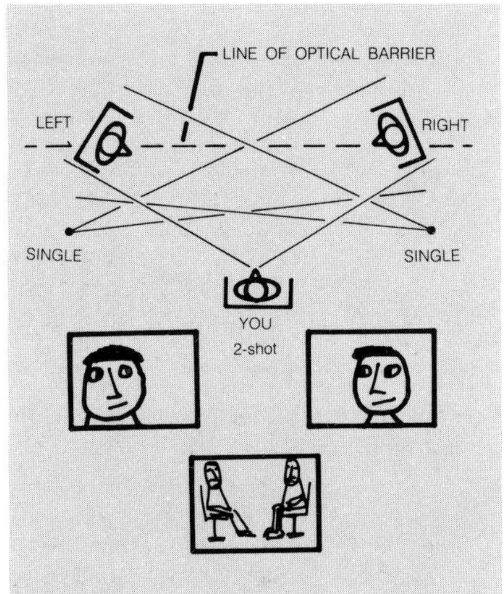

If you are shooting the conversation on film, you might shoot an establishing two shot from your position, and two close-ups, also from your position. This gives you three shots, in which your friends, Left and Right, are looking respectively right and left.

If you want better shots for the close-ups, you might choose to move the camera more on to the respective eyelines, to enable you to see both eyes. This would be rather similar to your leaning forward as you looked from one to the other. The imaginary line between Messrs. Left and Right is the **line**, or **optical barrier**. If you move the camera across that line, say for the close-up of friend Right, then he will appear to be looking to the right and so will friend Left!

If you cut the pictures together, they will appear to be talking, not to each other, but to some third party. This is because your camera crossed the line, and you are suddenly asking your audience to be in two places at once. This is the most basic example of line crossing.

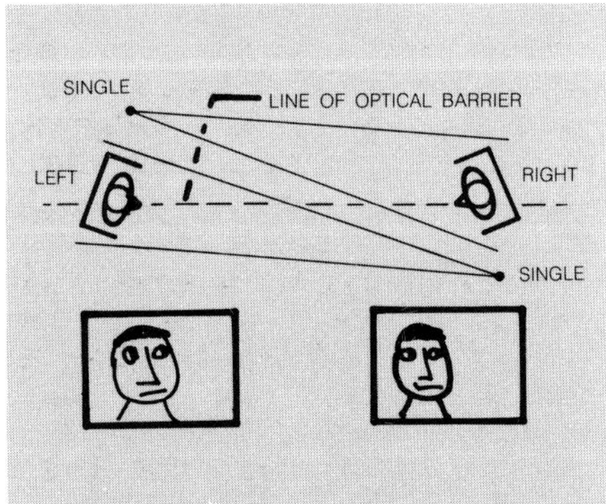

If you have four people spaced equally round the four sides of, say, a bridge table, shooting becomes quite complicated. The camera, in effect, goes into a fifth place, as observer. At any one time, it will only see two of the players in anything like full face: the two players opposite the camera. If they talk to each other then they go into profile, too.

Suppose the camera starts between players South and East with a four shot (in pos.1). If the other two, West and North look at each other, then they create a line between themselves, and the camera can move round in much the same way as it did for Left and Right, and can safely take close-ups (to pos.2 and 3).

If North and West now look at East, something interesting happens. On their **close-ups**, they are now looking out of the other side of their respective frames.

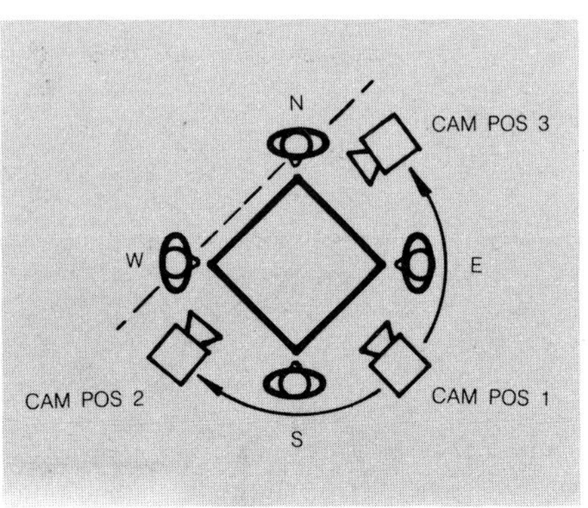

If we cut back to the original four shot, West appears to change the direction he is looking (that is, from the left to the right), and North will not. She will look on both shots to the right of frame.

The editor can therefore cut from North's close-up back to the four shot, but not from West's.

If we see on West's close-up, how his look to East crosses the camera lens, and we wish to go from that shot (with West looking frame left) to a close-up of East, she will have to appear to

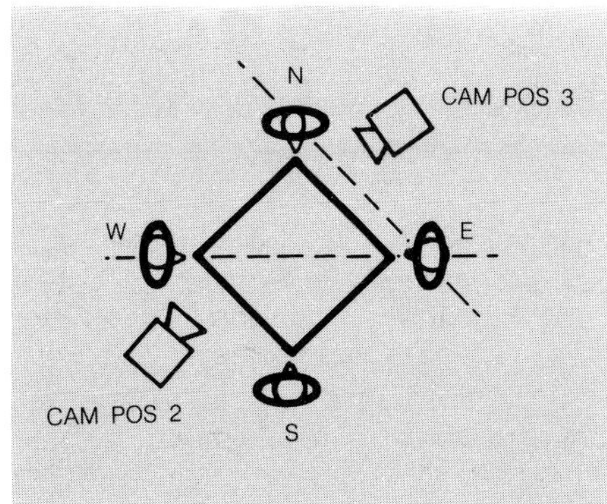

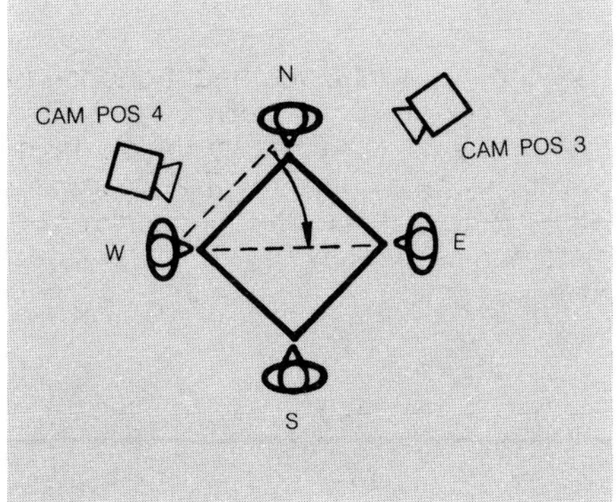

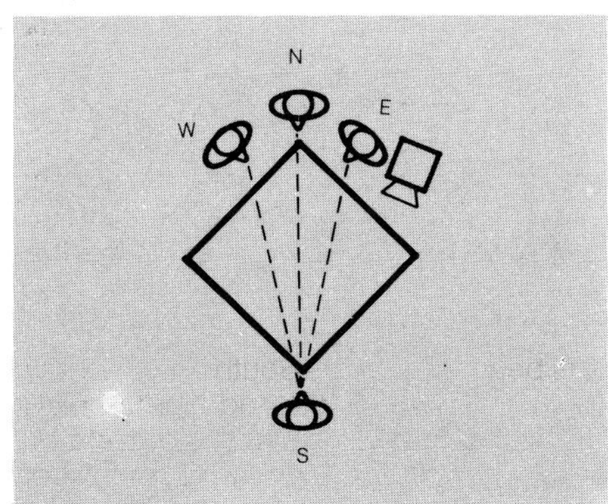

be looking frame right. This can only be achieved by moving the camera — perhaps between West and North (pos.4).

We have not even considered South! Try working it out for yourself.

Suppose the whole hand has been covered in a master-shot from our first position, and you plan to use it several times. Where would you put the camera to take a close-up of South when:

He is talking to West?
He is talking to North?
He is talking to East?

The real problems come when South's eyeline switches from one to the other and back. There are ways, other than shooting every line from all possible angles. You could, for instance, move the other three players very close together and put the camera next to East's left shoulder. South's eyeline will then stay to the right of frame, and you should have a clear, not-too-profiley shot of him, whomever he is addressing.

Another approach would be to abandon the master-shot, and use a combination of two-shots and singles that follow on one from another, as the need arises.

Try working out how you would shoot the conversation next time you have coffee with your friends. The criteria are very difficult to set down on paper.

It is very easy to get confused. You must try and understand the principles, even though the decisions will be made by the director in consultation with the cameraman. As a last resort, some really problematic shots may have to be done twice for safety, with an each-way eyeline.

The director needs to know from your notes: who is looking which way at what point; when do head-turns occur in relation to dialogue and other action. In other words, if in doubt, go back to basic principles.

Further into the maze

More complications occur with any kind of movement. If a car is driving to Sheffield and it is first seen travelling left to right, then, unless direction of travel changes within a shot, all subsequent shots should show the car travelling left to right. If the car is then shown coming back from Sheffield, then it is a filmic convention that it should be seen travelling the other way — right to left.

If Romeo is on his way to meet Juliet, and she is on her way to meet him, then one should travel camera left to right, and the other, right to left. If they do not, they could appear to be moving apart or to be pursuing one another.

These principles hold good for any motion, by people, birds, aircraft, ships or even ants. Failure to stick to them is likely to result

Eyelines

in another version of crossing the Line. In this case, the Line is that between the subject, and whatever it is moving towards.

Another version of the **line** is the **look**. If you have an actor looking at an object, like a mirror, then the direction of that look forms a line. If the camera travels across the line, on a track, all is well. If you cut from one side to the other, a nasty jump is the likely result.

Incidentally, shots of people in mirrors raise whole new areas of problems. If in doubt, draw a little map. Normally, the actor should do the natural thing — should be taking the eyeline he would normally take. The eyeline the camera should be concerned with is the real one, not the one that appears to be correct simply because the mirror is there.

CAM POS 2
LINE OF MOTION
R
J
CAM POS 1

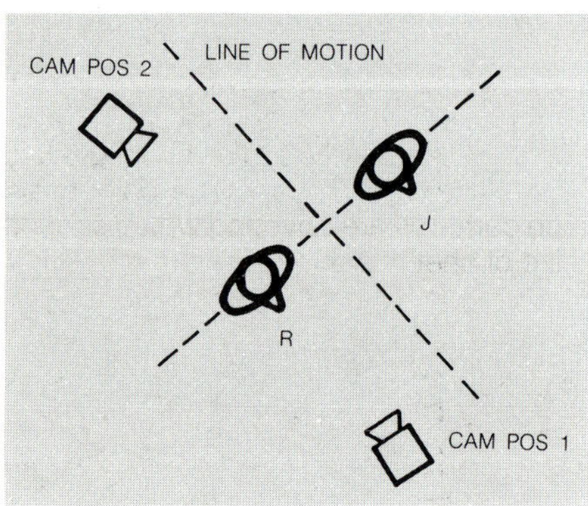

Four actors — four sets of actions to check

EXCEPTIONS

There are many occasions when the line has been crossed with little ill effect. If the audience does not become disoriented, all may be well. If the desire is that the audience is disoriented, all may still be well.

Then we have the **reverse cut**.

Let us suppose that Romeo has met Juliet and they are walking hand in hand towards us. The line is apparently between them. It is perfectly proper, however, to move the camera 180° behind them and see them disappearing into the sunset.

If the motion is not directly towards camera, then the camera will have to move less than 180°, and stay on the correct side of the line of motion.

If there are two lines, one of motion, and one of looking, as of Juliet waving farewell to departing Romeo, be careful. The better Line to observe may be the one of motion, not the more obvious Line between the lovers!

These are, once again, only guidelines. The answer for the director is simply this — if it works, do it.

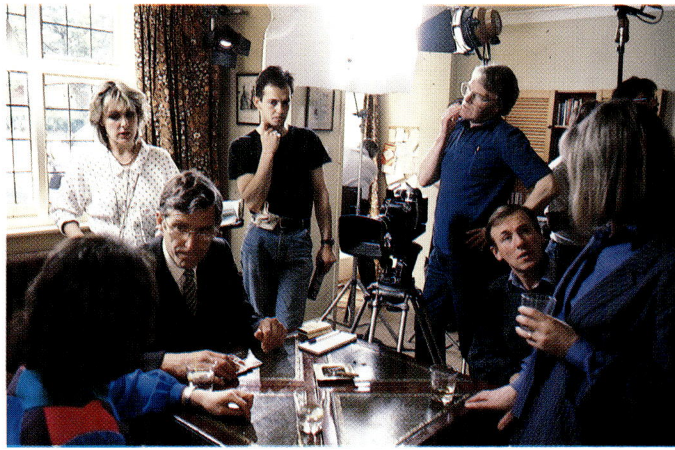

Other Problems

Quite often, a close-up or two will get everyone out of trouble — because there are fewer things in close-ups that affect continuity. Two shots that would not work if cut directly together, may be fine with a bridging close-up. This comment applies not only to the unpredictable factors within this section, but on almost any sort of sequence. Pay close attention to head angle and direction of movement, as well as to expression in these cases.

Music

If there is music in the action, you again need to be careful. If music is to be played back, then action and dialogue need to be consistent. The point at which, say, the radio is switched off, is most important. Life will be difficult, especially for the editor and dubbing mixer, if there are supposed to be several intercut shots in such a sequence. It would then normally be better to dub the sound.

If there is a dance sequence, clearly the dancers have to work to playback. However, since their movements are closely tied to the music, there should not be too much of a problem, provided the music is pre-recorded, and is therefore a constant.

A common system involves the use of playback, which is then recorded with each slate as a guide track. The editor then lays down a copy of the complete piece and cuts the pictures, matching the guide to his master track.

If there is speech in the middle of a waltz, then the actors may have to hold a rhythm in their minds for a time. It should all work.

If the music has to be 'live', then it is probably best to use several cameras. The only problem then is getting the pictures in sync with the sound. This is a technical question, moving away from the responsibility of a continuity assistant. The point to be noted then becomes which cameras are covering which section of the music, and what size of shot they have.

Children

The vagaries of children have been mentioned. The fact that their permitted working hours are strictly limited, combined with a lack of life experience and the ability to pace themselves, can mean that there is not time to do retakes for the smaller matters of continuity. It also means that there is often little point in being as fastidious as one would be with adults, as the freshness of performance tails off rapidly. Shooting re-takes becomes counter-productive and there is a greater need, usually, to compromise. Mind you, working with small groups of children can be great fun.

Animals

Animals present similar problems. Their concentration span can be short. Short shots and lots of cutaways help matters enormously. Again, working with animals can be fun. A good trainer and careful planning make the difference between fun and purgatory.

Other Problems

Visual Effects

If your project involves visual effects, there is one point to remember. Each effect has been brought to your location for the particular circumstances as a tailor made, one-off item. To expect several takes or a precise re-run of the first take, can therefore be optimistic, to say the least. Thorough planning and contingency planning are, as always, vital.

Water

Water plays havoc with continuity. Hair and wigs get wet at the wrong moment, clothes that should be wet look dry, and those that should be dry look soaked.

Water also plays havoc with continuity notes. Plastic covers on notes and script help, but you cannot write through them. Avoid water soluble ink — that is if you cannot avoid water altogether.

SO REMEMBER ...

The first time you go out on location, you may well find some continuity problem not covered in this book. We hope, though, that there is sufficient information to provide a guide to the likely hazards, and to ways of coping with them.

You will come across new problems, or new combinations of old ones, and you will doubtless find your own solutions to both — and to the ordinary everyday problems.

There is one more thing to remember when you are out on a windy, wet day in November, half a boggy mile from the location caterers, filming two children and an electronic goat — filming can be fun!

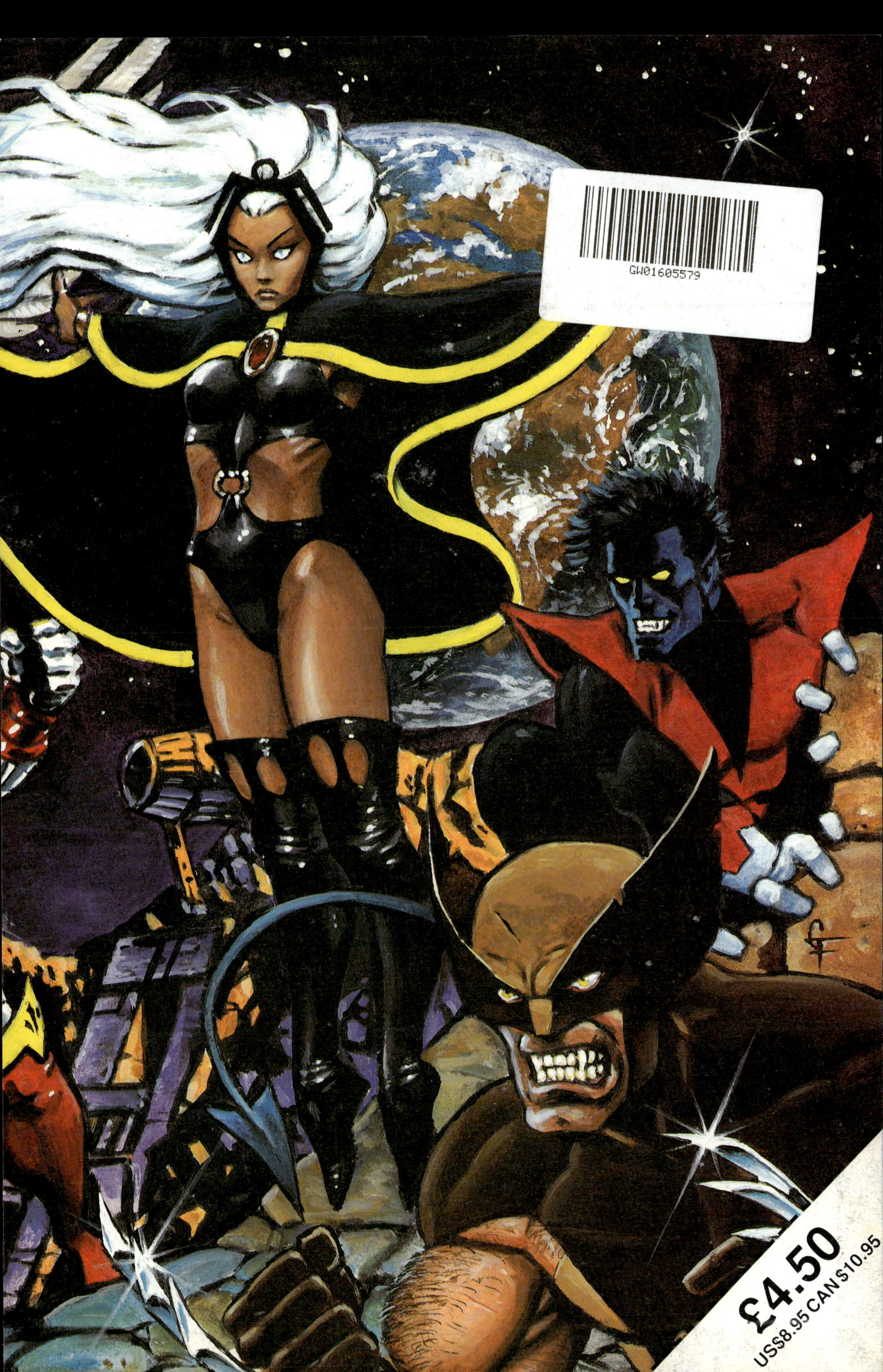
GW01605579
£4.50
US$8.95 CAN $10.95

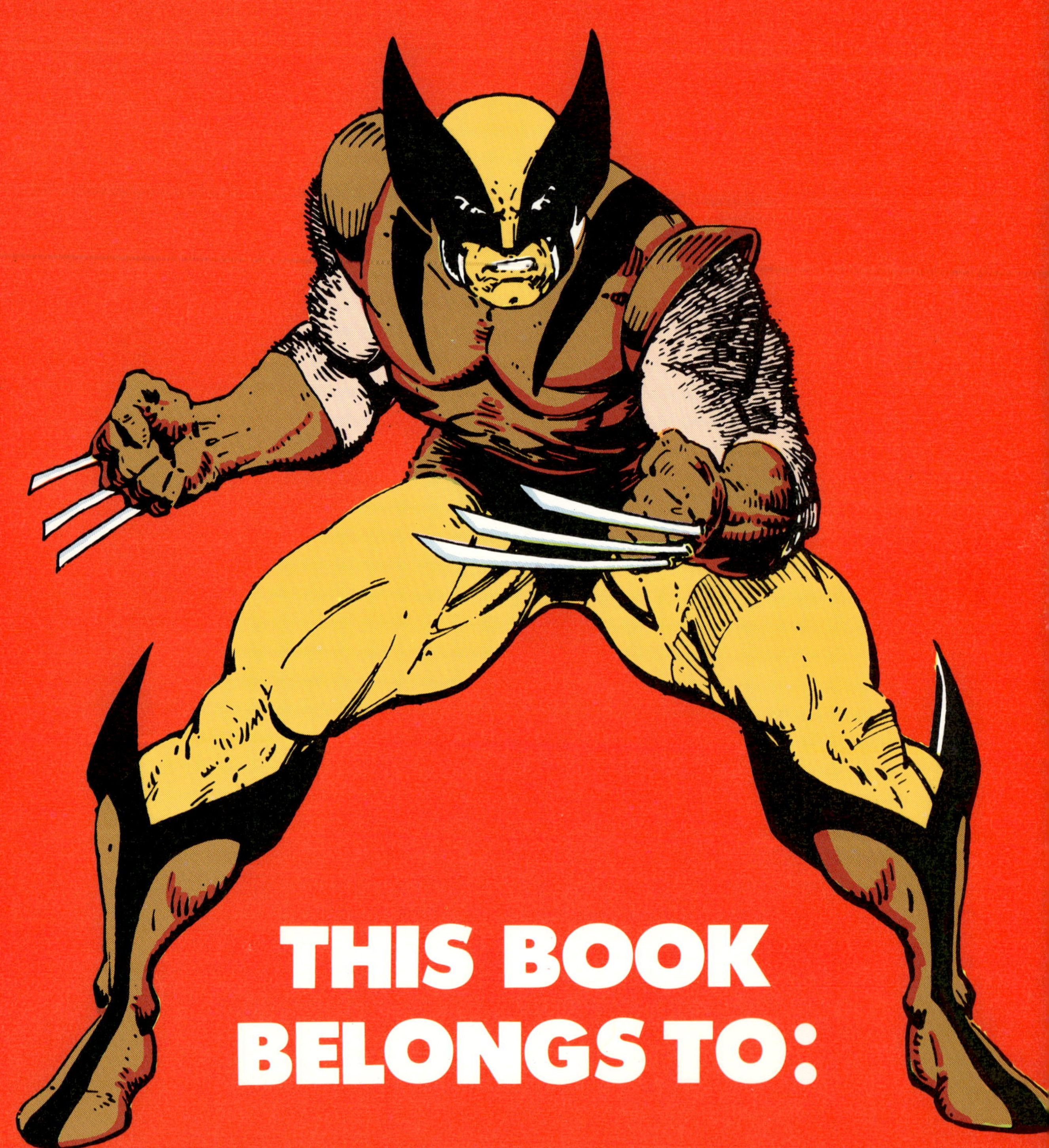

THIS BOOK BELONGS TO:

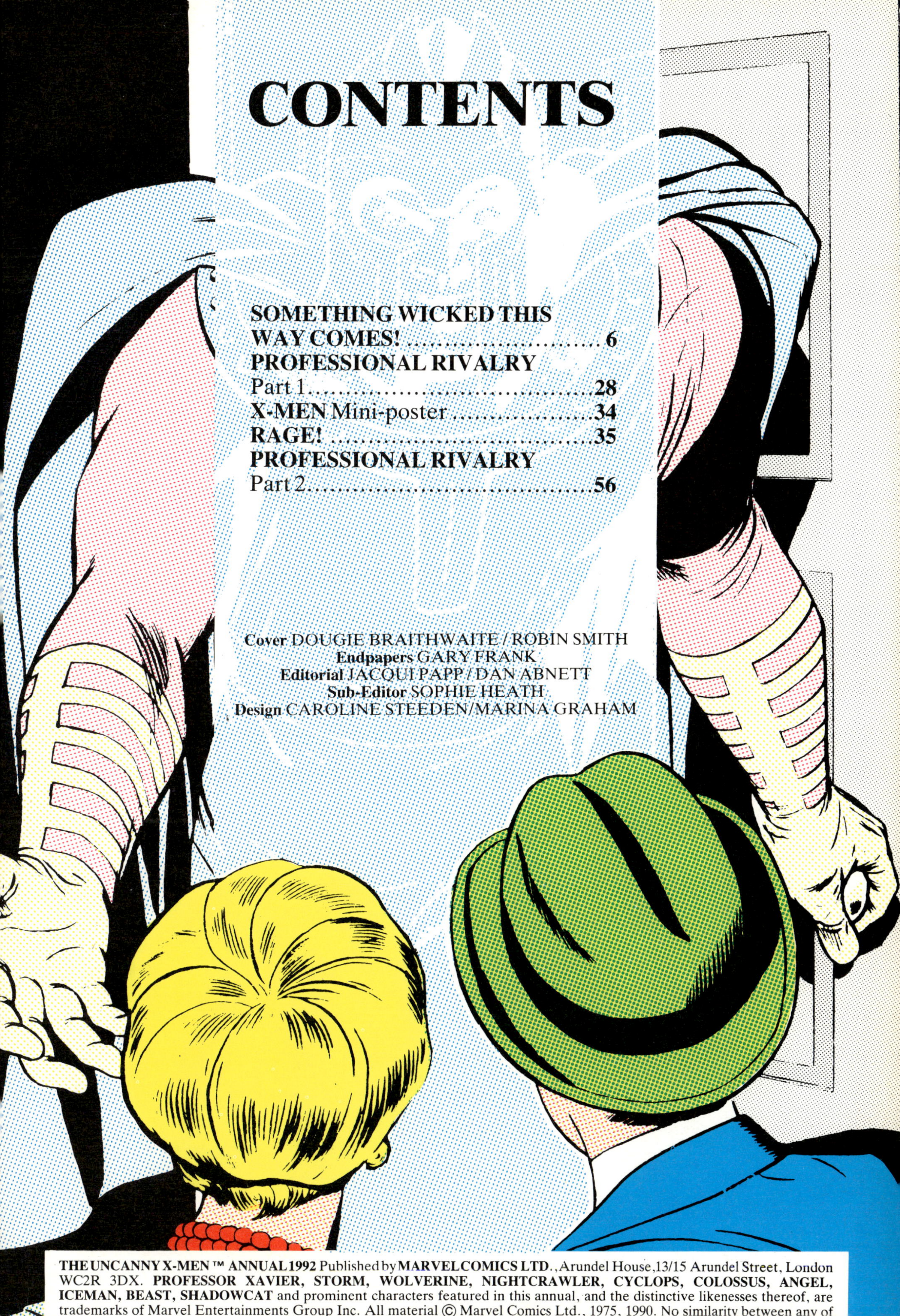

CONTENTS

Cover DOUGIE BRAITHWAITE / ROBIN SMITH
Endpapers GARY FRANK
Editorial JACQUI PAPP / DAN ABNETT
Sub-Editor SOPHIE HEATH
Design CAROLINE STEEDEN/MARINA GRAHAM

THE UNCANNY X-MEN ™ ANNUAL 1992 Published by **MARVEL COMICS LTD.**, Arundel House, 13/15 Arundel Street, London WC2R 3DX.

Cyclops. Storm. Nightcrawler. Wolverine. Colossus. Children of the atom, students of Charles Xavier, MUTANTS — feared and hated by the world they have sworn to protect. These are the STRANGEST heroes of all!

Stan Lee PRESENTS:

THE UNCANNY X-MEN!™

CHRIS CLAREMONT WRITER | JOHN BYRNE PLOT-PENCILS | TERRY AUSTIN INKER | TOM ORZECHOWSKI, letterer GLYNIS WEIN, colourist | BOB HARRAS EDITOR | TOM DEFALCO Ed. in CHIEF

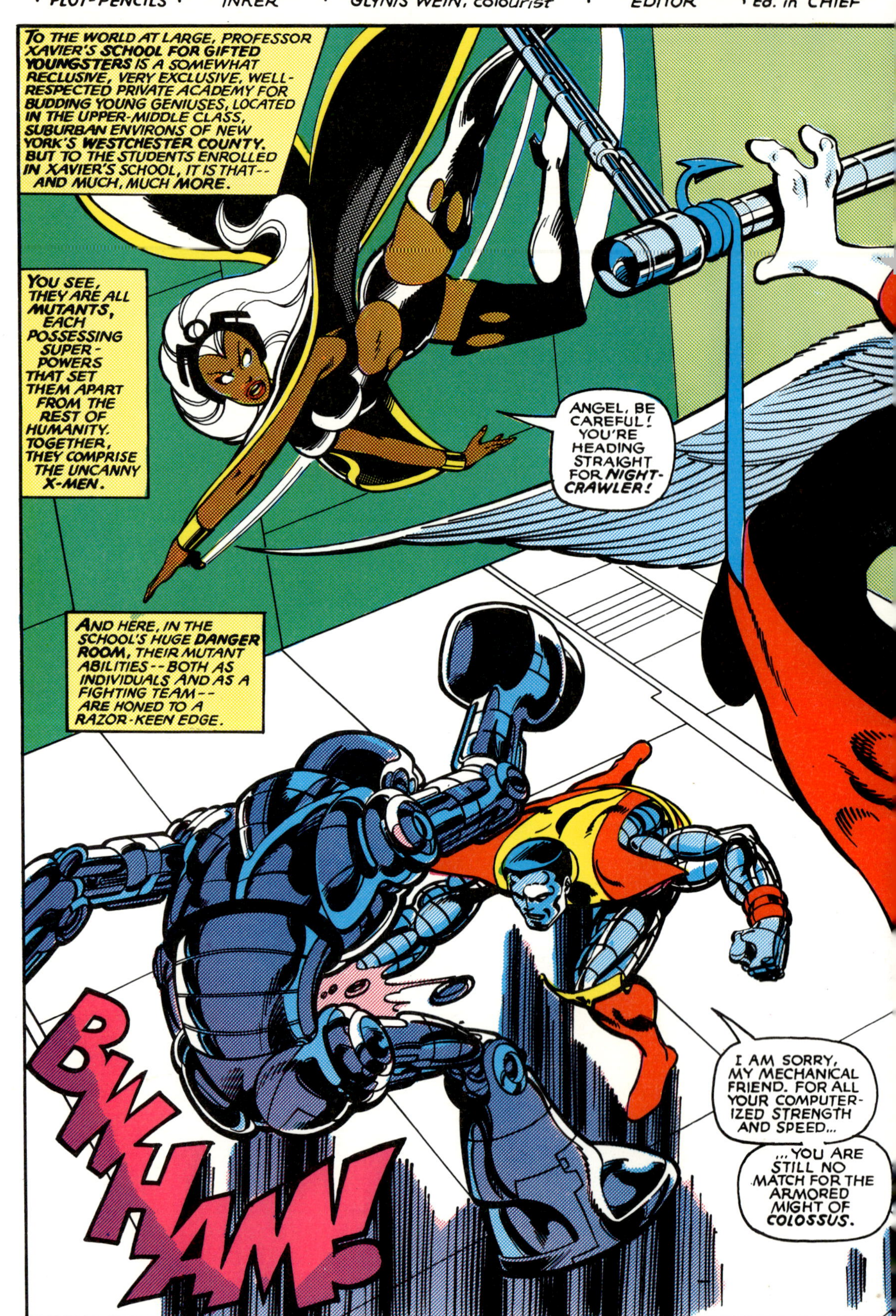

...SOMETHING WICKED THIS WAY COMES!

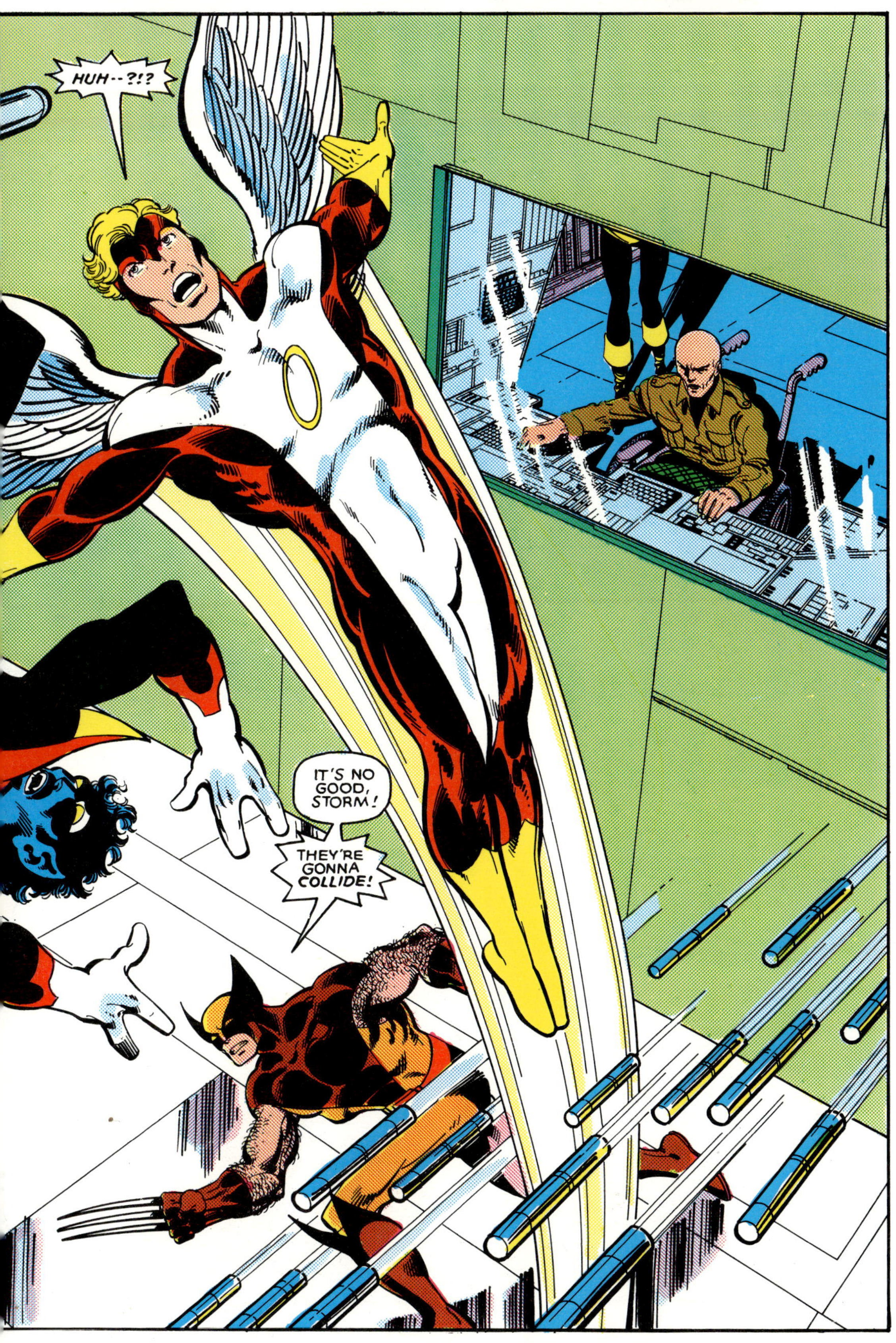

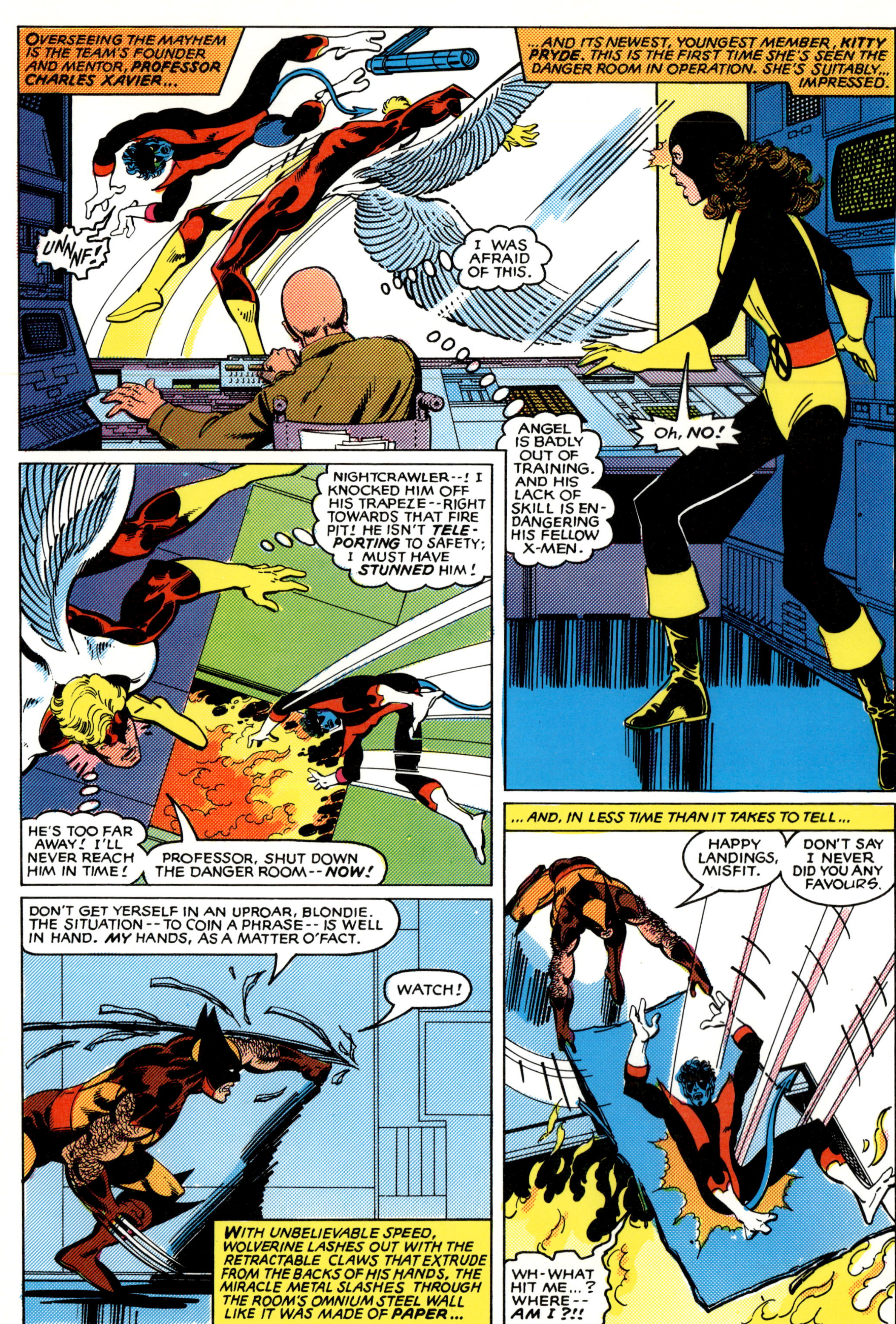

OVERSEEING THE MAYHEM IS THE TEAM'S FOUNDER AND MENTOR, PROFESSOR CHARLES XAVIER...
...AND ITS NEWEST, YOUNGEST MEMBER, KITTY PRYDE. THIS IS THE FIRST TIME SHE'S SEEN THE DANGER ROOM IN OPERATION. SHE'S SUITABLY... IMPRESSED.
UNNNF!
I WAS AFRAID OF THIS.
ANGEL IS BADLY OUT OF TRAINING. AND HIS LACK OF SKILL IS ENDANGERING HIS FELLOW X-MEN.
Oh, NO!
NIGHTCRAWLER--! I KNOCKED HIM OFF HIS TRAPEZE--RIGHT TOWARDS THAT FIRE PIT! HE ISN'T TELE-PORTING TO SAFETY; I MUST HAVE STUNNED HIM!
HE'S TOO FAR AWAY! I'LL NEVER REACH HIM IN TIME!
PROFESSOR, SHUT DOWN THE DANGER ROOM--NOW!
DON'T GET YERSELF IN AN UPROAR, BLONDIE. THE SITUATION--TO COIN A PHRASE--IS WELL IN HAND. MY HANDS, AS A MATTER O'FACT.
WATCH!
WITH UNBELIEVABLE SPEED, WOLVERINE LASHES OUT WITH THE RETRACTABLE CLAWS THAT EXTRUDE FROM THE BACKS OF HIS HANDS. THE MIRACLE METAL SLASHES THROUGH THE ROOM'S OMNIUM STEEL WALL LIKE IT WAS MADE OF PAPER...
...AND, IN LESS TIME THAN IT TAKES TO TELL...
HAPPY LANDINGS, MISFIT.
DON'T SAY I NEVER DID YOU ANY FAVOURS.
WH-WHAT HIT ME...? WHERE--AM I?!!

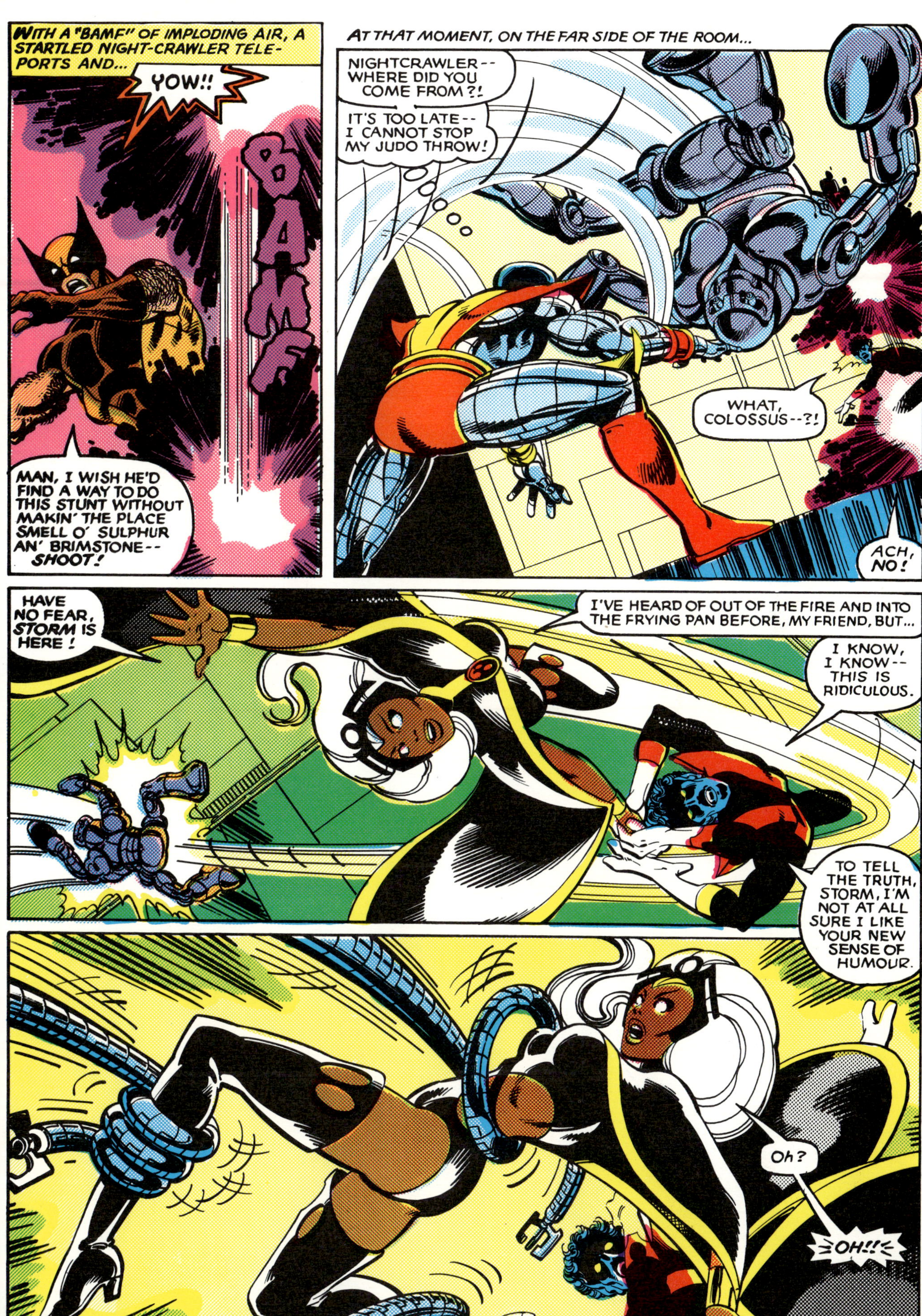
WITH A "BAMF" OF IMPLODING AIR, A STARTLED NIGHT-CRAWLER TELE-PORTS AND...
YOW!!
BAMF
MAN, I WISH HE'D FIND A WAY TO DO THIS STUNT WITHOUT MAKIN' THE PLACE SMELL O' SULPHUR AN' BRIMSTONE-- SHOOT!
AT THAT MOMENT, ON THE FAR SIDE OF THE ROOM...
NIGHTCRAWLER-- WHERE DID YOU COME FROM?!
IT'S TOO LATE-- I CANNOT STOP MY JUDO THROW!
WHAT, COLOSSUS--?!
ACH, NO!
HAVE NO FEAR, STORM IS HERE!
I'VE HEARD OF OUT OF THE FIRE AND INTO THE FRYING PAN BEFORE, MY FRIEND, BUT...
I KNOW, I KNOW-- THIS IS RIDICULOUS.
TO TELL THE TRUTH, STORM, I'M NOT AT ALL SURE I LIKE YOUR NEW SENSE OF HUMOUR.
Oh?
OH!!

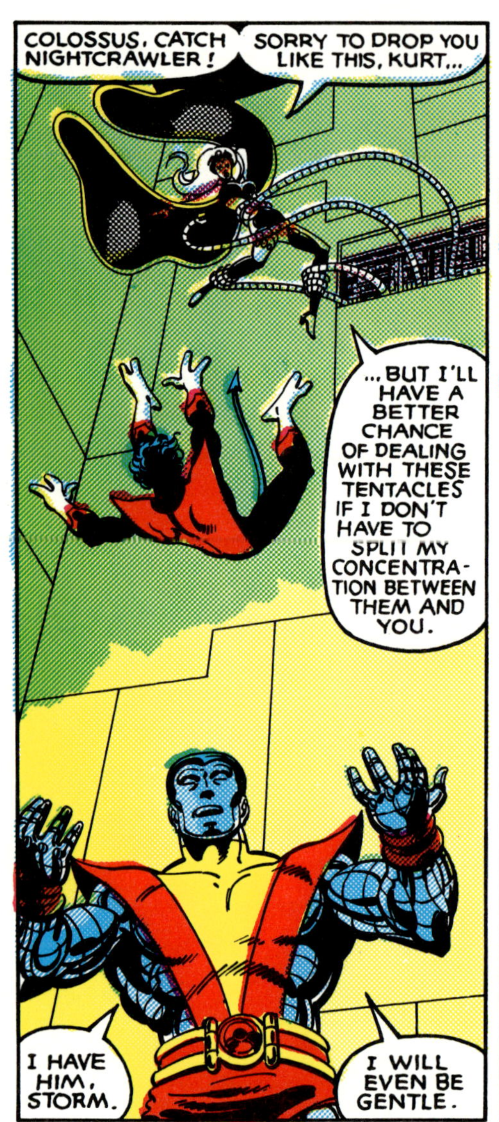
COLOSSUS, CATCH NIGHTCRAWLER!
SORRY TO DROP YOU LIKE THIS, KURT...
...BUT I'LL HAVE A BETTER CHANCE OF DEALING WITH THESE TENTACLES IF I DON'T HAVE TO SPLIT MY CONCENTRA-TION BETWEEN THEM AND YOU.
I HAVE HIM, STORM.
I WILL EVEN BE GENTLE.

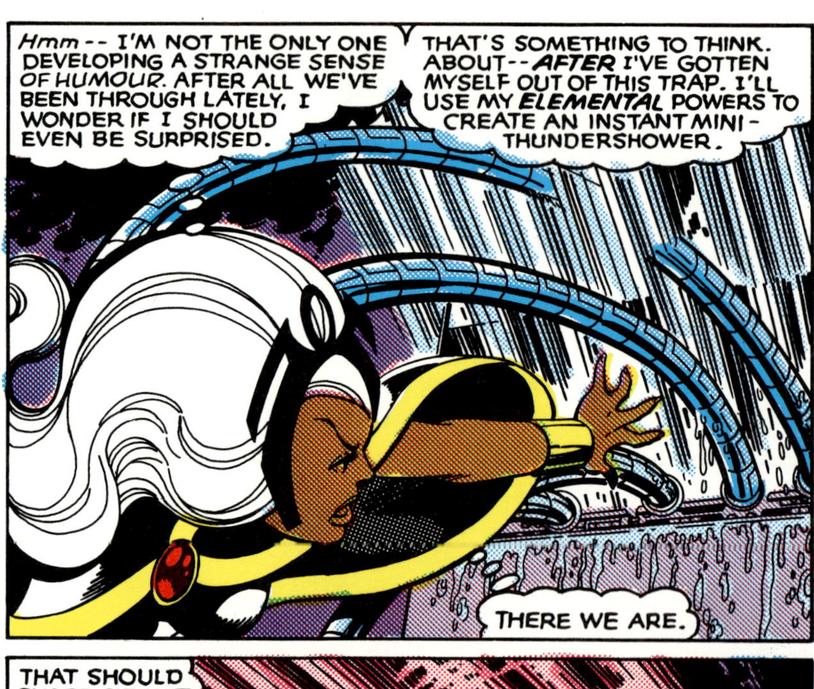
Hmm -- I'M NOT THE ONLY ONE DEVELOPING A STRANGE SENSE OF HUMOUR. AFTER ALL WE'VE BEEN THROUGH LATELY, I WONDER IF I SHOULD EVEN BE SURPRISED.
THAT'S SOMETHING TO THINK ABOUT--AFTER I'VE GOTTEN MYSELF OUT OF THIS TRAP. I'LL USE MY ELEMENTAL POWERS TO CREATE AN INSTANT MINI-THUNDERSHOWER.
THERE WE ARE.

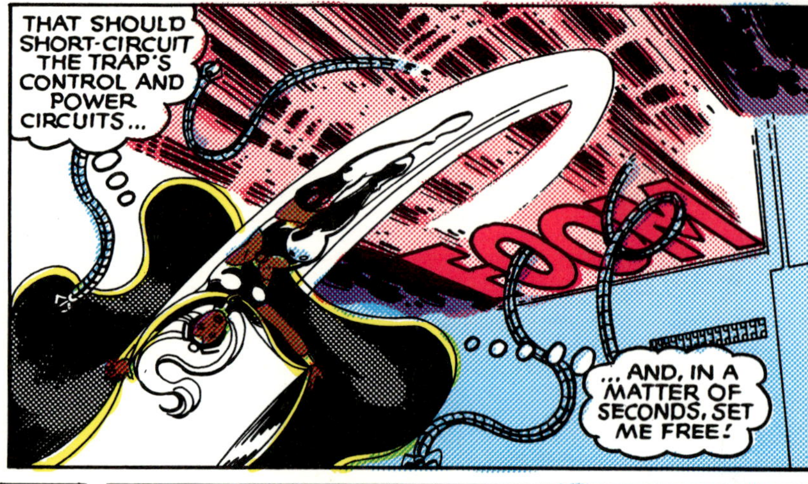
THAT SHOULD SHORT-CIRCUIT THE TRAP'S CONTROL AND POWER CIRCUITS...
...AND, IN A MATTER OF SECONDS, SET ME FREE!

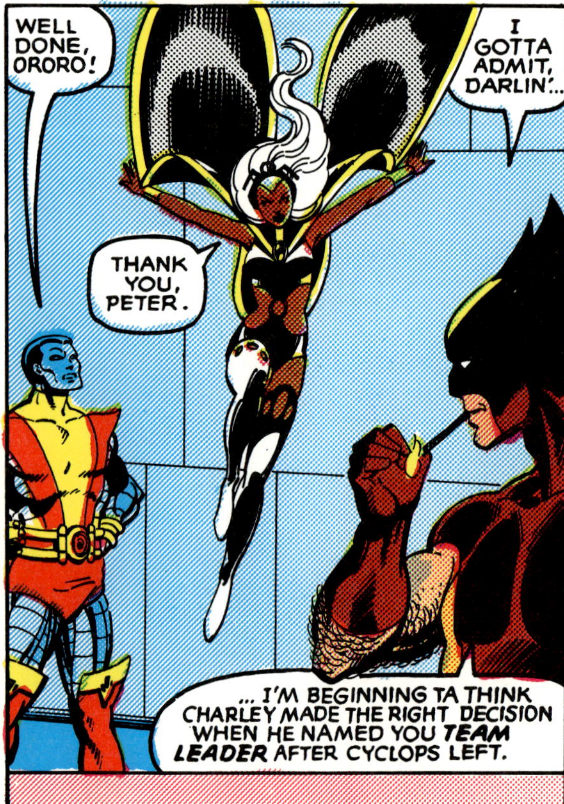
WELL DONE, ORORO!
THANK YOU, PETER.
I GOTTA ADMIT, DARLIN'...
...I'M BEGINNING TA THINK CHARLEY MADE THE RIGHT DECISION WHEN HE NAMED YOU TEAM LEADER AFTER CYCLOPS LEFT.

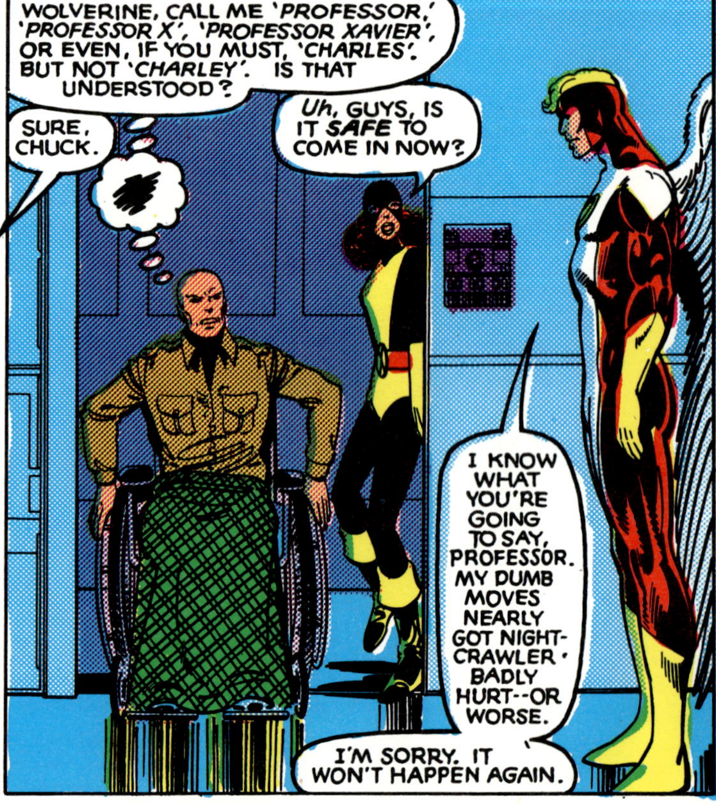
WOLVERINE, CALL ME 'PROFESSOR,' 'PROFESSOR X', 'PROFESSOR XAVIER', OR EVEN, IF YOU MUST, 'CHARLES'. BUT NOT 'CHARLEY'. IS THAT UNDERSTOOD?
SURE, CHUCK.
Uh, GUYS, IS IT SAFE TO COME IN NOW?
I KNOW WHAT YOU'RE GOING TO SAY, PROFESSOR. MY DUMB MOVES NEARLY GOT NIGHT-CRAWLER BADLY HURT--OR WORSE.
I'M SORRY. IT WON'T HAPPEN AGAIN.

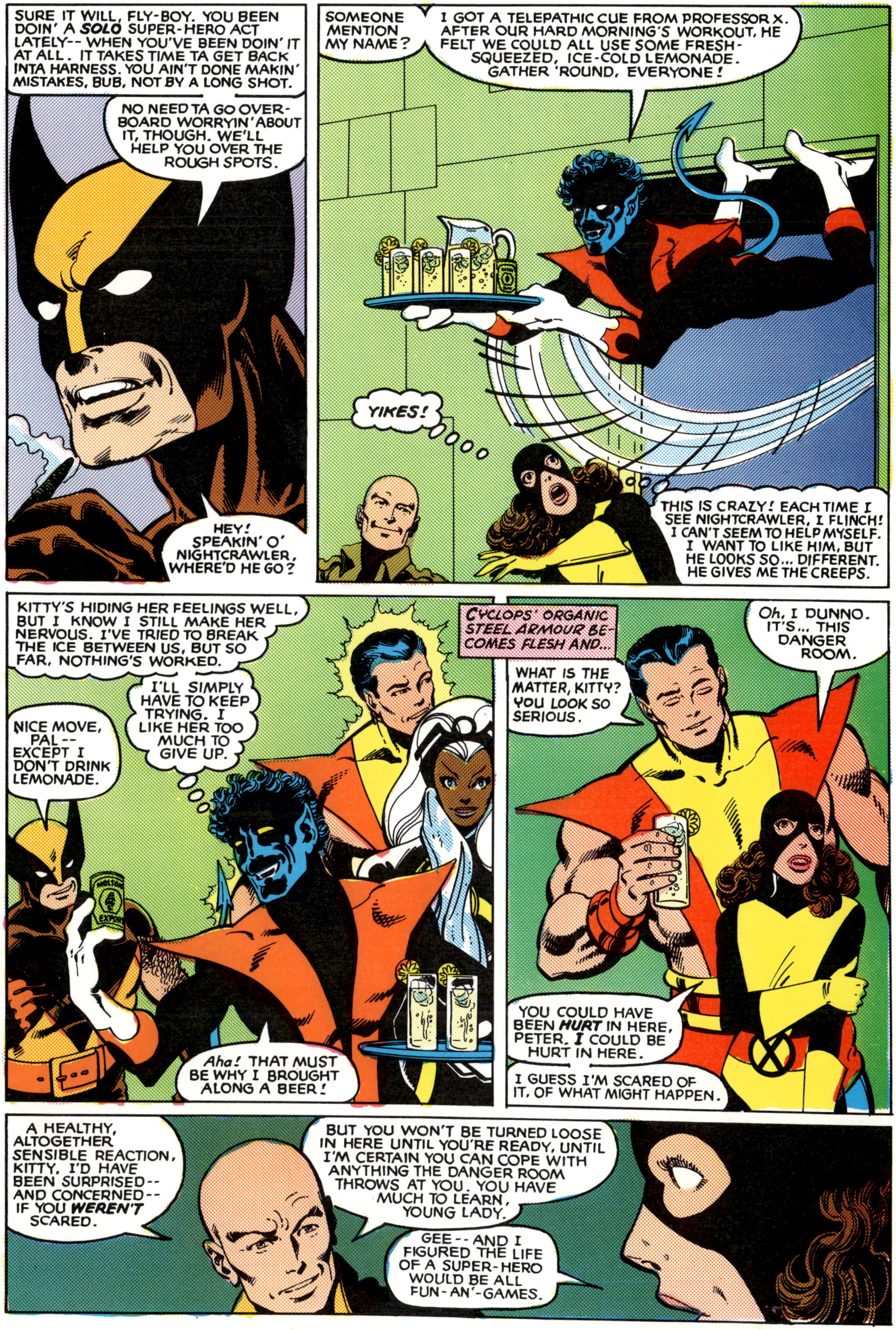

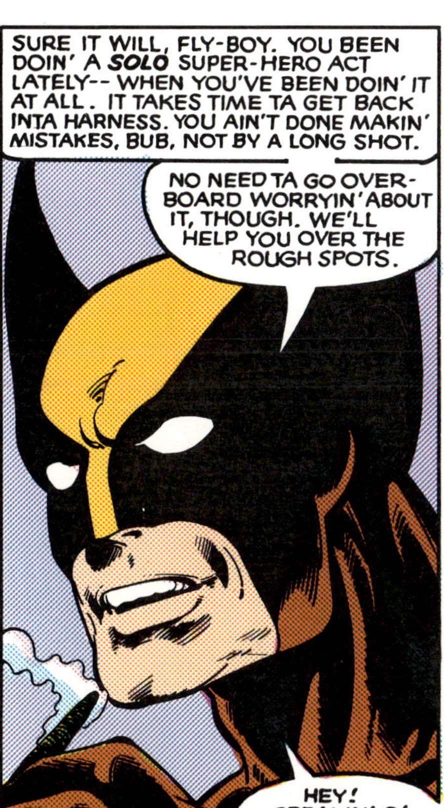
SURE IT WILL, FLY-BOY. YOU BEEN DOIN' A **SOLO** SUPER-HERO ACT LATELY-- WHEN YOU'VE BEEN DOIN' IT AT ALL. IT TAKES TIME TA GET BACK INTA HARNESS. YOU AIN'T DONE MAKIN' MISTAKES, BUB, NOT BY A LONG SHOT.
NO NEED TA GO OVERBOARD WORRYIN' ABOUT IT, THOUGH. WE'LL HELP YOU OVER THE ROUGH SPOTS.
HEY! SPEAKIN' O' NIGHTCRAWLER, WHERE'D HE GO?

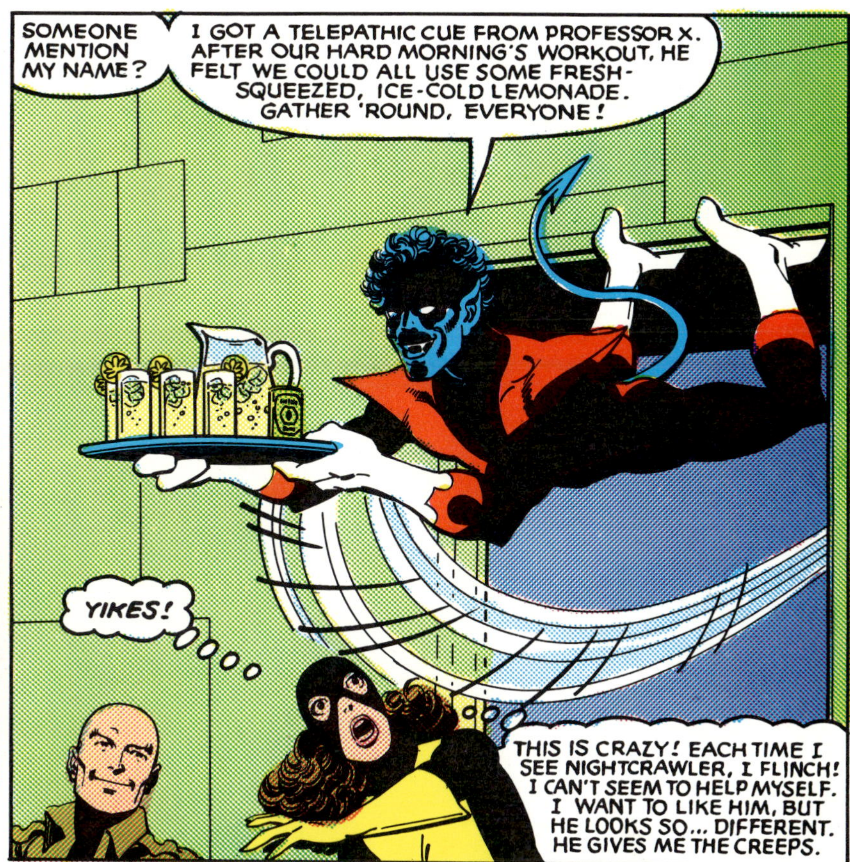
SOMEONE MENTION MY NAME?
I GOT A TELEPATHIC CUE FROM PROFESSOR X. AFTER OUR HARD MORNING'S WORKOUT, HE FELT WE COULD ALL USE SOME FRESH-SQUEEZED, ICE-COLD LEMONADE. GATHER 'ROUND, EVERYONE!
YIKES!
THIS IS CRAZY! EACH TIME I SEE NIGHTCRAWLER, I FLINCH! I CAN'T SEEM TO HELP MYSELF. I WANT TO LIKE HIM, BUT HE LOOKS SO... DIFFERENT. HE GIVES ME THE CREEPS.
KITTY'S HIDING HER FEELINGS WELL, BUT I KNOW I STILL MAKE HER NERVOUS. I'VE TRIED TO BREAK THE ICE BETWEEN US, BUT SO FAR, NOTHING'S WORKED.
I'LL SIMPLY HAVE TO KEEP TRYING. I LIKE HER TOO MUCH TO GIVE UP.
NICE MOVE, PAL-- EXCEPT I DON'T DRINK LEMONADE.
Aha! THAT MUST BE WHY I BROUGHT ALONG A BEER!
CYCLOPS' ORGANIC STEEL ARMOUR BECOMES FLESH AND...
WHAT IS THE MATTER, KITTY? YOU LOOK SO SERIOUS.
Oh, I DUNNO. IT'S... THIS DANGER ROOM.
YOU COULD HAVE BEEN **HURT** IN HERE, PETER. **I** COULD BE HURT IN HERE.
I GUESS I'M SCARED OF IT, OF WHAT MIGHT HAPPEN.
A HEALTHY, ALTOGETHER SENSIBLE REACTION, KITTY. I'D HAVE BEEN SURPRISED-- AND CONCERNED-- IF YOU **WEREN'T** SCARED.
BUT YOU WON'T BE TURNED LOOSE IN HERE UNTIL YOU'RE READY, UNTIL I'M CERTAIN YOU CAN COPE WITH ANYTHING THE DANGER ROOM THROWS AT YOU. YOU HAVE MUCH TO LEARN, YOUNG LADY.
GEE-- AND I FIGURED THE LIFE OF A SUPER-HERO WOULD BE ALL FUN-AN'-GAMES.

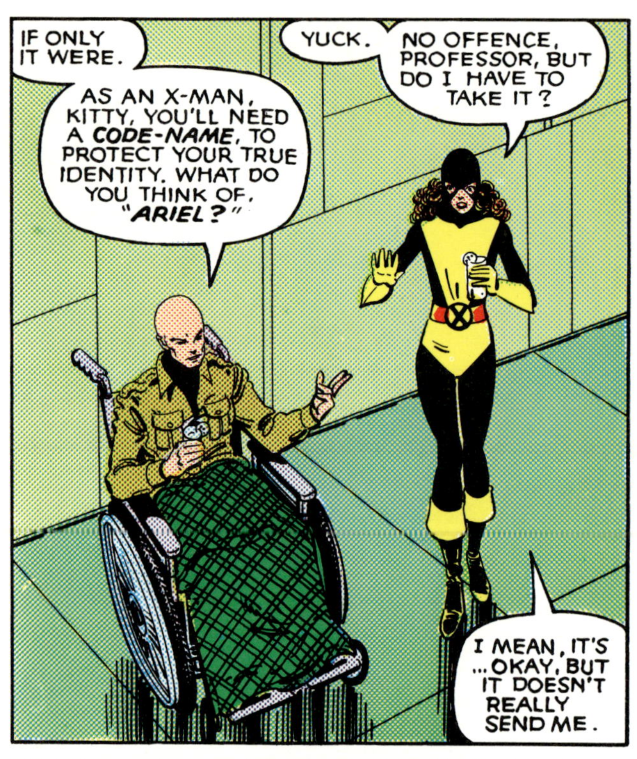
IF ONLY IT WERE.
AS AN X-MAN, KITTY, YOU'LL NEED A CODE-NAME, TO PROTECT YOUR TRUE IDENTITY. WHAT DO YOU THINK OF, "ARIEL?"
YUCK.
NO OFFENCE, PROFESSOR, BUT DO I HAVE TO TAKE IT?
I MEAN, IT'S ...OKAY, BUT IT DOESN'T REALLY SEND ME.

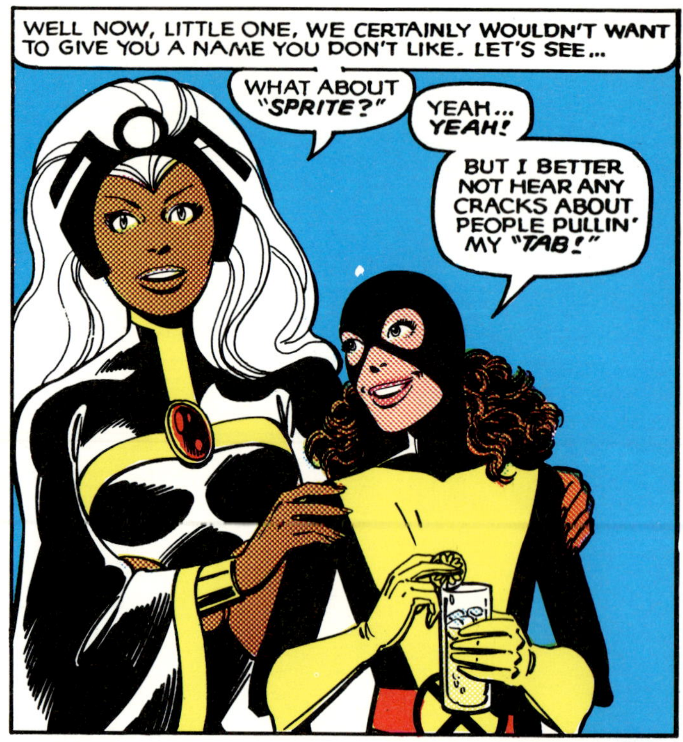
WELL NOW, LITTLE ONE, WE CERTAINLY WOULDN'T WANT TO GIVE YOU A NAME YOU DON'T LIKE. LET'S SEE...
WHAT ABOUT "SPRITE?"
YEAH... YEAH!
BUT I BETTER NOT HEAR ANY CRACKS ABOUT PEOPLE PULLIN' MY "TAB!"

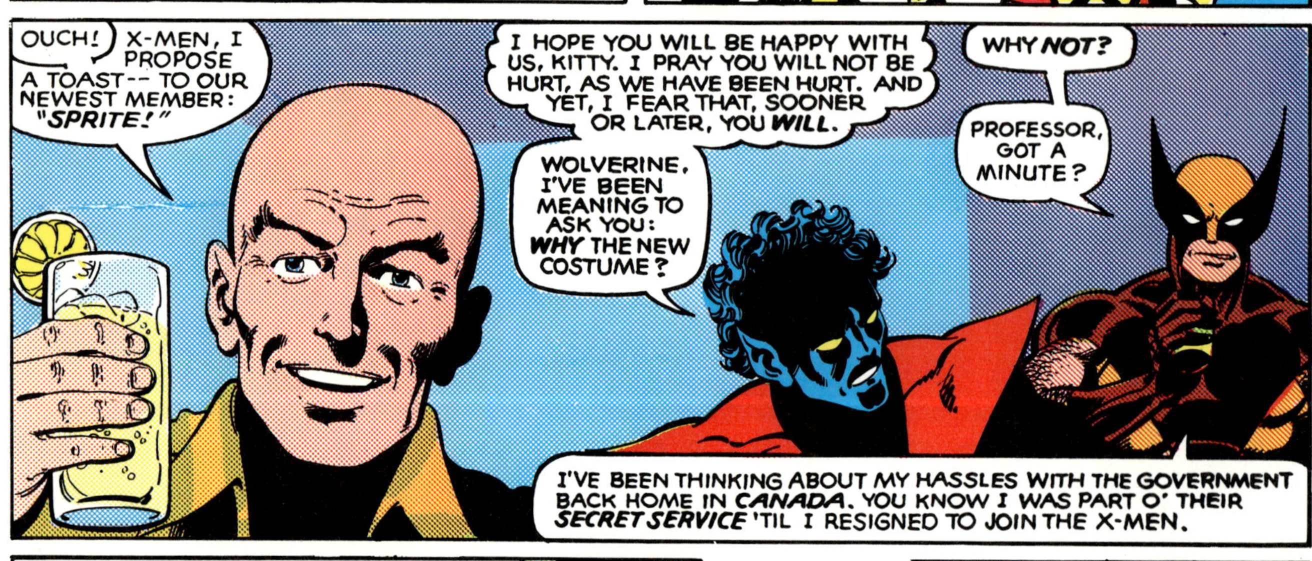
OUCH!
X-MEN, I PROPOSE A TOAST-- TO OUR NEWEST MEMBER: "SPRITE!"
I HOPE YOU WILL BE HAPPY WITH US, KITTY. I PRAY YOU WILL NOT BE HURT, AS WE HAVE BEEN HURT. AND YET, I FEAR THAT, SOONER OR LATER, YOU WILL.
WOLVERINE, I'VE BEEN MEANING TO ASK YOU: WHY THE NEW COSTUME?
WHY NOT?
PROFESSOR, GOT A MINUTE?
I'VE BEEN THINKING ABOUT MY HASSLES WITH THE GOVERNMENT BACK HOME IN CANADA. YOU KNOW I WAS PART O' THEIR SECRET SERVICE 'TIL I RESIGNED TO JOIN THE X-MEN.

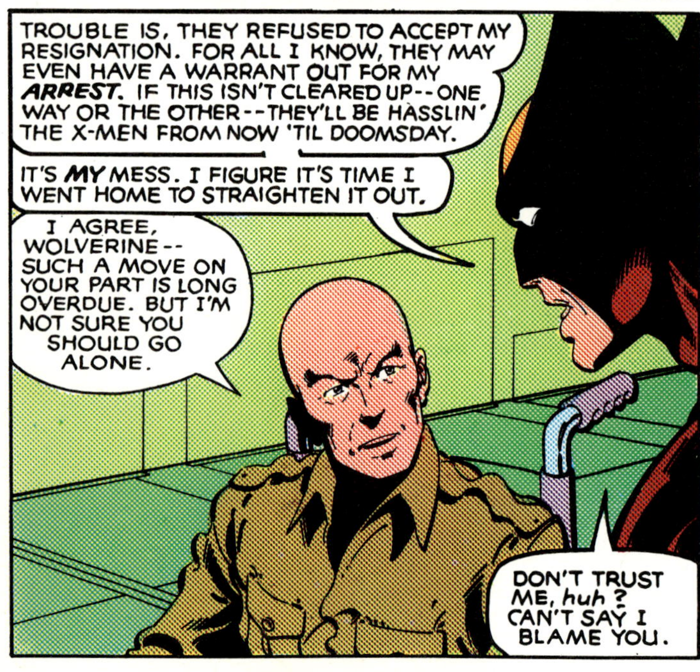
TROUBLE IS, THEY REFUSED TO ACCEPT MY RESIGNATION. FOR ALL I KNOW, THEY MAY EVEN HAVE A WARRANT OUT FOR MY ARREST. IF THIS ISN'T CLEARED UP--ONE WAY OR THE OTHER--THEY'LL BE HASSLIN' THE X-MEN FROM NOW 'TIL DOOMSDAY.
IT'S MY MESS. I FIGURE IT'S TIME I WENT HOME TO STRAIGHTEN IT OUT.
I AGREE, WOLVERINE-- SUCH A MOVE ON YOUR PART IS LONG OVERDUE. BUT I'M NOT SURE YOU SHOULD GO ALONE.
DON'T TRUST ME, huh? CAN'T SAY I BLAME YOU.

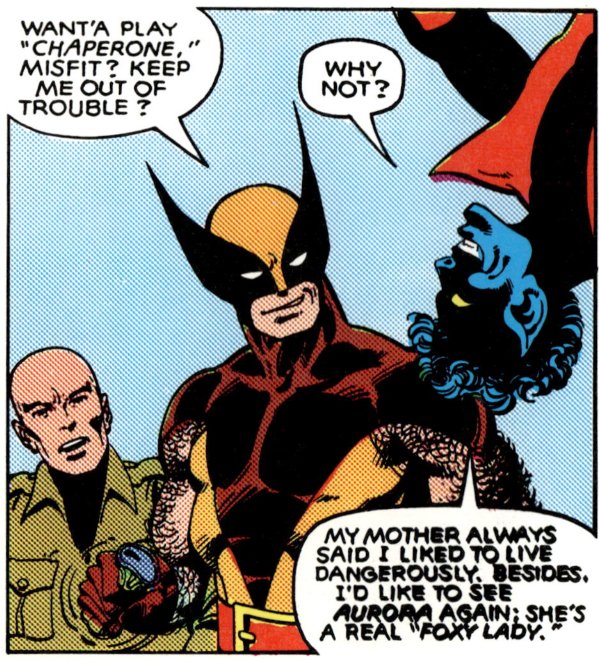
WANT'A PLAY "CHAPERONE," MISFIT? KEEP ME OUT OF TROUBLE?
WHY NOT?
MY MOTHER ALWAYS SAID I LIKED TO LIVE DANGEROUSLY. BESIDES, I'D LIKE TO SEE AURORA AGAIN; SHE'S A REAL "FOXY LADY."

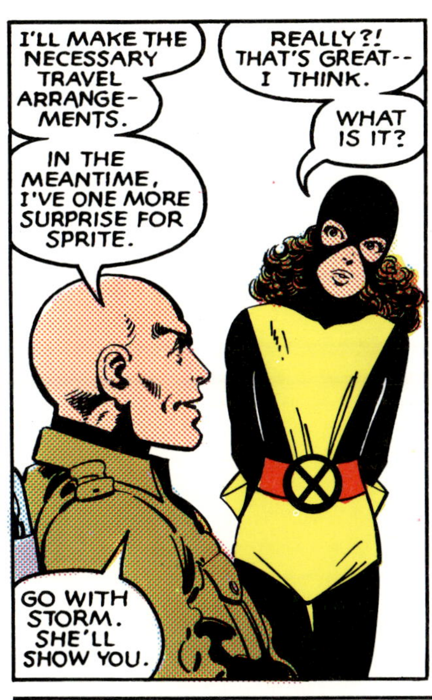
I'LL MAKE THE NECESSARY TRAVEL ARRANGE-MENTS.
REALLY?! THAT'S GREAT-- I THINK.
IN THE MEANTIME, I'VE ONE MORE SURPRISE FOR SPRITE.
WHAT IS IT?
GO WITH STORM. SHE'LL SHOW YOU.

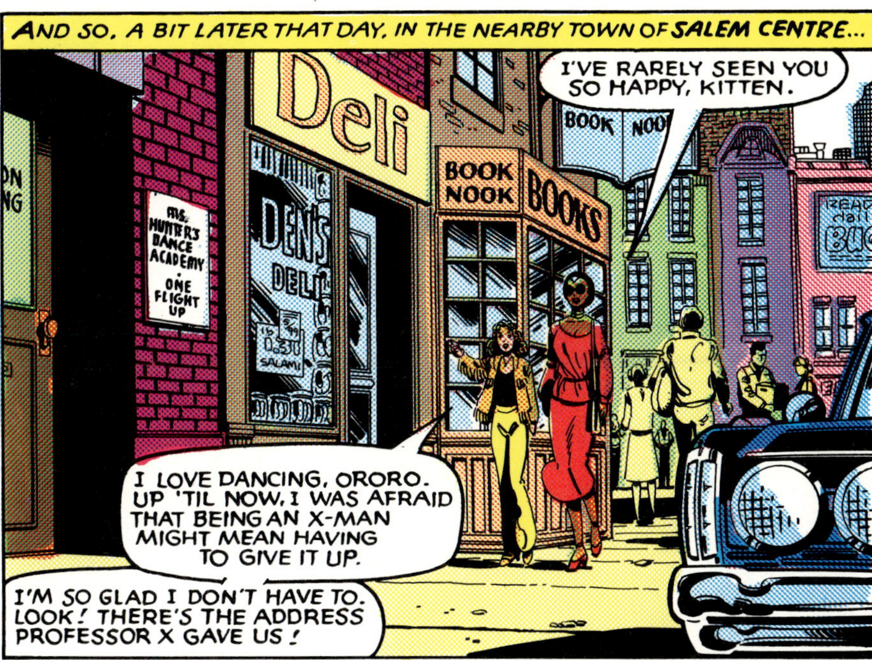
AND SO, A BIT LATER THAT DAY, IN THE NEARBY TOWN OF SALEM CENTRE...
I'VE RARELY SEEN YOU SO HAPPY, KITTEN.
Deli
BOOK NOOK
BOOKS
MS. HUNTER'S DANCE ACADEMY • ONE FLIGHT UP
DEN'S DELI
I LOVE DANCING, ORORO. UP 'TIL NOW, I WAS AFRAID THAT BEING AN X-MAN MIGHT MEAN HAVING TO GIVE IT UP.
I'M SO GLAD I DON'T HAVE TO. LOOK! THERE'S THE ADDRESS PROFESSOR X GAVE US!

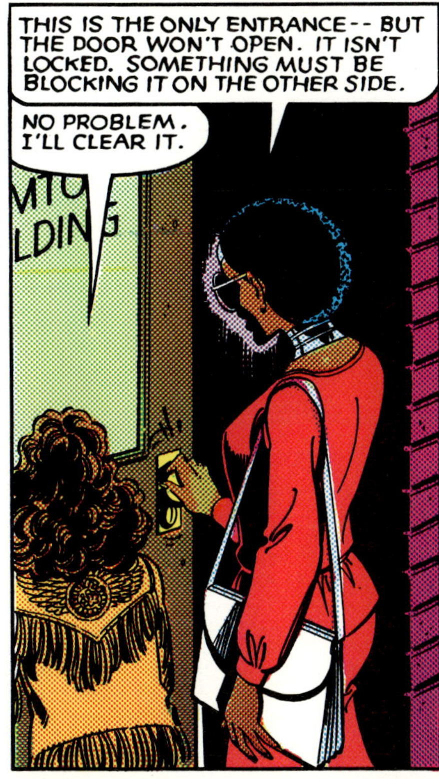
THIS IS THE ONLY ENTRANCE-- BUT THE DOOR WON'T OPEN. IT ISN'T LOCKED. SOMETHING MUST BE BLOCKING IT ON THE OTHER SIDE.
NO PROBLEM. I'LL CLEAR IT.

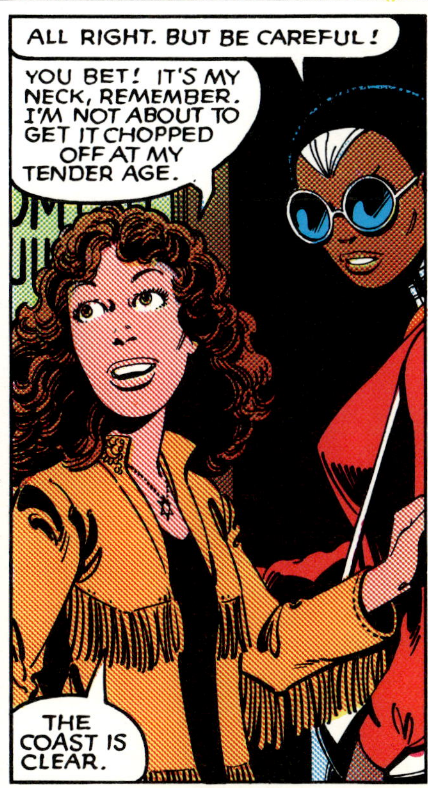
ALL RIGHT. BUT BE CAREFUL!
YOU BET! IT'S MY NECK, REMEMBER. I'M NOT ABOUT TO GET IT CHOPPED OFF AT MY TENDER AGE.
THE COAST IS CLEAR.

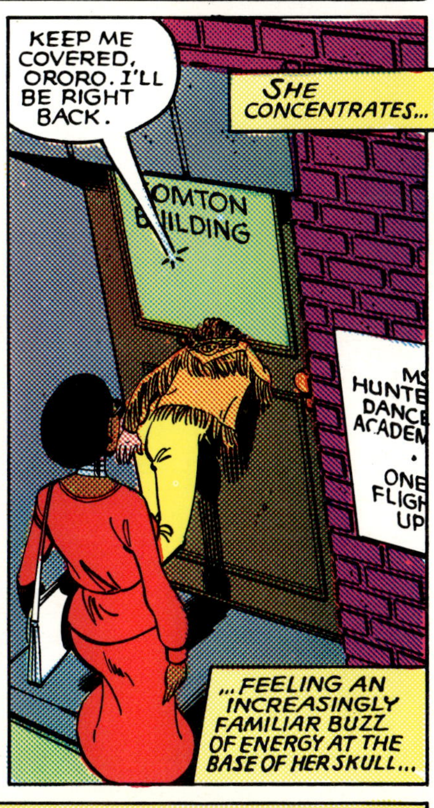
KEEP ME COVERED, ORORO. I'LL BE RIGHT BACK.
SHE CONCENTRATES...
COMTON BUILDING
...FEELING AN INCREASINGLY FAMILIAR BUZZ OF ENERGY AT THE BASE OF HER SKULL...

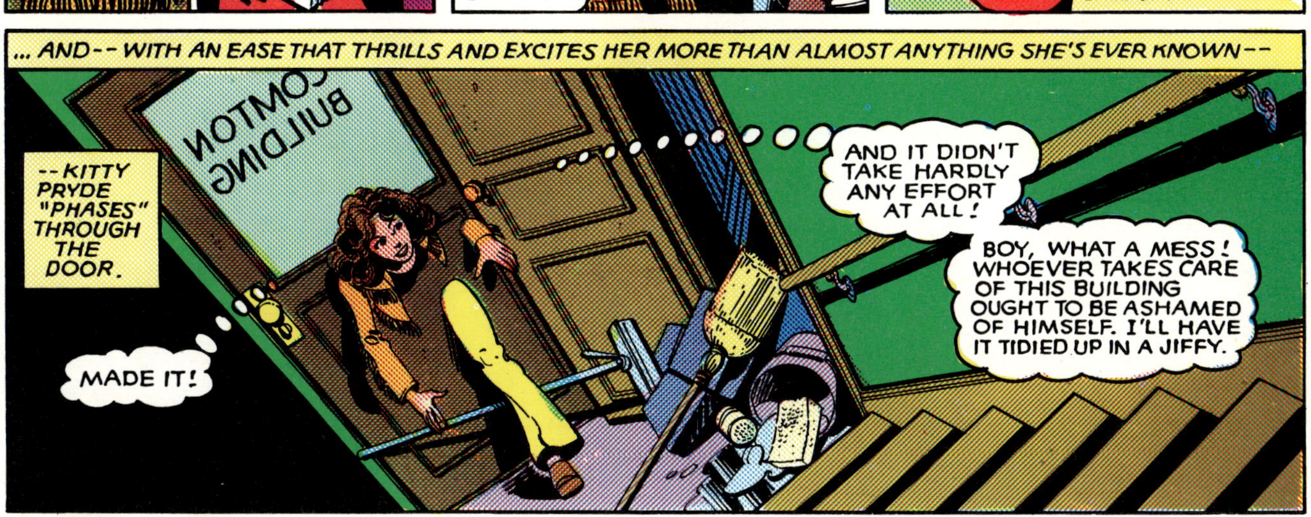
... AND-- WITH AN EASE THAT THRILLS AND EXCITES HER MORE THAN ALMOST ANYTHING SHE'S EVER KNOWN--
--KITTY PRYDE "PHASES" THROUGH THE DOOR.
AND IT DIDN'T TAKE HARDLY ANY EFFORT AT ALL!
BOY, WHAT A MESS! WHOEVER TAKES CARE OF THIS BUILDING OUGHT TO BE ASHAMED OF HIMSELF. I'LL HAVE IT TIDIED UP IN A JIFFY.
MADE IT!

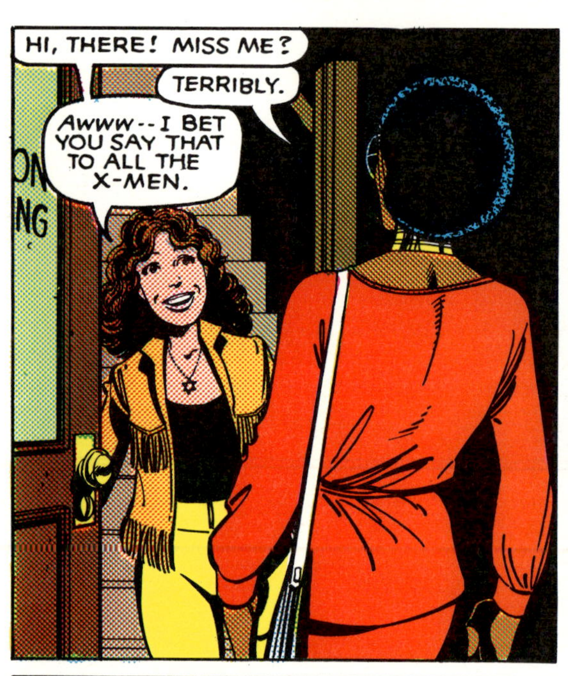
HI, THERE! MISS ME?
TERRIBLY.
AWWW--I BET YOU SAY THAT TO ALL THE X-MEN.

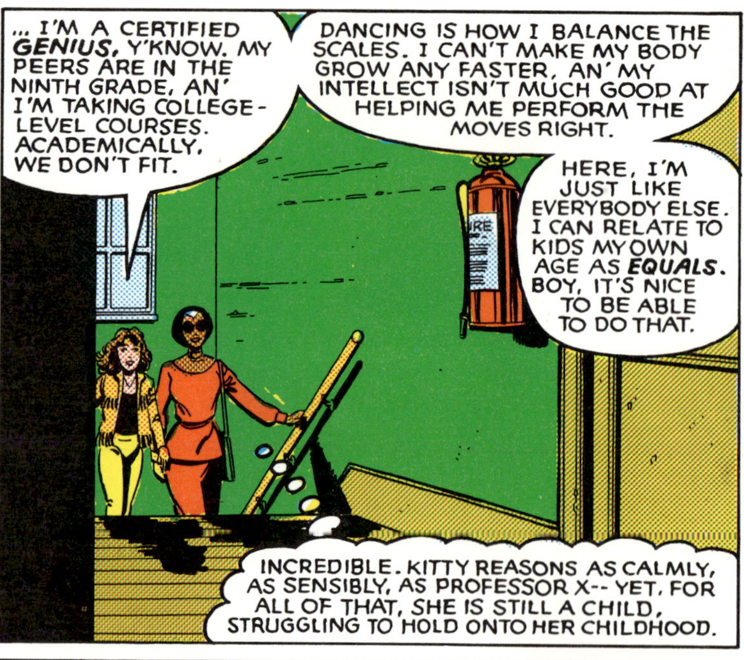
...I'M A CERTIFIED **GENIUS**, Y'KNOW. MY PEERS ARE IN THE NINTH GRADE, AN' I'M TAKING COLLEGE-LEVEL COURSES. ACADEMICALLY, WE DON'T FIT.
DANCING IS HOW I BALANCE THE SCALES. I CAN'T MAKE MY BODY GROW ANY FASTER, AN' MY INTELLECT ISN'T MUCH GOOD AT HELPING ME PERFORM THE MOVES RIGHT.
HERE, I'M JUST LIKE EVERYBODY ELSE. I CAN RELATE TO KIDS MY OWN AGE AS **EQUALS**. BOY, IT'S NICE TO BE ABLE TO DO THAT.
INCREDIBLE. KITTY REASONS AS CALMLY, AS SENSIBLY, AS PROFESSOR X-- YET, FOR ALL OF THAT, SHE IS STILL A CHILD, STRUGGLING TO HOLD ONTO HER CHILDHOOD.

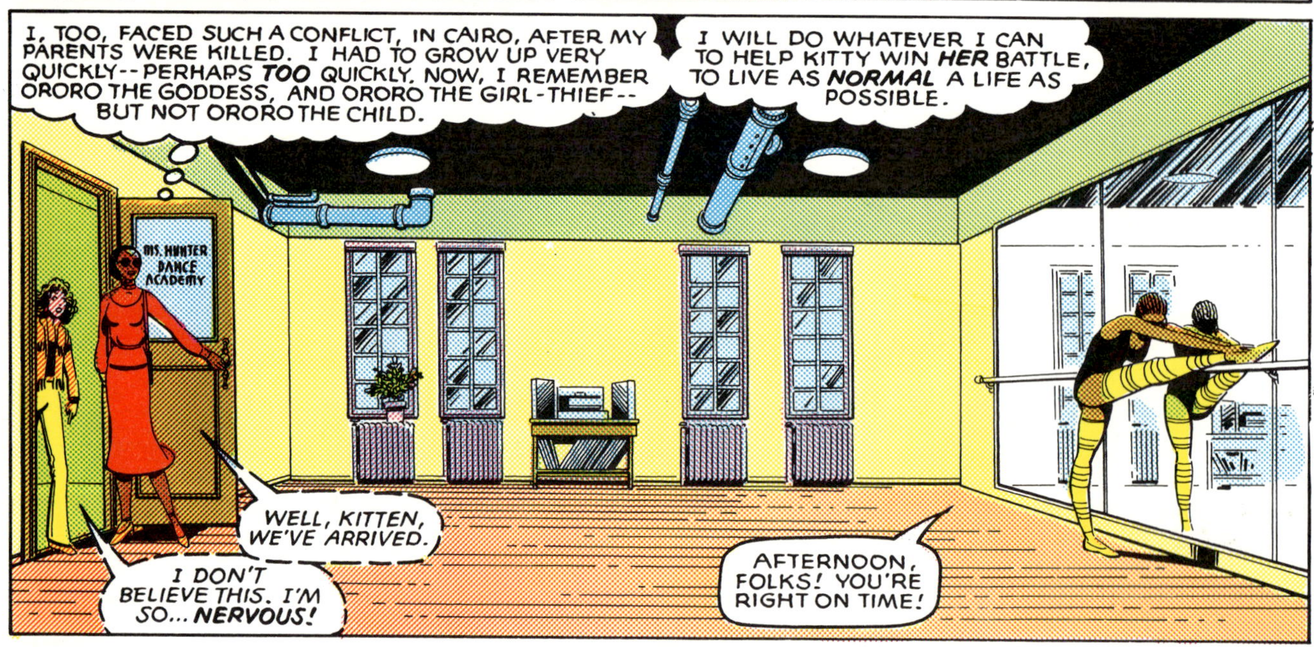
I, TOO, FACED SUCH A CONFLICT, IN CAIRO, AFTER MY PARENTS WERE KILLED. I HAD TO GROW UP VERY QUICKLY--PERHAPS **TOO** QUICKLY. NOW, I REMEMBER ORORO THE GODDESS, AND ORORO THE GIRL-THIEF-- BUT NOT ORORO THE CHILD.
I WILL DO WHATEVER I CAN TO HELP KITTY WIN **HER** BATTLE, TO LIVE AS **NORMAL** A LIFE AS POSSIBLE.
MS. HUNTER DANCE ACADEMY
WELL, KITTEN, WE'VE ARRIVED.
I DON'T BELIEVE THIS. I'M SO... **NERVOUS!**
AFTERNOON, FOLKS! YOU'RE RIGHT ON TIME!

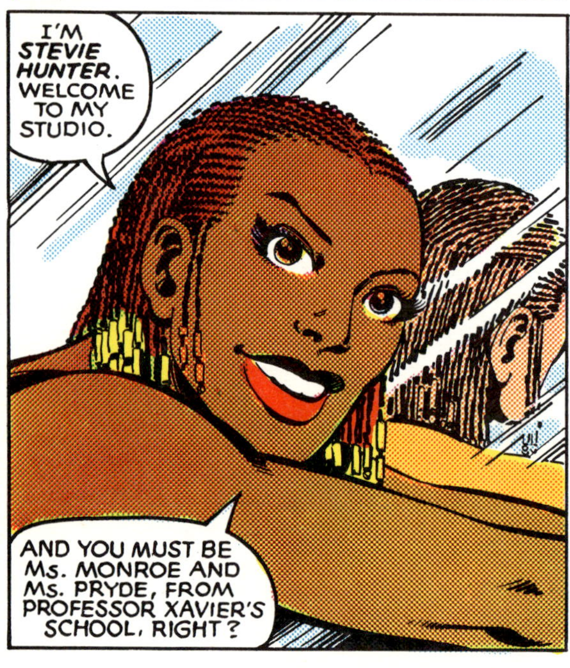
I'M **STEVIE HUNTER**. WELCOME TO MY STUDIO.
AND YOU MUST BE Ms. MONROE AND Ms. PRYDE, FROM PROFESSOR XAVIER'S SCHOOL, RIGHT?

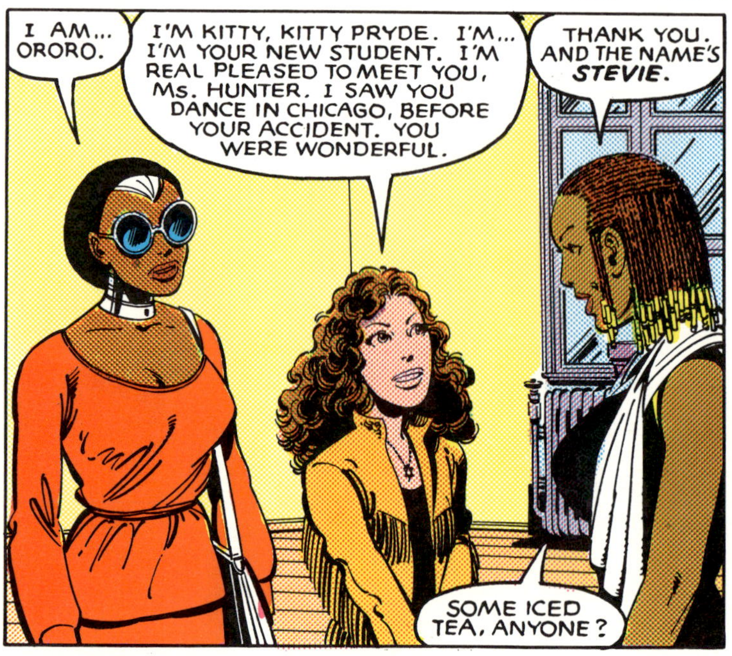
I AM... ORORO.
I'M KITTY, KITTY PRYDE. I'M... I'M YOUR NEW STUDENT. I'M REAL PLEASED TO MEET YOU, Ms. HUNTER. I SAW YOU DANCE IN CHICAGO, BEFORE YOUR ACCIDENT. YOU WERE WONDERFUL.
THANK YOU. AND THE NAME'S **STEVIE**.
SOME ICED TEA, ANYONE?

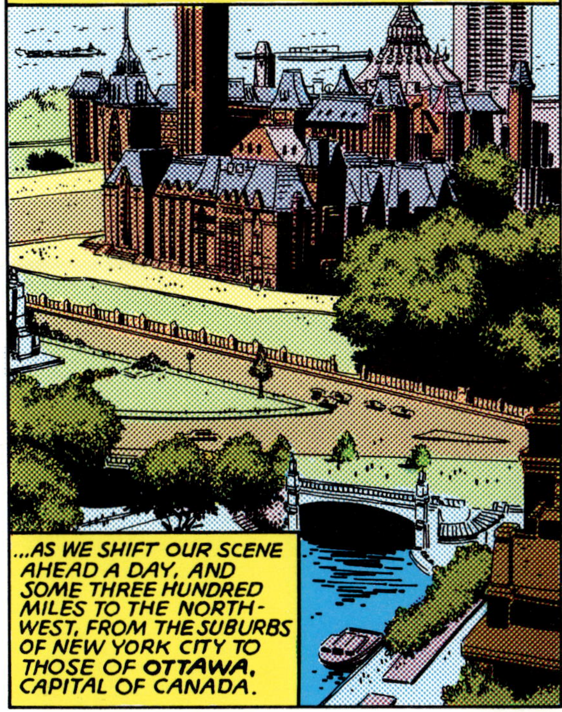
WITH THAT, AN EFFERVESCENT, ENTHUSIASTIC KITTY, AND SURPRISINGLY, A SLIGHTLY WARY STORM, GET TO KNOW KITTY'S NEW DANCE TEACHER OVER A POT OF ICED HERBAL TEA...
...AS WE SHIFT OUR SCENE AHEAD A DAY, AND SOME THREE HUNDRED MILES TO THE NORTH-WEST, FROM THE SUBURBS OF NEW YORK CITY TO THOSE OF OTTAWA, CAPITAL OF CANADA.

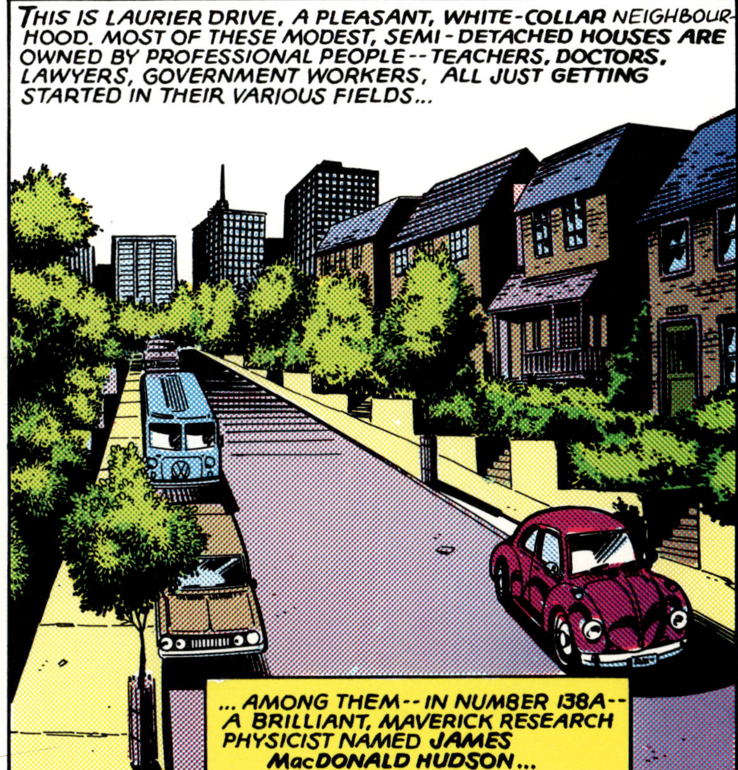
THIS IS LAURIER DRIVE, A PLEASANT, WHITE-COLLAR NEIGHBOURHOOD. MOST OF THESE MODEST, SEMI-DETACHED HOUSES ARE OWNED BY PROFESSIONAL PEOPLE--TEACHERS, DOCTORS, LAWYERS, GOVERNMENT WORKERS, ALL JUST GETTING STARTED IN THEIR VARIOUS FIELDS...
...AMONG THEM--IN NUMBER 138A--A BRILLIANT, MAVERICK RESEARCH PHYSICIST NAMED JAMES MacDONALD HUDSON...

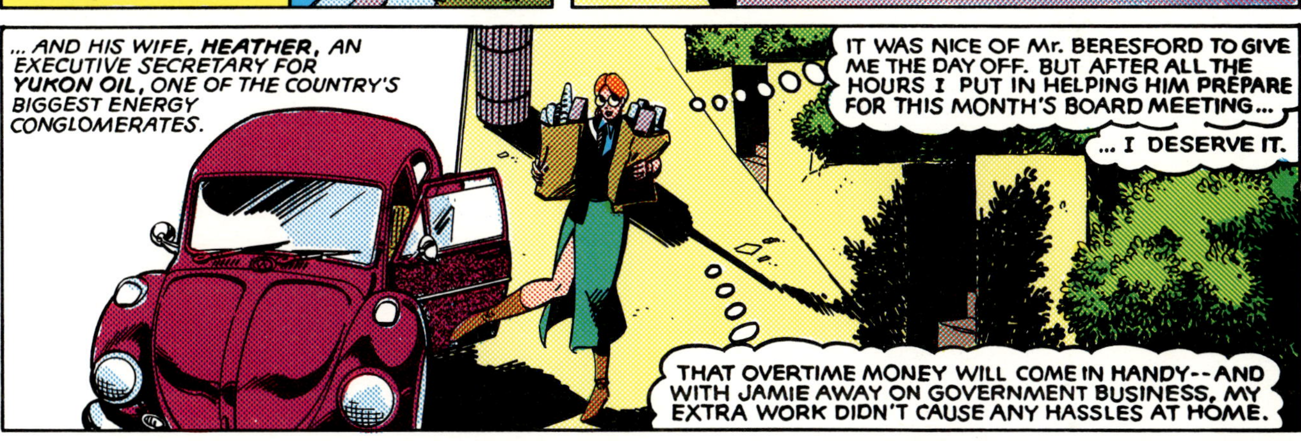
...AND HIS WIFE, HEATHER, AN EXECUTIVE SECRETARY FOR YUKON OIL, ONE OF THE COUNTRY'S BIGGEST ENERGY CONGLOMERATES.
IT WAS NICE OF Mr. BERESFORD TO GIVE ME THE DAY OFF. BUT AFTER ALL THE HOURS I PUT IN HELPING HIM PREPARE FOR THIS MONTH'S BOARD MEETING...
...I DESERVE IT.
THAT OVERTIME MONEY WILL COME IN HANDY--AND WITH JAMIE AWAY ON GOVERNMENT BUSINESS, MY EXTRA WORK DIDN'T CAUSE ANY HASSLES AT HOME.

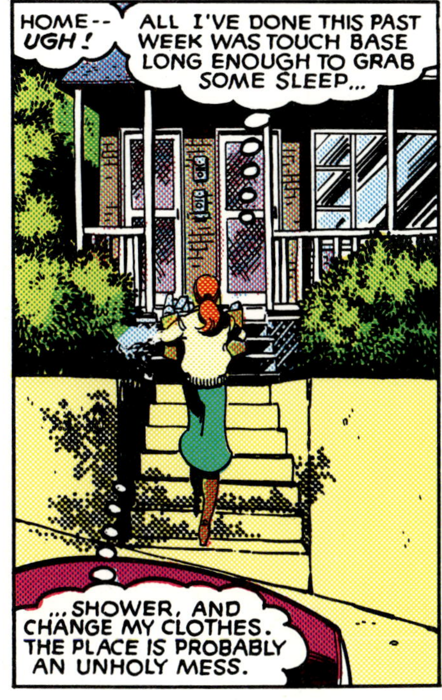
HOME--UGH!
ALL I'VE DONE THIS PAST WEEK WAS TOUCH BASE LONG ENOUGH TO GRAB SOME SLEEP...
...SHOWER, AND CHANGE MY CLOTHES. THE PLACE IS PROBABLY AN UNHOLY MESS.

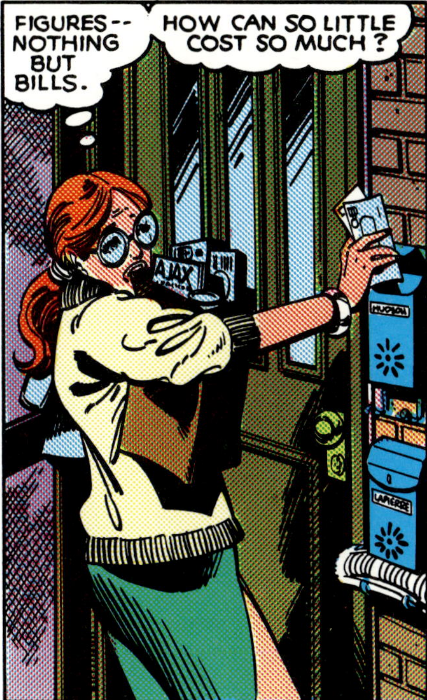
FIGURES--NOTHING BUT BILLS.
HOW CAN SO LITTLE COST SO MUCH?

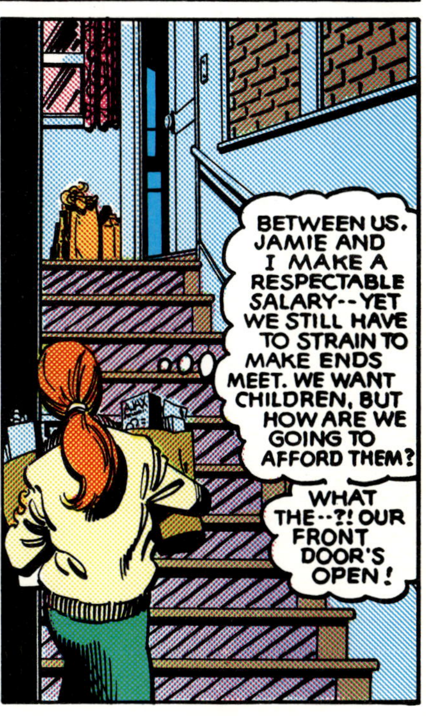
BETWEEN US, JAMIE AND I MAKE A RESPECTABLE SALARY--YET WE STILL HAVE TO STRAIN TO MAKE ENDS MEET. WE WANT CHILDREN, BUT HOW ARE WE GOING TO AFFORD THEM?
WHAT THE--?! OUR FRONT DOOR'S OPEN!

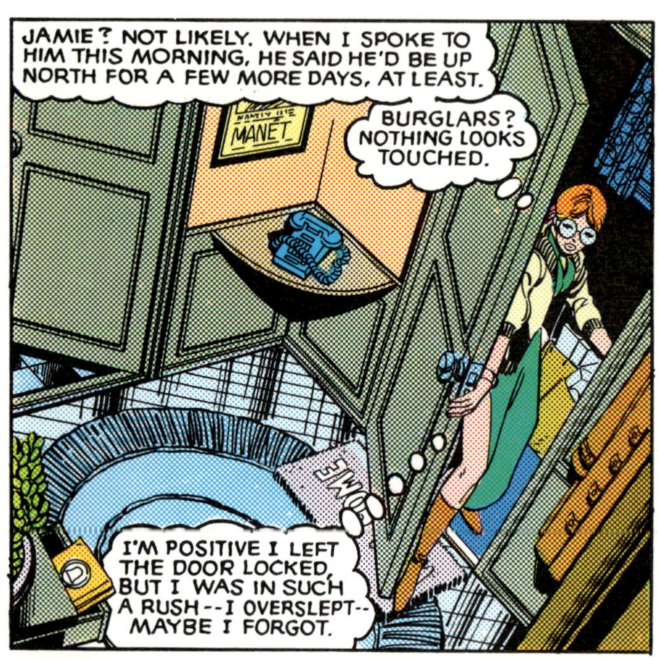
JAMIE? NOT LIKELY. WHEN I SPOKE TO HIM THIS MORNING, HE SAID HE'D BE UP NORTH FOR A FEW MORE DAYS, AT LEAST.
BURGLARS? NOTHING LOOKS TOUCHED.
MANET
I'M POSITIVE I LEFT THE DOOR LOCKED, BUT I WAS IN SUCH A RUSH--I OVERSLEPT--MAYBE I FORGOT.

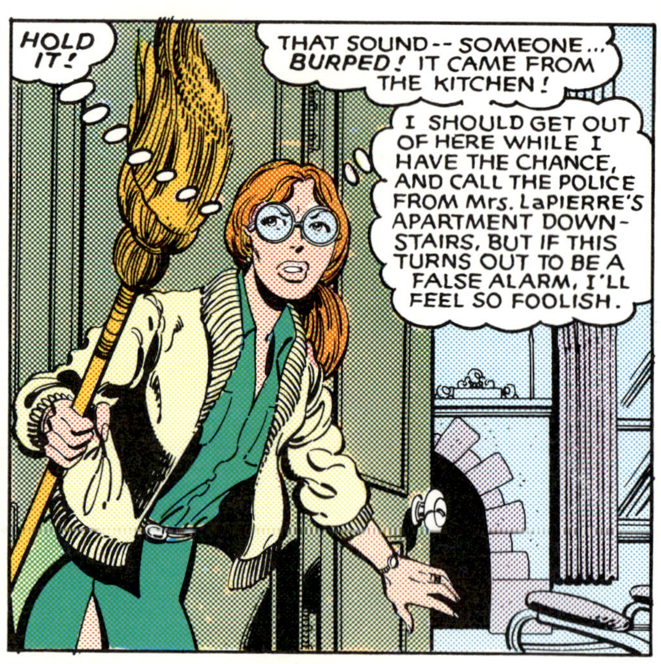
HOLD IT!
THAT SOUND--SOMEONE... BURPED! IT CAME FROM THE KITCHEN!
I SHOULD GET OUT OF HERE WHILE I HAVE THE CHANCE, AND CALL THE POLICE FROM Mrs. LaPIERRE'S APARTMENT DOWNSTAIRS. BUT IF THIS TURNS OUT TO BE A FALSE ALARM, I'LL FEEL SO FOOLISH.

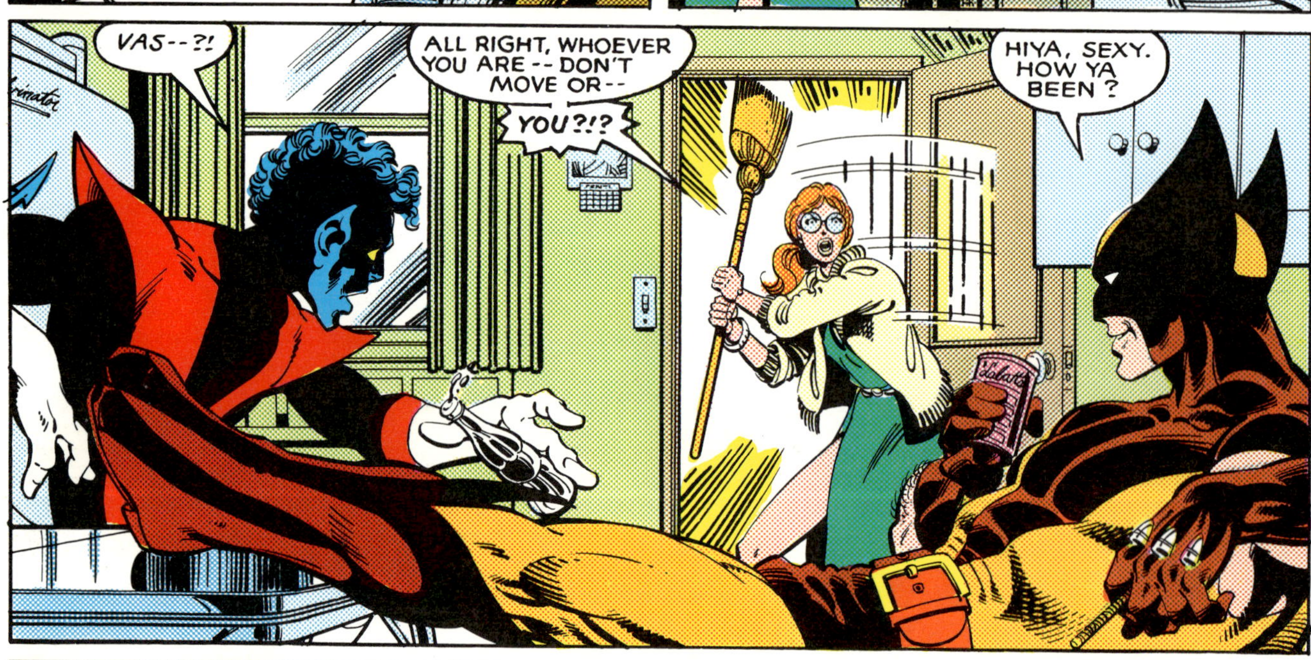
VAS--?!
ALL RIGHT, WHOEVER YOU ARE--DON'T MOVE OR--
YOU?!?
HIYA, SEXY. HOW YA BEEN?

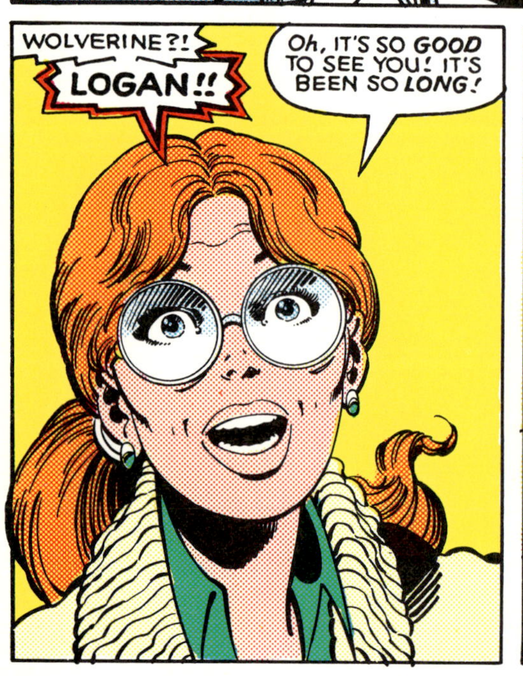
WOLVERINE?!
LOGAN!!
Oh, IT'S SO GOOD TO SEE YOU! IT'S BEEN SO LONG!

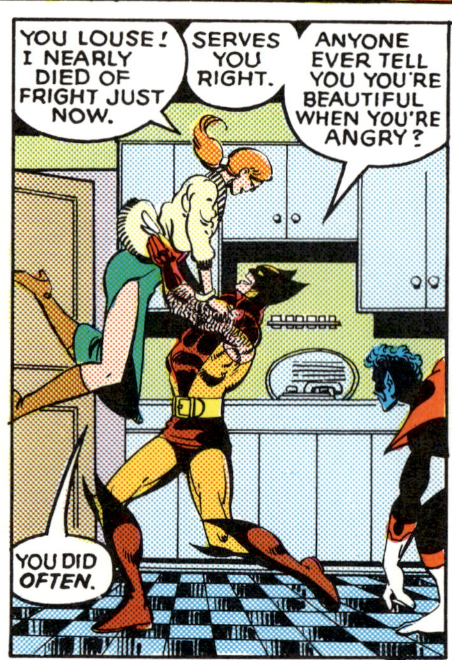
YOU LOUSE! I NEARLY DIED OF FRIGHT JUST NOW.
SERVES YOU RIGHT.
ANYONE EVER TELL YOU YOU'RE BEAUTIFUL WHEN YOU'RE ANGRY?
YOU DID OFTEN.

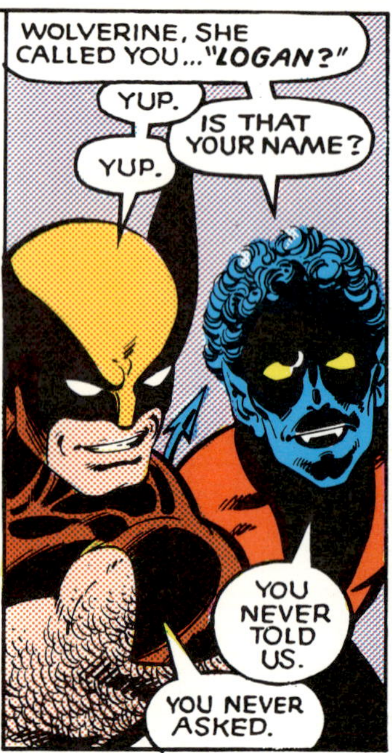
WOLVERINE, SHE CALLED YOU..."LOGAN?"
YUP.
IS THAT YOUR NAME?
YUP.
YOU NEVER TOLD US.
YOU NEVER ASKED.

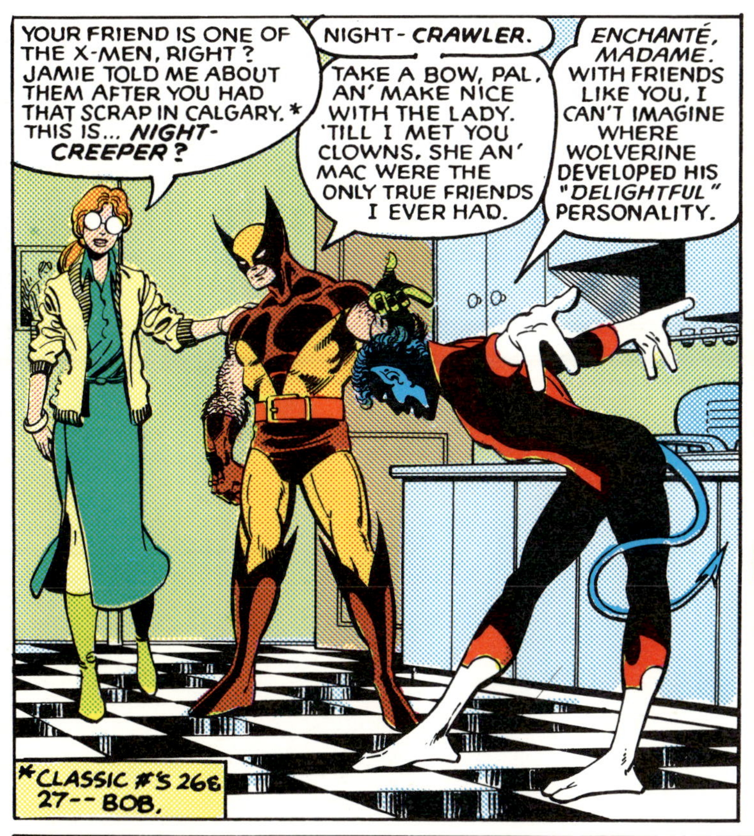
YOUR FRIEND IS ONE OF THE X-MEN, RIGHT? JAMIE TOLD ME ABOUT THEM AFTER YOU HAD THAT SCRAP IN CALGARY.* THIS IS... NIGHT-CREEPER?
NIGHT-CRAWLER.
TAKE A BOW, PAL, AN' MAKE NICE WITH THE LADY. 'TILL I MET YOU CLOWNS, SHE AN' MAC WERE THE ONLY TRUE FRIENDS I EVER HAD.
ENCHANTÉ, MADAME. WITH FRIENDS LIKE YOU, I CAN'T IMAGINE WHERE WOLVERINE DEVELOPED HIS "DELIGHTFUL" PERSONALITY.
*CLASSIC #'S 26 & 27-- BOB.

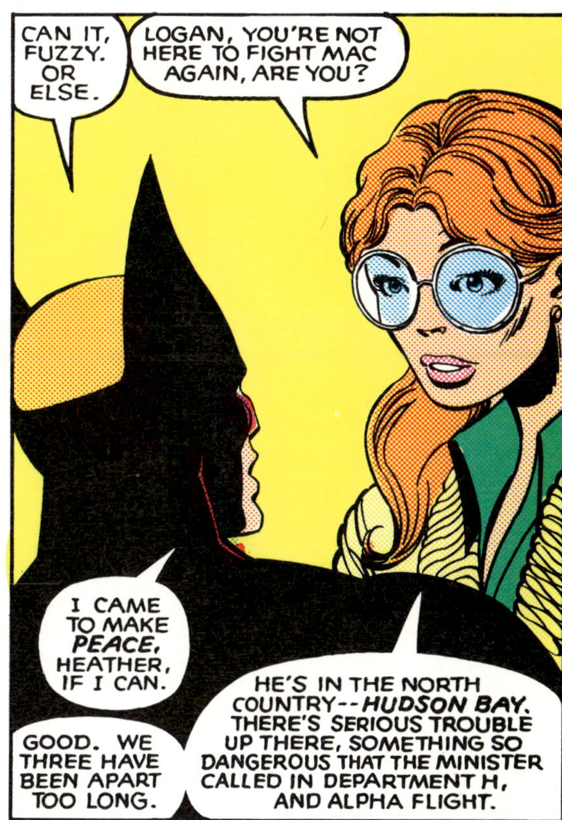
CAN IT, FUZZY. OR ELSE.
LOGAN, YOU'RE NOT HERE TO FIGHT MAC AGAIN, ARE YOU?
I CAME TO MAKE PEACE, HEATHER, IF I CAN.
HE'S IN THE NORTH COUNTRY--HUDSON BAY. THERE'S SERIOUS TROUBLE UP THERE, SOMETHING SO DANGEROUS THAT THE MINISTER CALLED IN DEPARTMENT H, AND ALPHA FLIGHT.
GOOD. WE THREE HAVE BEEN APART TOO LONG.

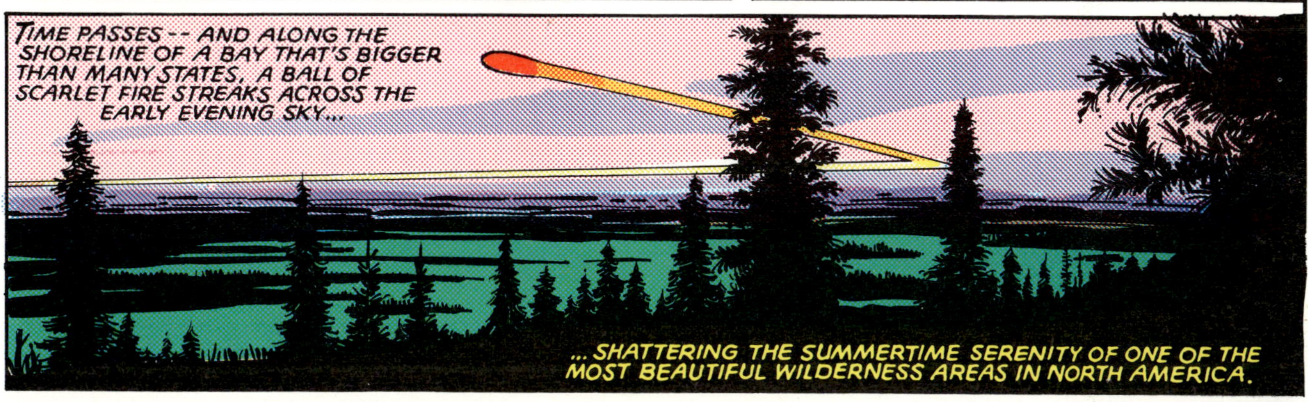
TIME PASSES -- AND ALONG THE SHORELINE OF A BAY THAT'S BIGGER THAN MANY STATES, A BALL OF SCARLET FIRE STREAKS ACROSS THE EARLY EVENING SKY...
...SHATTERING THE SUMMERTIME SERENITY OF ONE OF THE MOST BEAUTIFUL WILDERNESS AREAS IN NORTH AMERICA.

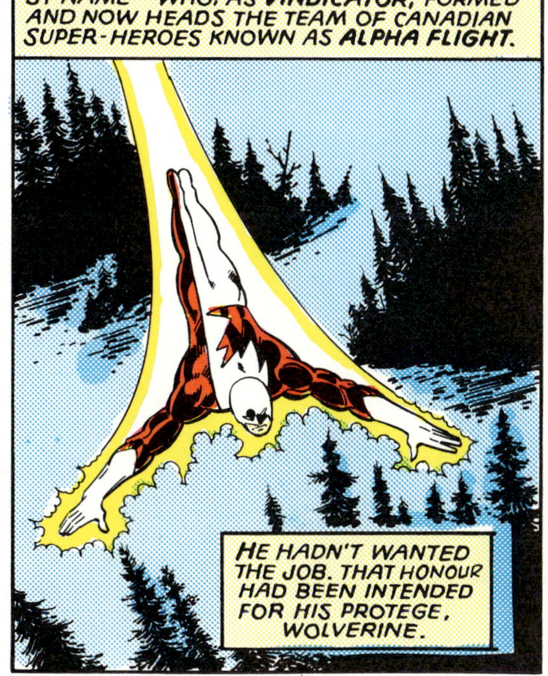
IT IS A MAN -- JAMES MacDONALD HUDSON, BY NAME -- WHO, AS VINDICATOR, FORMED AND NOW HEADS THE TEAM OF CANADIAN SUPER-HEROES KNOWN AS ALPHA FLIGHT.
HE HADN'T WANTED THE JOB. THAT HONOUR HAD BEEN INTENDED FOR HIS PROTEGE, WOLVERINE.

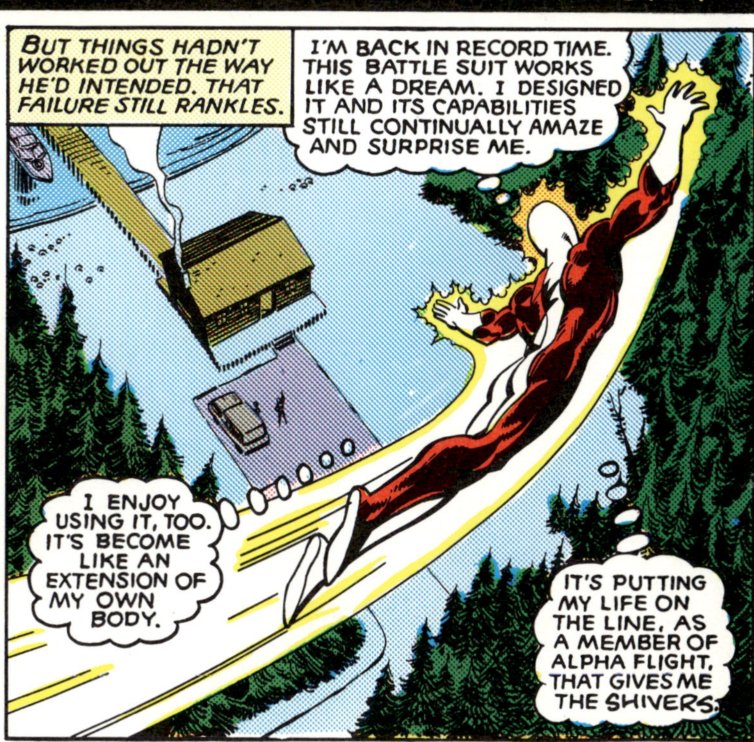
BUT THINGS HADN'T WORKED OUT THE WAY HE'D INTENDED. THAT FAILURE STILL RANKLES.
I'M BACK IN RECORD TIME. THIS BATTLE SUIT WORKS LIKE A DREAM. I DESIGNED IT AND ITS CAPABILITIES STILL CONTINUALLY AMAZE AND SURPRISE ME.
I ENJOY USING IT, TOO. IT'S BECOME LIKE AN EXTENSION OF MY OWN BODY.
IT'S PUTTING MY LIFE ON THE LINE, AS A MEMBER OF ALPHA FLIGHT, THAT GIVES ME THE SHIVERS.

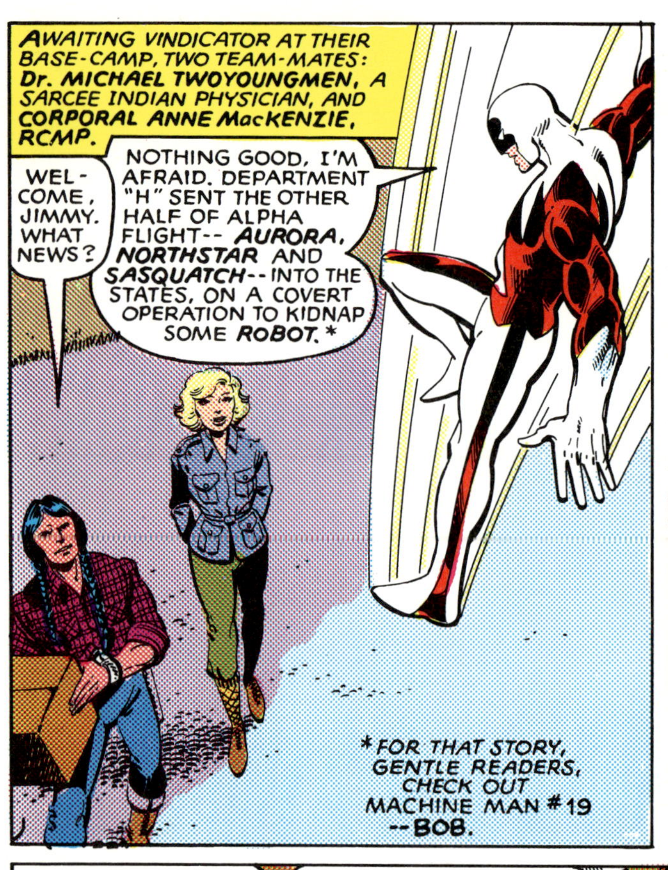
AWAITING VINDICATOR AT THEIR BASE-CAMP, TWO TEAM-MATES: Dr. MICHAEL TWOYOUNGMEN, A SARCEE INDIAN PHYSICIAN, AND CORPORAL ANNE MacKENZIE, RCMP.
WEL-COME, JIMMY. WHAT NEWS?
NOTHING GOOD, I'M AFRAID. DEPARTMENT "H" SENT THE OTHER HALF OF ALPHA FLIGHT-- AURORA, NORTHSTAR AND SASQUATCH-- INTO THE STATES, ON A COVERT OPERATION TO KIDNAP SOME ROBOT.*
*FOR THAT STORY, GENTLE READERS, CHECK OUT MACHINE MAN #19 --BOB.

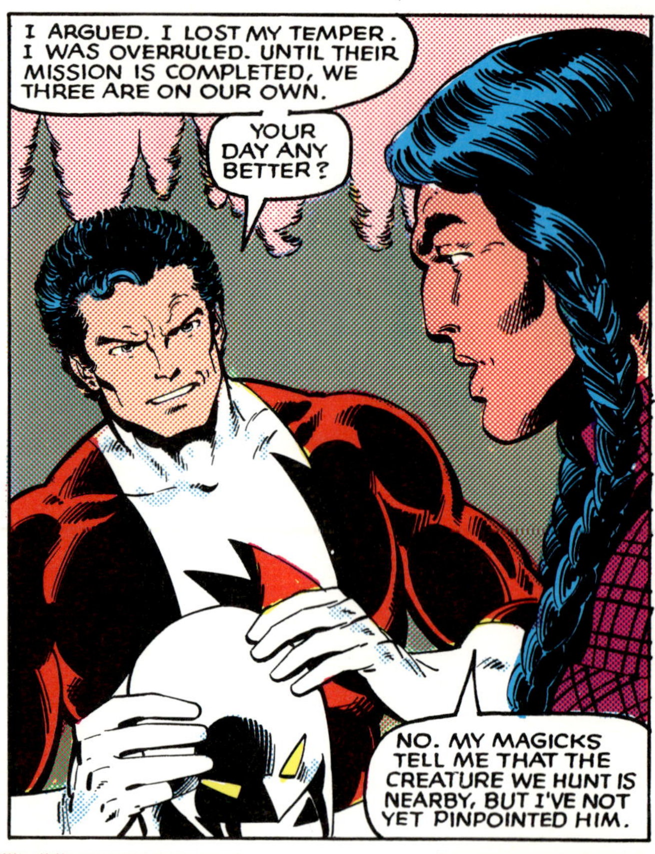
I ARGUED. I LOST MY TEMPER. I WAS OVERRULED. UNTIL THEIR MISSION IS COMPLETED, WE THREE ARE ON OUR OWN.
YOUR DAY ANY BETTER?
NO. MY MAGICKS TELL ME THAT THE CREATURE WE HUNT IS NEARBY, BUT I'VE NOT YET PINPOINTED HIM.

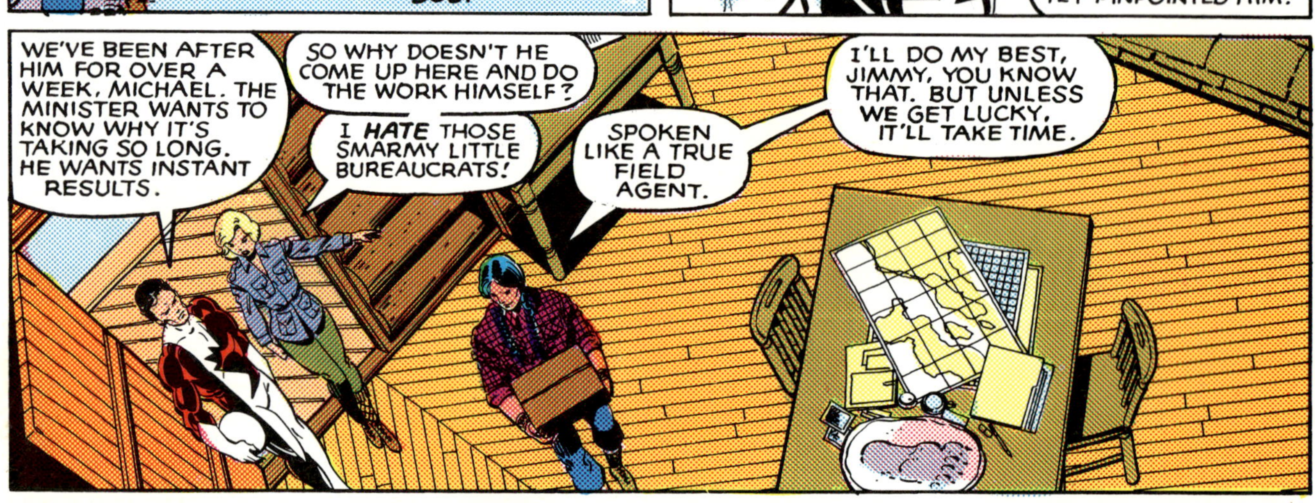
WE'VE BEEN AFTER HIM FOR OVER A WEEK, MICHAEL. THE MINISTER WANTS TO KNOW WHY IT'S TAKING SO LONG. HE WANTS INSTANT RESULTS.
SO WHY DOESN'T HE COME UP HERE AND DO THE WORK HIMSELF?
I HATE THOSE SMARMY LITTLE BUREAUCRATS!
SPOKEN LIKE A TRUE FIELD AGENT.
I'LL DO MY BEST, JIMMY, YOU KNOW THAT. BUT UNLESS WE GET LUCKY, IT'LL TAKE TIME.

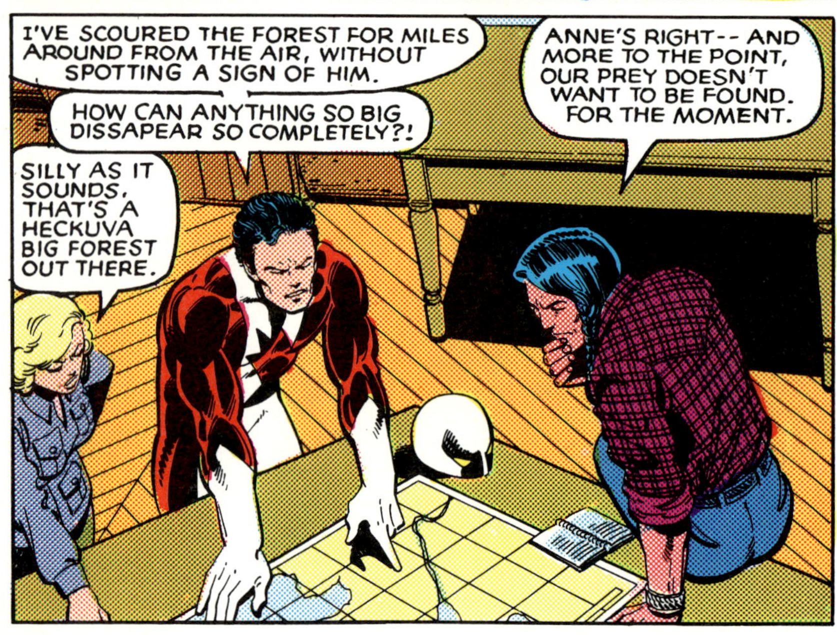
I'VE SCOURED THE FOREST FOR MILES AROUND FROM THE AIR, WITHOUT SPOTTING A SIGN OF HIM.
HOW CAN ANYTHING SO BIG DISSAPEAR SO COMPLETELY?!
SILLY AS IT SOUNDS, THAT'S A HECKUVA BIG FOREST OUT THERE.
ANNE'S RIGHT-- AND MORE TO THE POINT, OUR PREY DOESN'T WANT TO BE FOUND. FOR THE MOMENT.

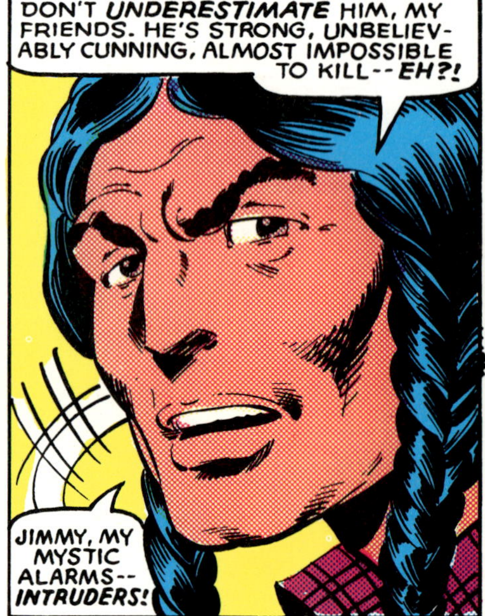
DON'T UNDERESTIMATE HIM, MY FRIENDS. HE'S STRONG, UNBELIEV-ABLY CUNNING, ALMOST IMPOSSIBLE TO KILL-- EH?!
JIMMY, MY MYSTIC ALARMS-- INTRUDERS!

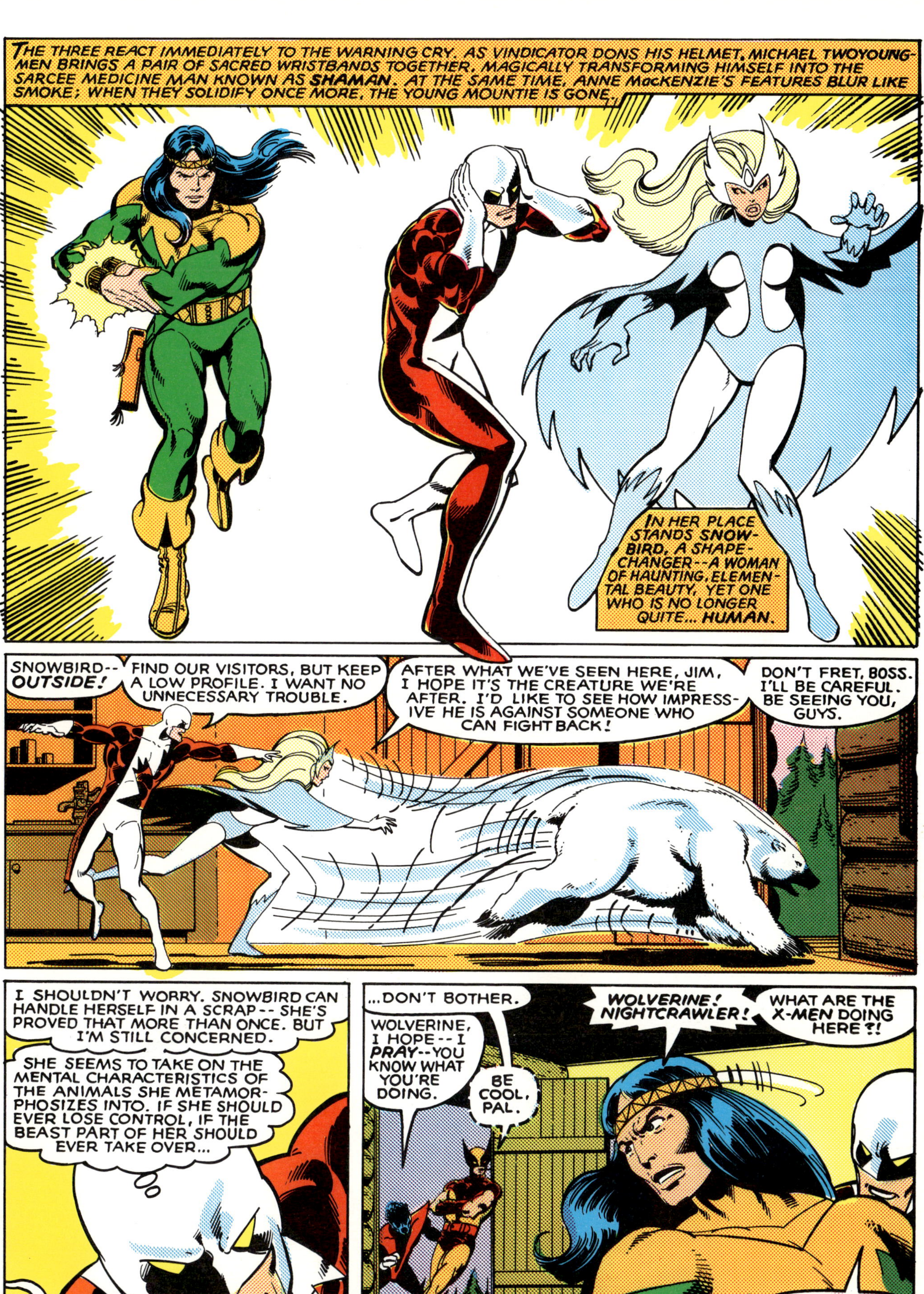
THE THREE REACT IMMEDIATELY TO THE WARNING CRY. AS VINDICATOR DONS HIS HELMET, MICHAEL TWOYOUNG-MEN BRINGS A PAIR OF SACRED WRISTBANDS TOGETHER, MAGICALLY TRANSFORMING HIMSELF INTO THE SARCEE MEDICINE MAN KNOWN AS SHAMAN. AT THE SAME TIME, ANNE MacKENZIE'S FEATURES BLUR LIKE SMOKE; WHEN THEY SOLIDIFY ONCE MORE, THE YOUNG MOUNTIE IS GONE...
IN HER PLACE STANDS SNOWBIRD, A SHAPE-CHANGER--A WOMAN OF HAUNTING, ELEMENTAL BEAUTY, YET ONE WHO IS NO LONGER QUITE... HUMAN.
SNOWBIRD-- OUTSIDE!
FIND OUR VISITORS, BUT KEEP A LOW PROFILE. I WANT NO UNNECESSARY TROUBLE.
AFTER WHAT WE'VE SEEN HERE, JIM, I HOPE IT'S THE CREATURE WE'RE AFTER. I'D LIKE TO SEE HOW IMPRESSIVE HE IS AGAINST SOMEONE WHO CAN FIGHT BACK!
DON'T FRET, BOSS. I'LL BE CAREFUL. BE SEEING YOU, GUYS.
I SHOULDN'T WORRY. SNOWBIRD CAN HANDLE HERSELF IN A SCRAP -- SHE'S PROVED THAT MORE THAN ONCE. BUT I'M STILL CONCERNED.
SHE SEEMS TO TAKE ON THE MENTAL CHARACTERISTICS OF THE ANIMALS SHE METAMORPHOSIZES INTO. IF SHE SHOULD EVER LOSE CONTROL, IF THE BEAST PART OF HER SHOULD EVER TAKE OVER...
HEY, MAC-- IF ALL THIS FUSS IS ON OUR ACCOUNT...
WHAT--?!
...DON'T BOTHER.
WOLVERINE, I HOPE -- I PRAY--YOU KNOW WHAT YOU'RE DOING.
BE COOL, PAL.
WOLVERINE! NIGHTCRAWLER!
WHAT ARE THE X-MEN DOING HERE?!
I HAVEN'T THE FOGGIEST, SHAMAN. BUT IF IT'S TO SETTLE OLD SCORES, THEY'LL FIND US READY FOR THEM!

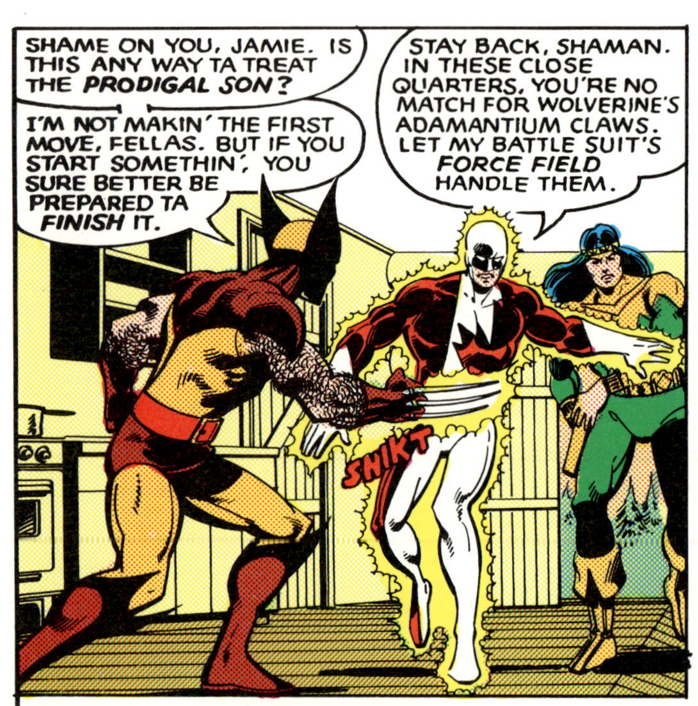
SHAME ON YOU, JAMIE. IS THIS ANY WAY TA TREAT THE *PRODIGAL SON?*
I'M NOT MAKIN' THE FIRST MOVE, FELLAS. BUT IF YOU START SOMETHIN', YOU SURE BETTER BE PREPARED TA *FINISH* IT.
STAY BACK, SHAMAN. IN THESE CLOSE QUARTERS, YOU'RE NO MATCH FOR WOLVERINE'S ADAMANTIUM CLAWS. LET MY BATTLE SUIT'S *FORCE FIELD* HANDLE THEM.
SHIKT

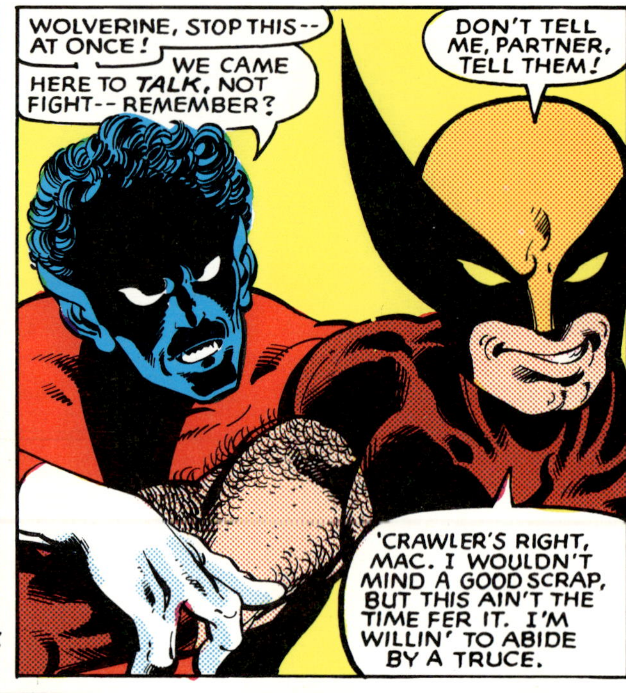
WOLVERINE, STOP THIS-- AT ONCE!
WE CAME HERE TO *TALK*, NOT FIGHT-- REMEMBER?
DON'T TELL ME, PARTNER, TELL THEM!
'CRAWLER'S RIGHT, MAC. I WOULDN'T MIND A GOOD SCRAP, BUT THIS AIN'T THE TIME FER IT. I'M WILLIN' TO ABIDE BY A TRUCE.

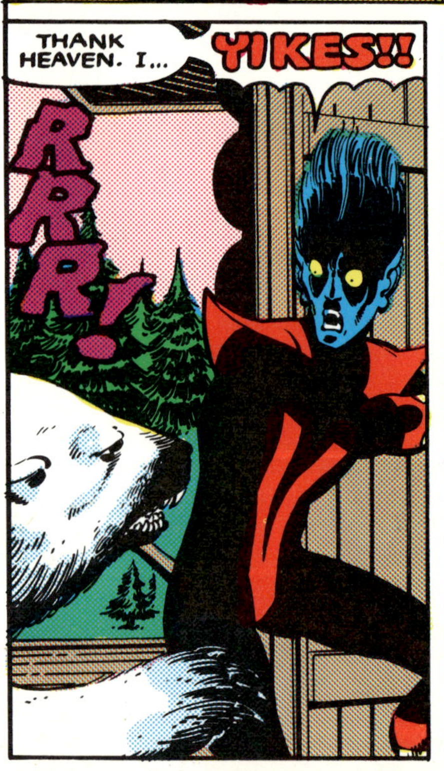
THANK HEAVEN. I...
YIKES!!
RRR!

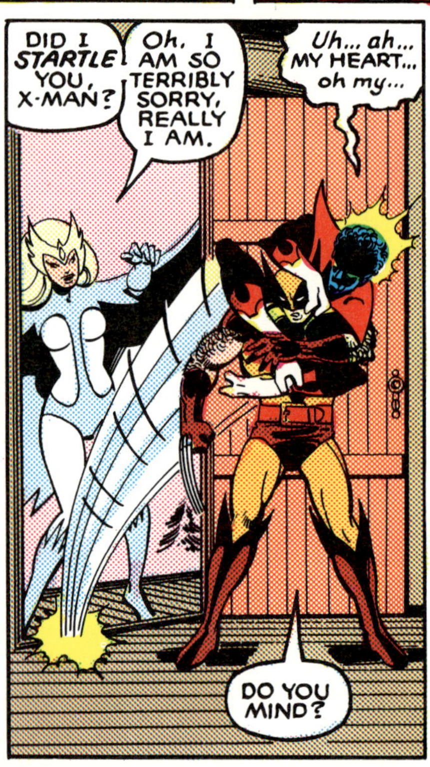
DID I *STARTLE* YOU, X-MAN?
Oh, I AM SO TERRIBLY SORRY, REALLY I AM.
Uh... ah... MY HEART... oh my...
DO YOU MIND?

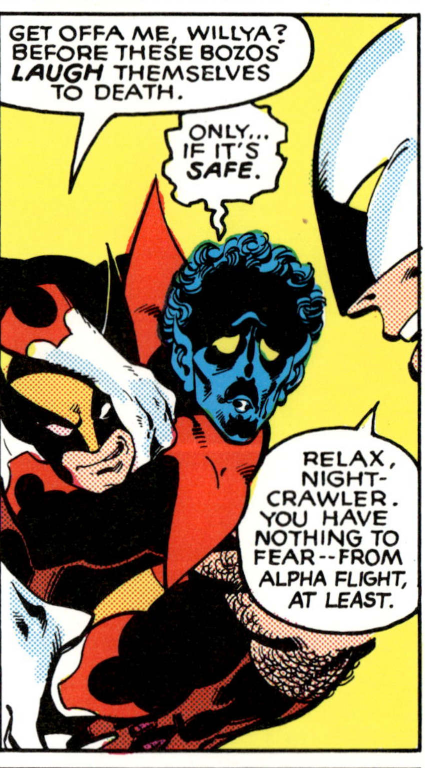
GET OFFA ME, WILLYA? BEFORE THESE BOZOS *LAUGH* THEMSELVES TO DEATH.
ONLY... IF IT'S *SAFE*.
RELAX, NIGHT-CRAWLER. YOU HAVE NOTHING TO FEAR--FROM ALPHA FLIGHT, AT LEAST.

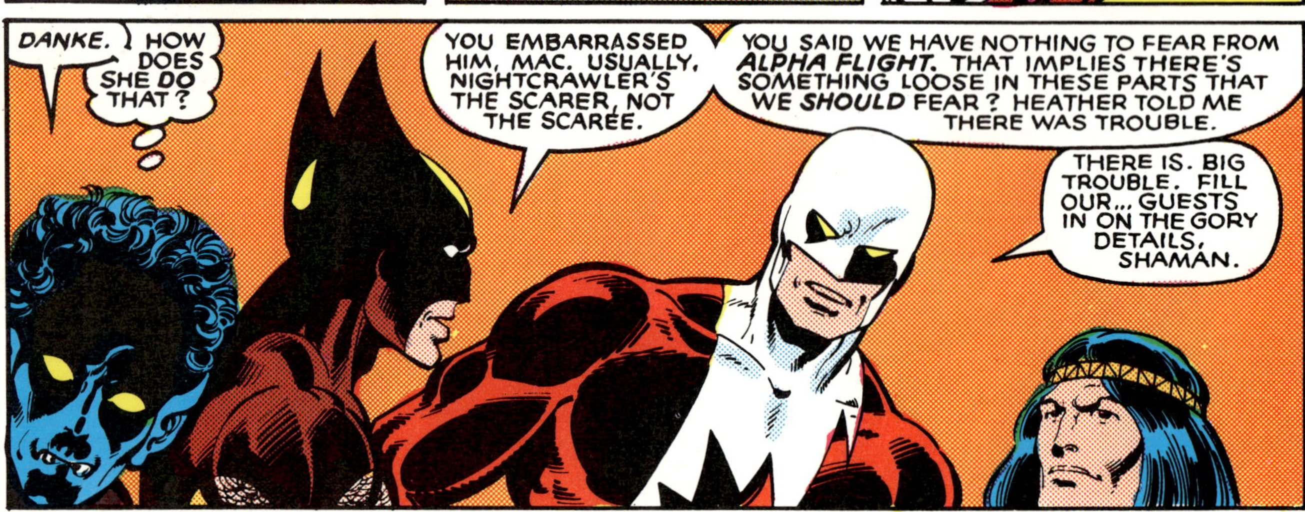
DANKE.
HOW DOES SHE *DO* THAT?
YOU EMBARRASSED HIM, MAC. USUALLY, NIGHTCRAWLER'S THE SCARER, NOT THE SCAREE.
YOU SAID WE HAVE NOTHING TO FEAR FROM *ALPHA FLIGHT*. THAT IMPLIES THERE'S SOMETHING LOOSE IN THESE PARTS THAT WE *SHOULD* FEAR? HEATHER TOLD ME THERE WAS TROUBLE.
THERE IS. BIG TROUBLE. FILL OUR... GUESTS IN ON THE GORY DETAILS, SHAMAN.

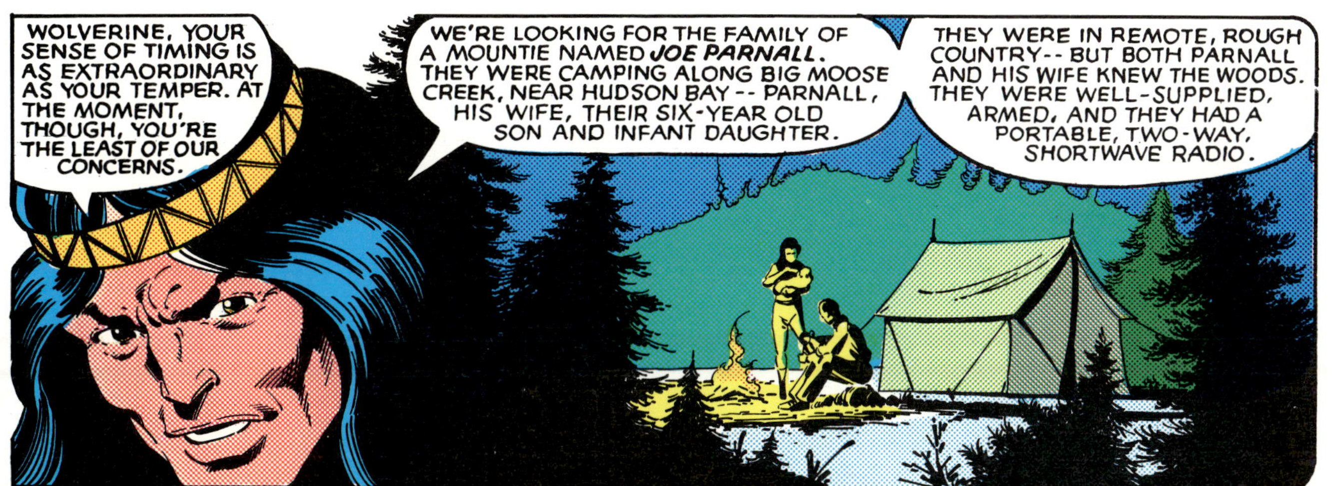
WOLVERINE, YOUR SENSE OF TIMING IS AS EXTRAORDINARY AS YOUR TEMPER. AT THE MOMENT, THOUGH, YOU'RE THE LEAST OF OUR CONCERNS.
WE'RE LOOKING FOR THE FAMILY OF A MOUNTIE NAMED **JOE PARNALL**. THEY WERE CAMPING ALONG BIG MOOSE CREEK, NEAR HUDSON BAY -- PARNALL, HIS WIFE, THEIR SIX-YEAR OLD SON AND INFANT DAUGHTER.
THEY WERE IN REMOTE, ROUGH COUNTRY -- BUT BOTH PARNALL AND HIS WIFE KNEW THE WOODS. THEY WERE WELL-SUPPLIED, ARMED, AND THEY HAD A PORTABLE, TWO-WAY, SHORTWAVE RADIO.

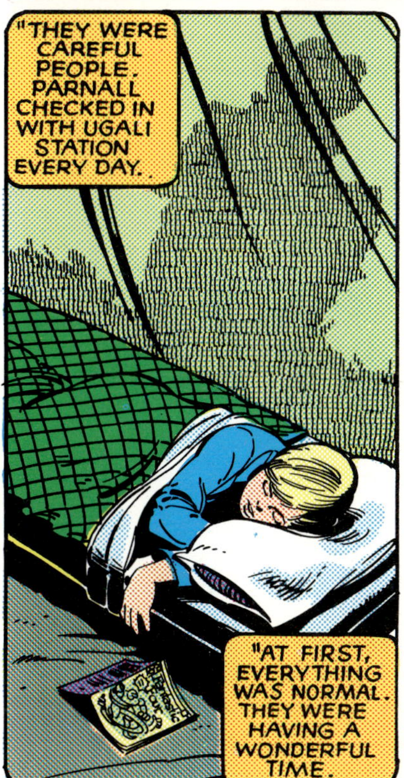
"THEY WERE CAREFUL PEOPLE. PARNALL CHECKED IN WITH UGALI STATION EVERY DAY.
"AT FIRST, EVERYTHING WAS NORMAL. THEY WERE HAVING A WONDERFUL TIME.

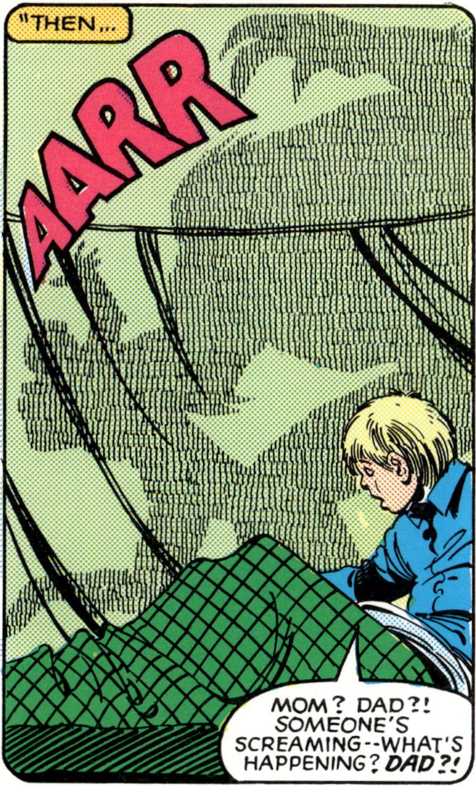
"THEN...
AARR
MOM? DAD?! SOMEONE'S SCREAMING--WHAT'S HAPPENING? **DAD?!**

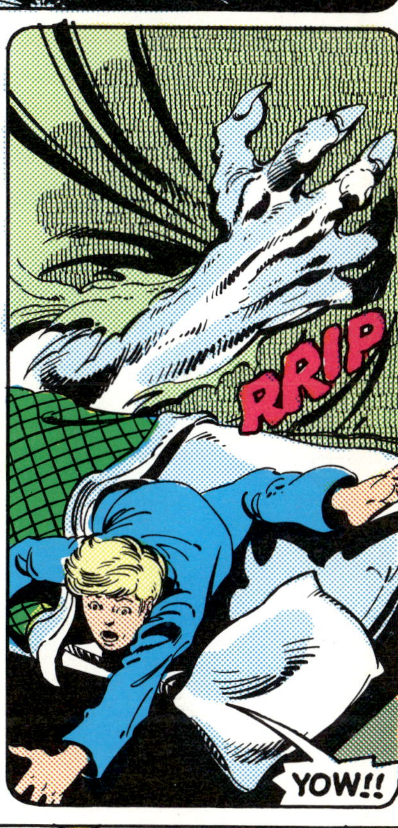
RRIP
YOW!!

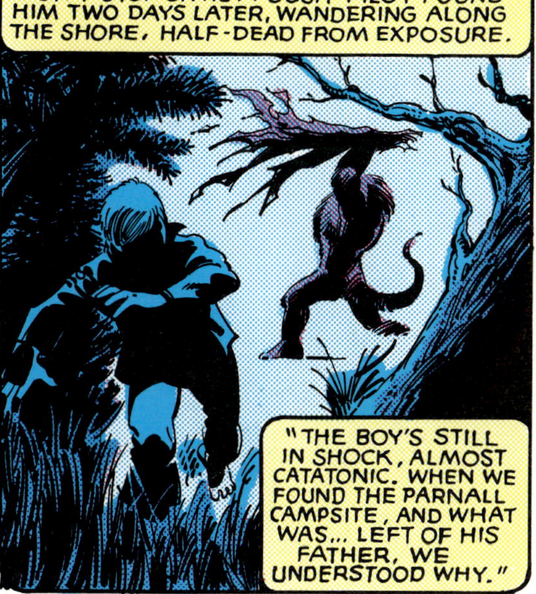
"TOMMY PARNALL RAN FOR HIS LIFE. HE DIDN'T STOP UNTIL A BUSH-PILOT FOUND HIM TWO DAYS LATER, WANDERING ALONG THE SHORE, HALF-DEAD FROM EXPOSURE.
"THE BOY'S STILL IN SHOCK, ALMOST CATATONIC. WHEN WE FOUND THE PARNALL CAMPSITE, AND WHAT WAS... LEFT OF HIS FATHER, WE UNDERSTOOD WHY."

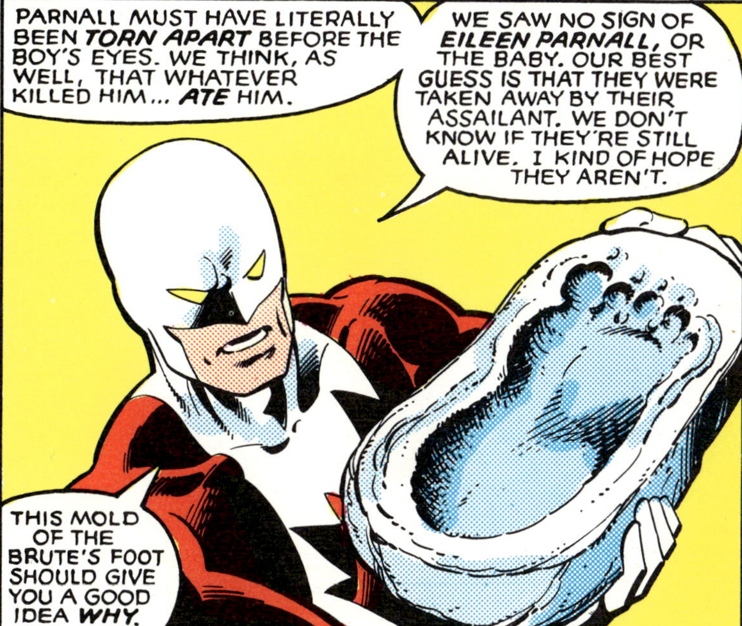
PARNALL MUST HAVE LITERALLY BEEN **TORN APART** BEFORE THE BOY'S EYES. WE THINK, AS WELL, THAT WHATEVER KILLED HIM... **ATE** HIM.
WE SAW NO SIGN OF **EILEEN PARNALL**, OR THE BABY. OUR BEST GUESS IS THAT THEY WERE TAKEN AWAY BY THEIR ASSAILANT. WE DON'T KNOW IF THEY'RE STILL ALIVE. I KIND OF HOPE THEY AREN'T.
THIS MOLD OF THE BRUTE'S FOOT SHOULD GIVE YOU A GOOD IDEA **WHY**.

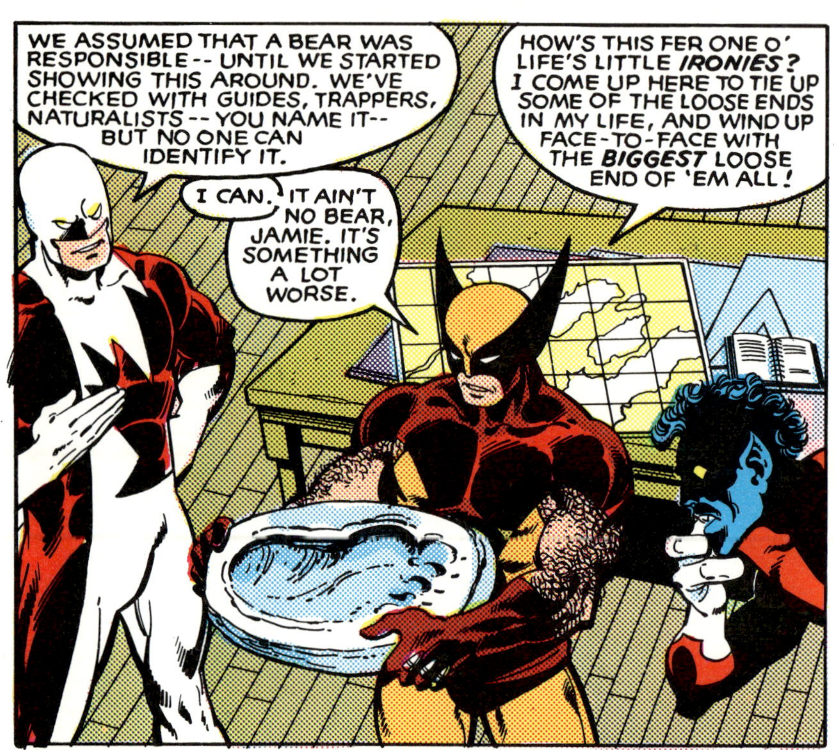
WE ASSUMED THAT A BEAR WAS RESPONSIBLE -- UNTIL WE STARTED SHOWING THIS AROUND. WE'VE CHECKED WITH GUIDES, TRAPPERS, NATURALISTS -- YOU NAME IT-- BUT NO ONE CAN IDENTIFY IT.
I CAN. IT AIN'T NO BEAR, JAMIE. IT'S SOMETHING A LOT WORSE.
HOW'S THIS FER ONE O' LIFE'S LITTLE *IRONIES?* I COME UP HERE TO TIE UP SOME OF THE LOOSE ENDS IN MY LIFE, AND WIND UP FACE-TO-FACE WITH THE *BIGGEST* LOOSE END OF 'EM ALL!

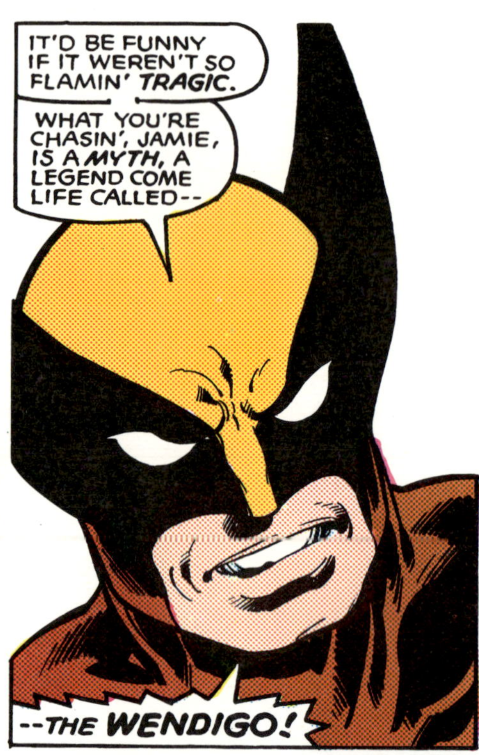
IT'D BE FUNNY IF IT WEREN'T SO FLAMIN' *TRAGIC.*
WHAT YOU'RE CHASIN', JAMIE, IS A *MYTH*, A LEGEND COME LIFE CALLED--
--THE *WENDIGO!*

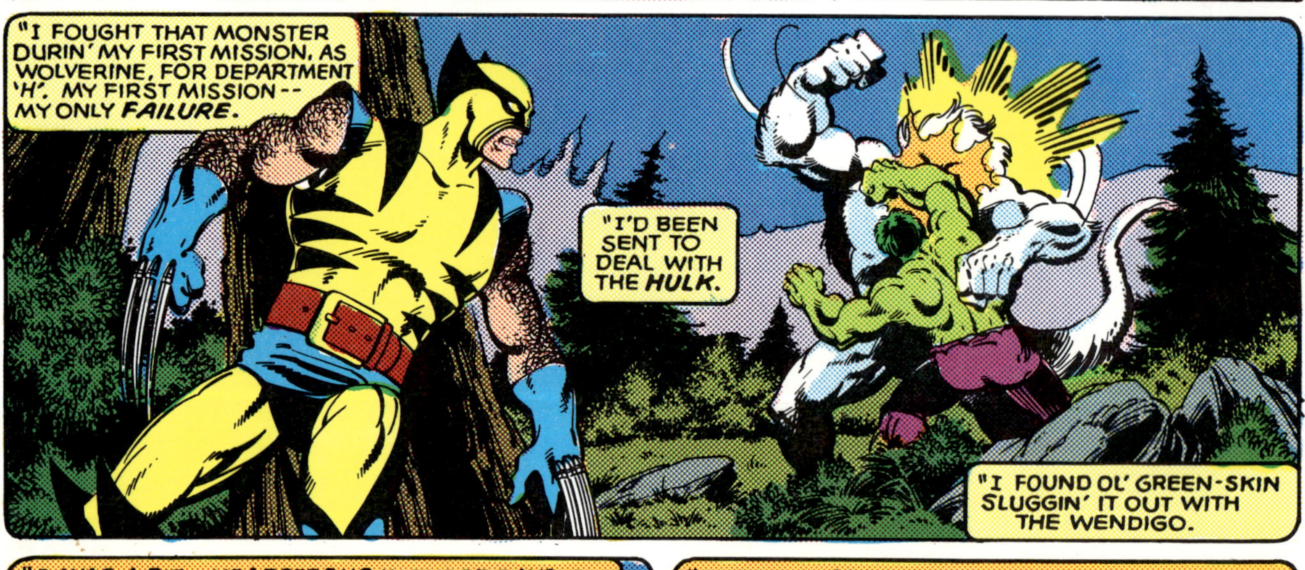
"I FOUGHT THAT MONSTER DURIN' MY FIRST MISSION, AS WOLVERINE, FOR DEPARTMENT 'H'. MY FIRST MISSION -- MY ONLY *FAILURE*.
"I'D BEEN SENT TO DEAL WITH THE *HULK*.
"I FOUND OL' GREEN-SKIN SLUGGIN' IT OUT WITH THE WENDIGO.

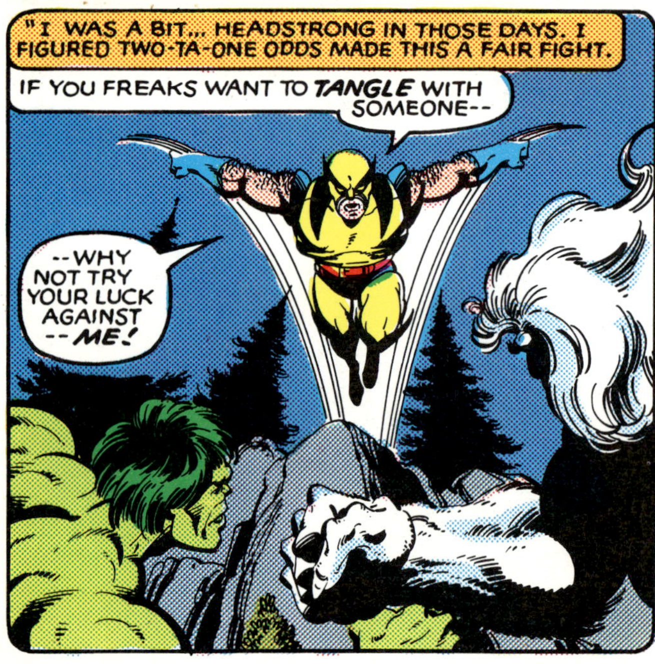
"I WAS A BIT... HEADSTRONG IN THOSE DAYS. I FIGURED TWO-TA-ONE ODDS MADE THIS A FAIR FIGHT.
IF YOU FREAKS WANT TO *TANGLE* WITH SOMEONE--
--WHY NOT TRY YOUR LUCK AGAINST --*ME!*

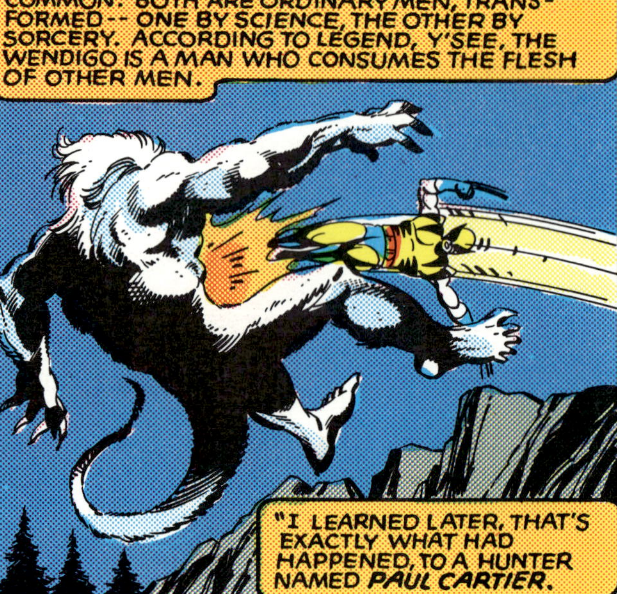
"THE HULK AN' THE WENDIGO HAVE A LOT IN COMMON. BOTH ARE ORDINARY MEN, TRANS-FORMED -- ONE BY SCIENCE, THE OTHER BY SORCERY. ACCORDING TO LEGEND, Y'SEE, THE WENDIGO IS A MAN WHO CONSUMES THE FLESH OF OTHER MEN.
"I LEARNED LATER, THAT'S EXACTLY WHAT HAD HAPPENED, TO A HUNTER NAMED *PAUL CARTIER*.

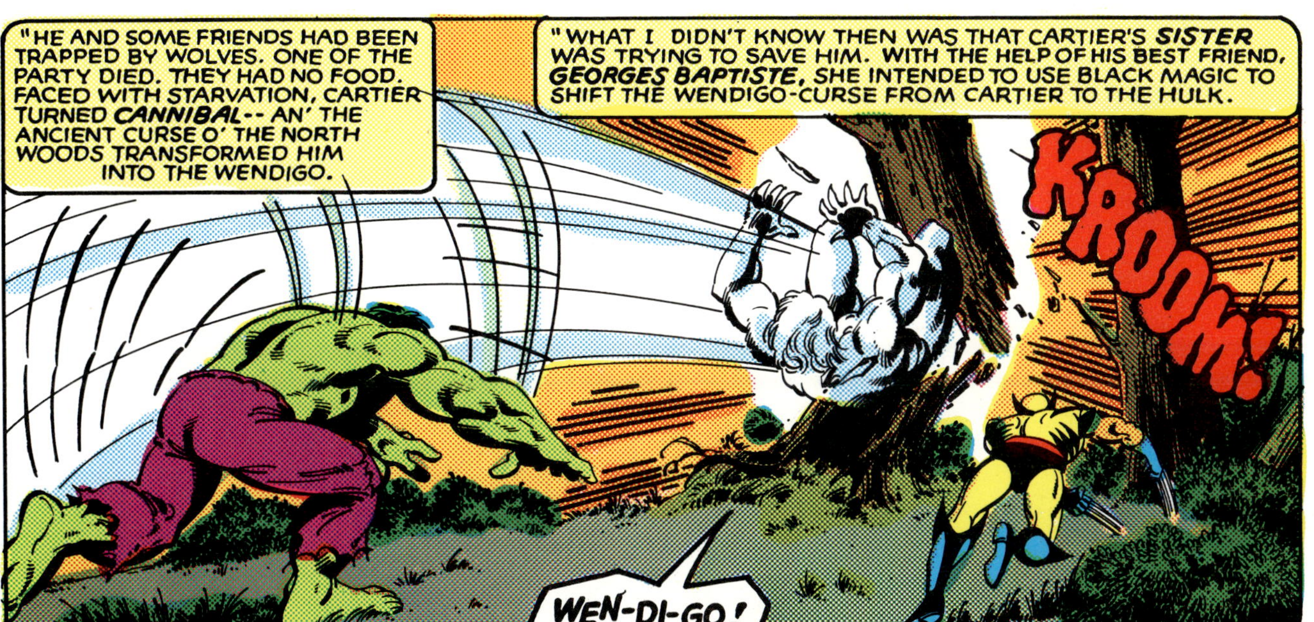
"HE AND SOME FRIENDS HAD BEEN TRAPPED BY WOLVES. ONE OF THE PARTY DIED. THEY HAD NO FOOD. FACED WITH STARVATION, CARTIER TURNED CANNIBAL-- AN' THE ANCIENT CURSE O' THE NORTH WOODS TRANSFORMED HIM INTO THE WENDIGO.
"WHAT I DIDN'T KNOW THEN WAS THAT CARTIER'S SISTER WAS TRYING TO SAVE HIM. WITH THE HELP OF HIS BEST FRIEND, GEORGES BAPTISTE, SHE INTENDED TO USE BLACK MAGIC TO SHIFT THE WENDIGO-CURSE FROM CARTIER TO THE HULK.
KROOM!
WEN-DI-GO!

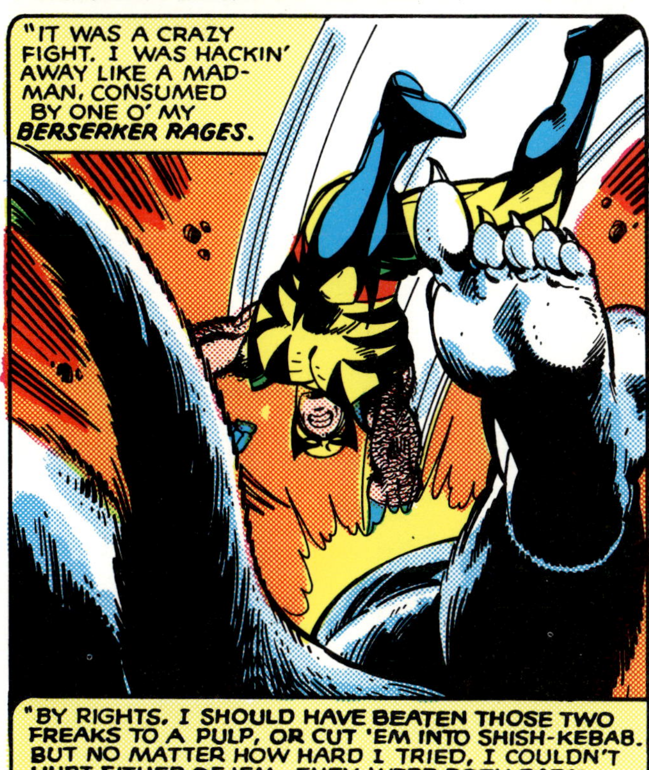
"IT WAS A CRAZY FIGHT. I WAS HACKIN' AWAY LIKE A MAD-MAN, CONSUMED BY ONE O' MY BERSERKER RAGES.
"BY RIGHTS, I SHOULD HAVE BEATEN THOSE TWO FREAKS TO A PULP, OR CUT 'EM INTO SHISH-KEBAB. BUT NO MATTER HOW HARD I TRIED, I COULDN'T HURT EITHER OF 'EM. THEY WERE BOTH DARN NEAR INVULNERABLE.

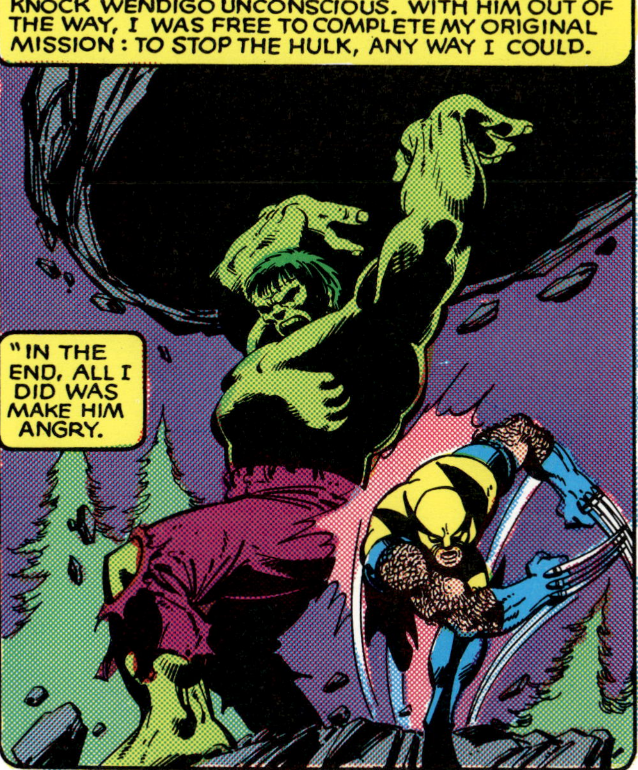
"BETWEEN ME AN' THE HULK, WE MANAGED TO KNOCK WENDIGO UNCONSCIOUS. WITH HIM OUT OF THE WAY, I WAS FREE TO COMPLETE MY ORIGINAL MISSION : TO STOP THE HULK, ANY WAY I COULD.
"IN THE END, ALL I DID WAS MAKE HIM ANGRY.

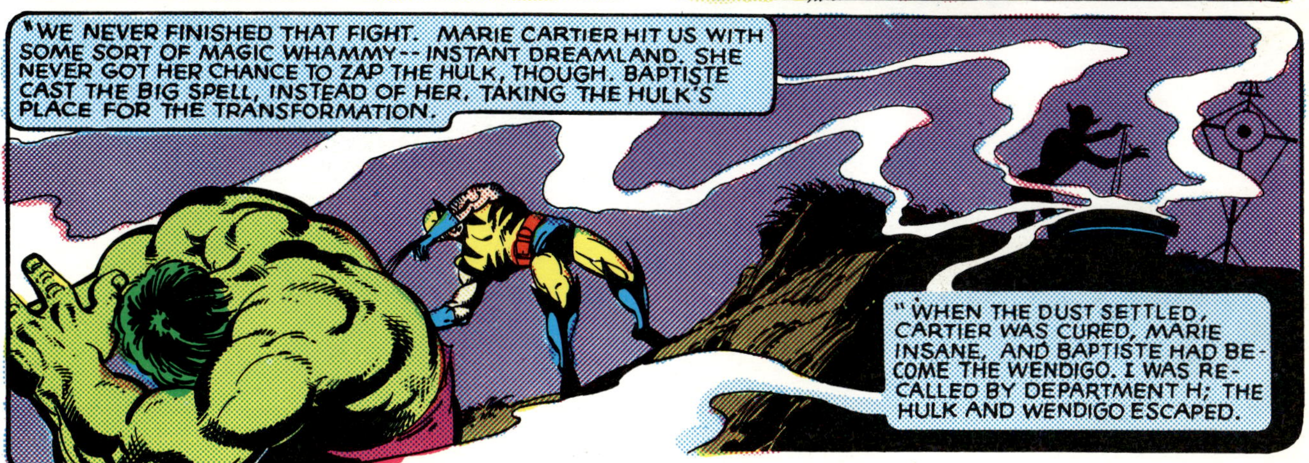
"WE NEVER FINISHED THAT FIGHT. MARIE CARTIER HIT US WITH SOME SORT OF MAGIC WHAMMY-- INSTANT DREAMLAND. SHE NEVER GOT HER CHANCE TO ZAP THE HULK, THOUGH. BAPTISTE CAST THE BIG SPELL, INSTEAD OF HER, TAKING THE HULK'S PLACE FOR THE TRANSFORMATION.
"WHEN THE DUST SETTLED, CARTIER WAS CURED, MARIE INSANE, AND BAPTISTE HAD BECOME THE WENDIGO. I WAS RECALLED BY DEPARTMENT H; THE HULK AND WENDIGO ESCAPED.

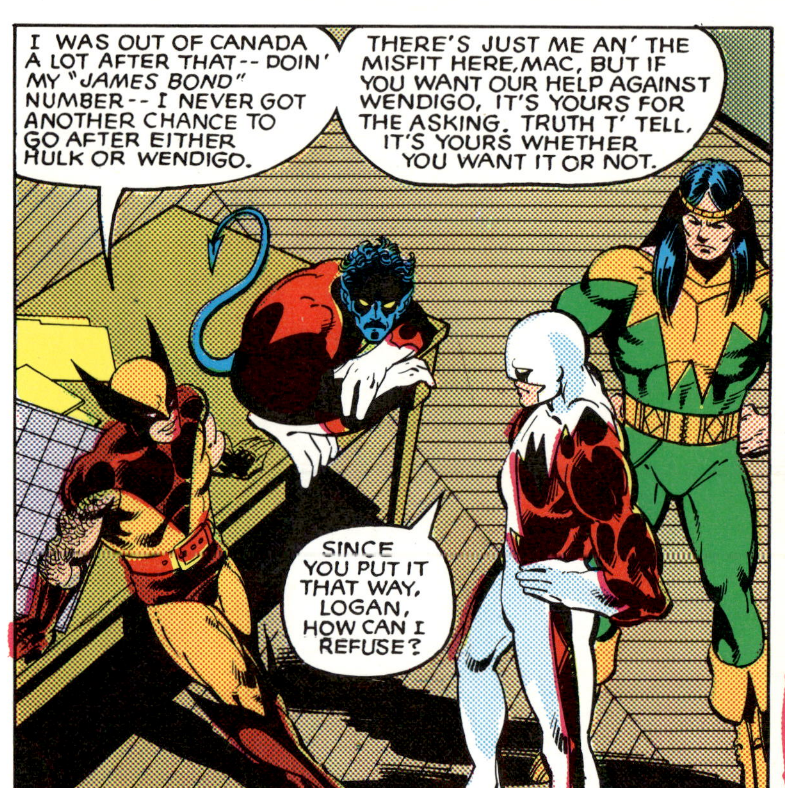
I WAS OUT OF CANADA A LOT AFTER THAT -- DOIN' MY "JAMES BOND" NUMBER -- I NEVER GOT ANOTHER CHANCE TO GO AFTER EITHER HULK OR WENDIGO.
THERE'S JUST ME AN' THE MISFIT HERE, MAC, BUT IF YOU WANT OUR HELP AGAINST WENDIGO, IT'S YOURS FOR THE ASKING. TRUTH T' TELL, IT'S YOURS WHETHER YOU WANT IT OR NOT.
SINCE YOU PUT IT THAT WAY, LOGAN, HOW CAN I REFUSE?

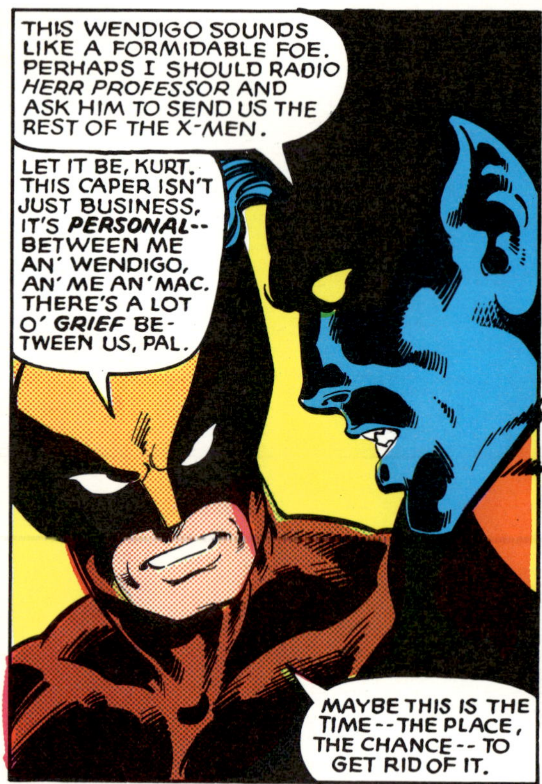
THIS WENDIGO SOUNDS LIKE A FORMIDABLE FOE. PERHAPS I SHOULD RADIO HERR PROFESSOR AND ASK HIM TO SEND US THE REST OF THE X-MEN.
LET IT BE, KURT. THIS CAPER ISN'T JUST BUSINESS, IT'S PERSONAL -- BETWEEN ME AN' WENDIGO, AN' ME AN' MAC. THERE'S A LOT O' GRIEF BETWEEN US, PAL.
MAYBE THIS IS THE TIME -- THE PLACE, THE CHANCE -- TO GET RID OF IT.

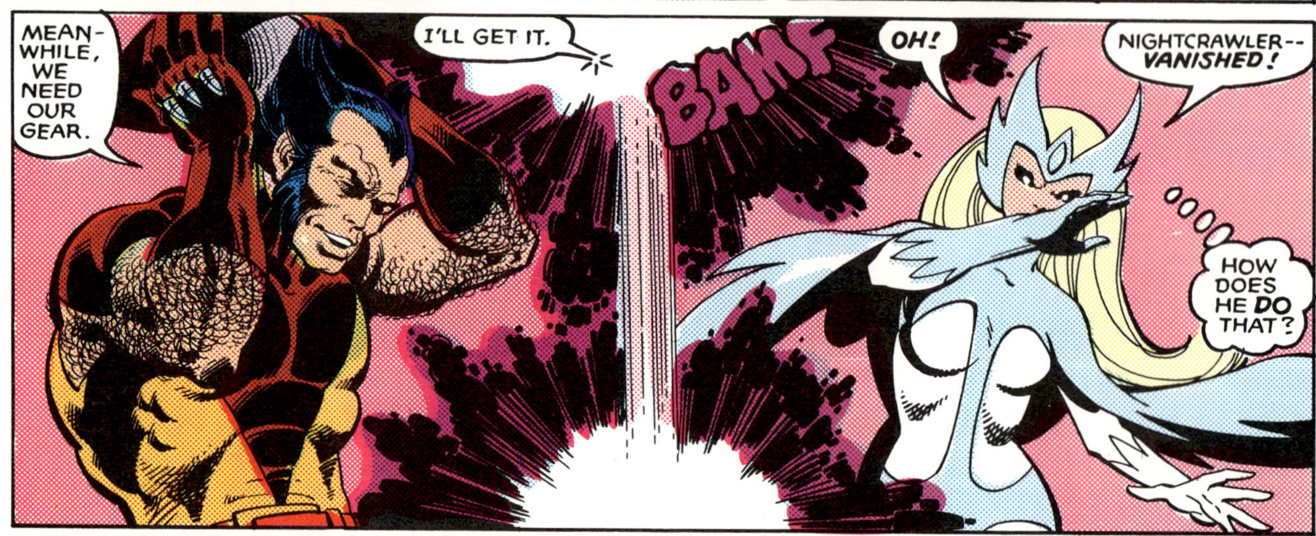
MEANWHILE, WE NEED OUR GEAR.
I'LL GET IT.
BAMF
OH!
NIGHTCRAWLER -- VANISHED!
HOW DOES HE DO THAT?

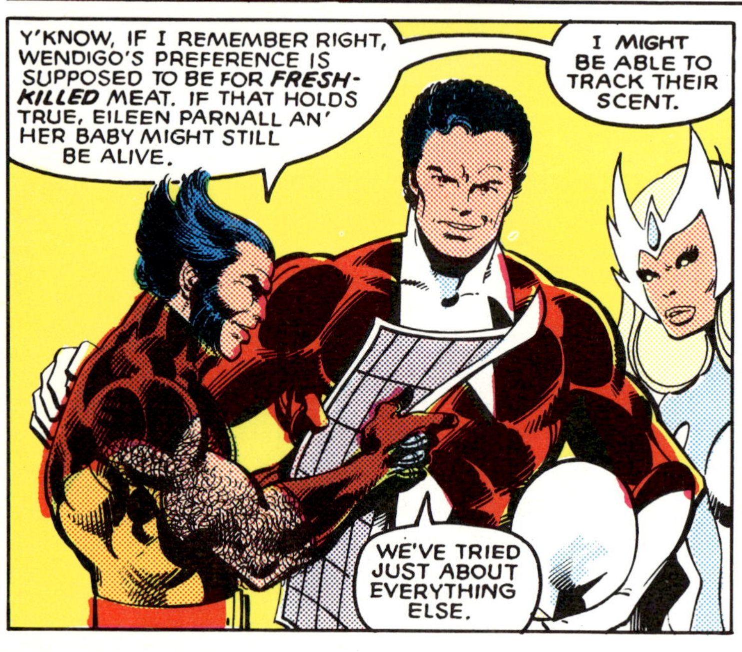
Y'KNOW, IF I REMEMBER RIGHT, WENDIGO'S PREFERENCE IS SUPPOSED TO BE FOR FRESH-KILLED MEAT. IF THAT HOLDS TRUE, EILEEN PARNALL AN' HER BABY MIGHT STILL BE ALIVE.
I MIGHT BE ABLE TO TRACK THEIR SCENT.
WE'VE TRIED JUST ABOUT EVERYTHING ELSE.

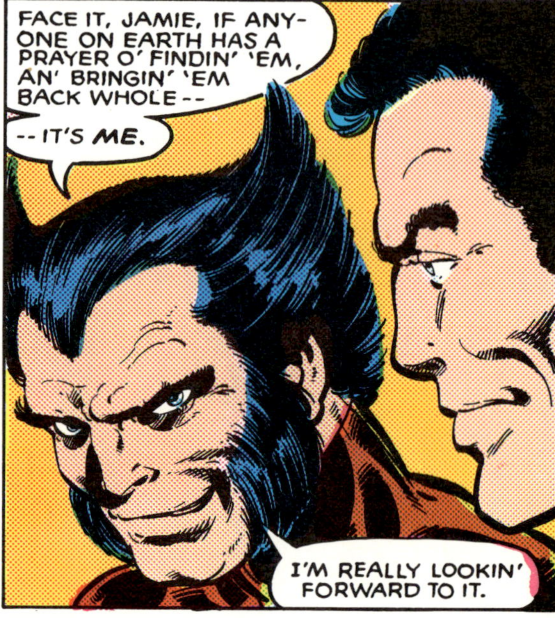
FACE IT, JAMIE, IF ANYONE ON EARTH HAS A PRAYER O' FINDIN' 'EM, AN' BRINGIN' 'EM BACK WHOLE --
-- IT'S ME.
I'M REALLY LOOKIN' FORWARD TO IT.

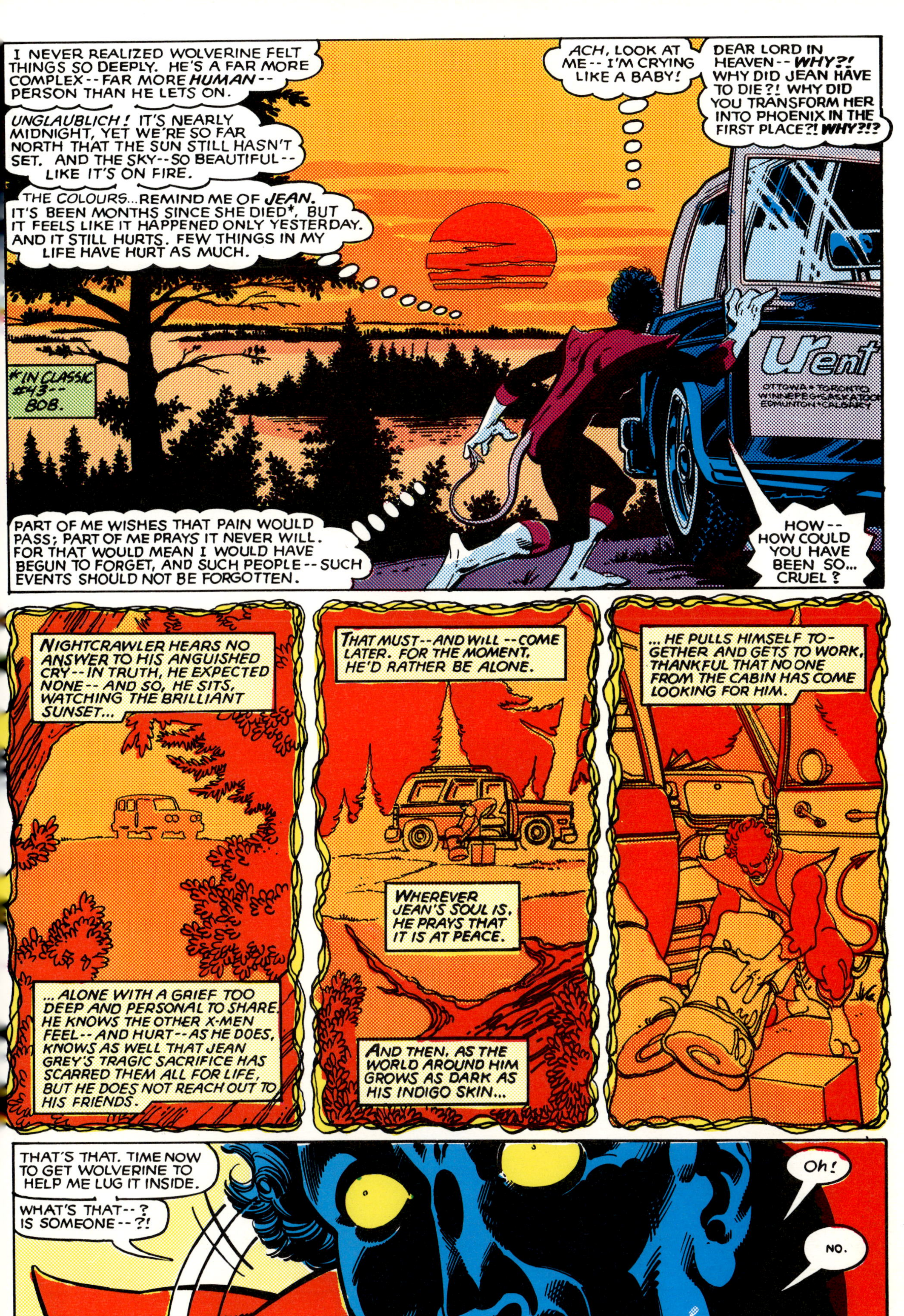
I NEVER REALIZED WOLVERINE FELT THINGS SO DEEPLY. HE'S A FAR MORE COMPLEX--FAR MORE HUMAN--PERSON THAN HE LETS ON.
UNGLAUBLICH! IT'S NEARLY MIDNIGHT, YET WE'RE SO FAR NORTH THAT THE SUN STILL HASN'T SET. AND THE SKY--SO BEAUTIFUL--LIKE IT'S ON FIRE.
THE COLOURS...REMIND ME OF JEAN. IT'S BEEN MONTHS SINCE SHE DIED*, BUT IT FEELS LIKE IT HAPPENED ONLY YESTERDAY. AND IT STILL HURTS. FEW THINGS IN MY LIFE HAVE HURT AS MUCH.
ACH, LOOK AT ME--I'M CRYING LIKE A BABY!
DEAR LORD IN HEAVEN--WHY?! WHY DID JEAN HAVE TO DIE?! WHY DID YOU TRANSFORM HER INTO PHOENIX IN THE FIRST PLACE?! WHY?!?
*IN CLASSIC #43--BOB.
U-rent
PART OF ME WISHES THAT PAIN WOULD PASS; PART OF ME PRAYS IT NEVER WILL. FOR THAT WOULD MEAN I WOULD HAVE BEGUN TO FORGET, AND SUCH PEOPLE--SUCH EVENTS SHOULD NOT BE FORGOTTEN.
HOW--HOW COULD YOU HAVE BEEN SO... CRUEL?
NIGHTCRAWLER HEARS NO ANSWER TO HIS ANGUISHED CRY--IN TRUTH, HE EXPECTED NONE--AND SO, HE SITS, WATCHING THE BRILLIANT SUNSET...
...ALONE WITH A GRIEF TOO DEEP AND PERSONAL TO SHARE. HE KNOWS THE OTHER X-MEN FEEL--AND HURT--AS HE DOES, KNOWS AS WELL THAT JEAN GREY'S TRAGIC SACRIFICE HAS SCARRED THEM ALL FOR LIFE, BUT HE DOES NOT REACH OUT TO HIS FRIENDS.
THAT MUST--AND WILL--COME LATER. FOR THE MOMENT, HE'D RATHER BE ALONE.
WHEREVER JEAN'S SOUL IS, HE PRAYS THAT IT IS AT PEACE.
AND THEN, AS THE WORLD AROUND HIM GROWS AS DARK AS HIS INDIGO SKIN...
...HE PULLS HIMSELF TOGETHER AND GETS TO WORK, THANKFUL THAT NO ONE FROM THE CABIN HAS COME LOOKING FOR HIM.
THAT'S THAT. TIME NOW TO GET WOLVERINE TO HELP ME LUG IT INSIDE.
WHAT'S THAT--? IS SOMEONE--?!
Oh!
NO.

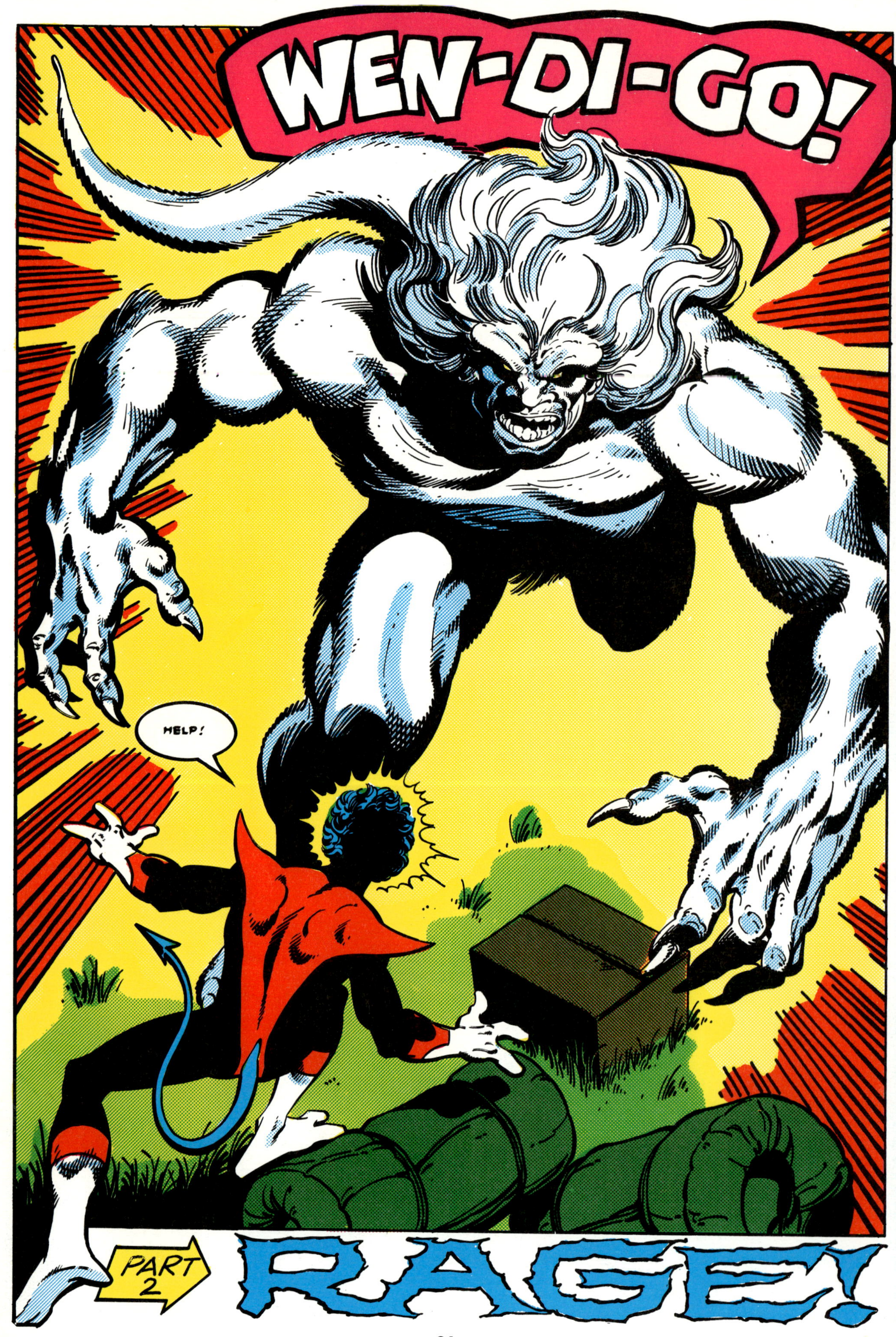
WEN-DI-GO!
HELP!
PART 2
RAGE!

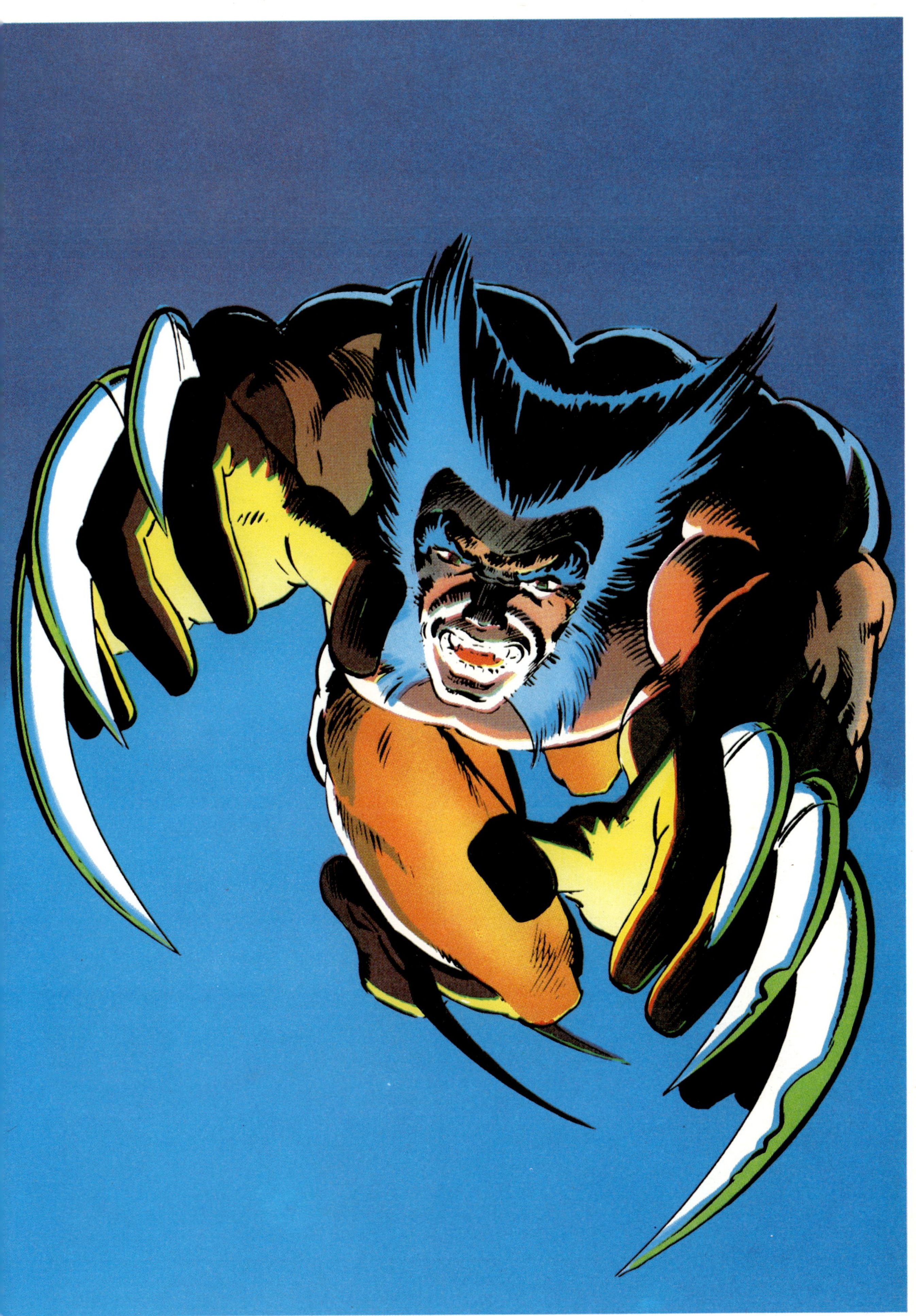

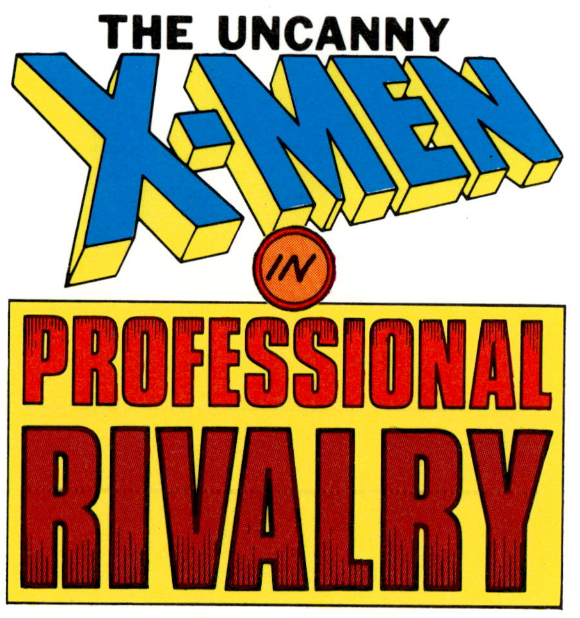

PART ONE

STORY: RIK HOSKIN
ART: GARY FRANK
COLOUR: EUAN PETERS

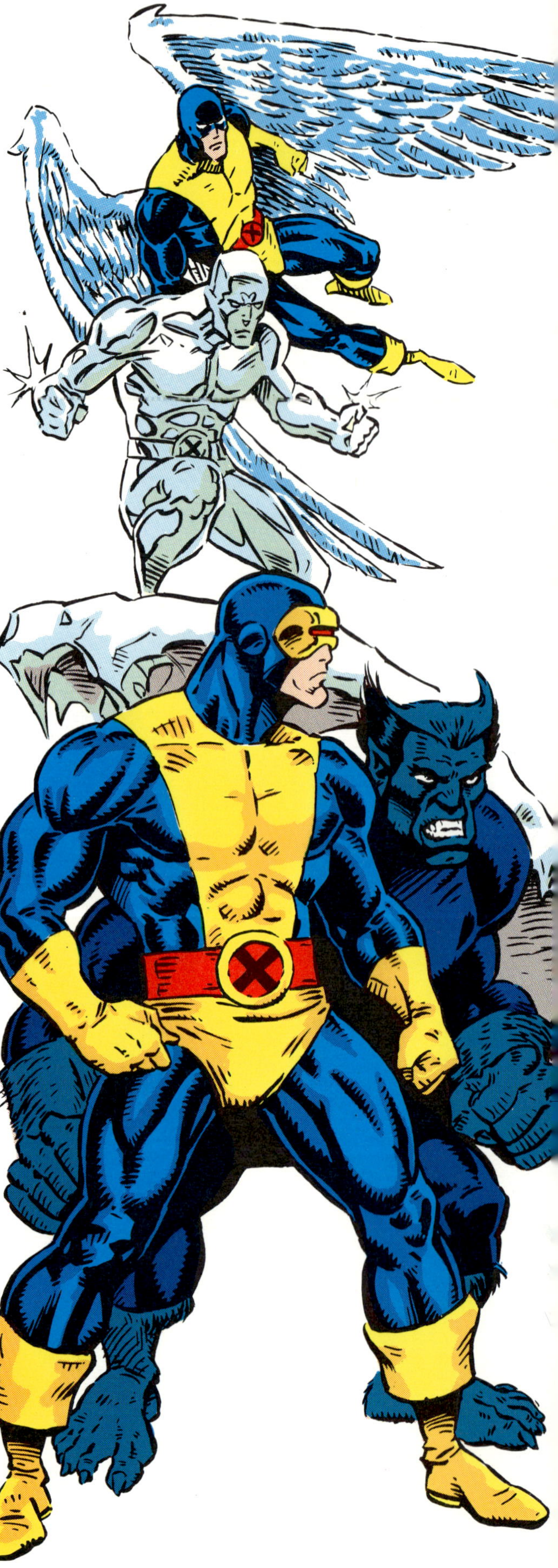

Following her strenuous dance lesson, there was nothing Kitty Pryde wanted more in the world than a hot shower, a cool drink and a nice relaxing afternoon by the X-Men's swimming pool.

. . . Of course, when you're a mutant, life is never *that* simple.

"I'm so glad Professor Xavier has finally accepted me as one of the X-Men, Ororo. I can't wait to see my folks' faces when I tell them . . ." Kitty's face was aglow as she and Ororo left Salem Centre in their Rolls Royce and headed back to 1407 Graymalkin Lane, also known as the X-Men mansion. "I just wish I'd been with the team at the beginning, like you."

The mutant windrider turned to her enthusiastic friend slowly, contemplating whether or not she should ruin the child's hero-worship dreams. "Kitty," said Storm at last, "life as an X-Man will not be easy for you. You are still inexperienced with your . . . gift and . . ."

"But you guys'll train me – soon I'll be as great as you." Kitty still had her head in the clouds.

Ah, the impetuousness of youth, thought Storm as she began to tell Kitty more of her comrades-to-be. "We are still quite inexperienced ourselves, Kitten. Myself and most of the others are relatively new recruits to the X-Men. Before us there were the Original X-Men – a band of young mutants bonded by a single goal – World Peace between man and mutant. That team, gathered together by Professor Xavier, were made up of the Angel, who you've already met, Cyclops, the Beast, Iceman and . . ." Ororo paused for a moment, then continued in a shaky voice, "Marvel Girl . . . Jean . . . who we all miss very much. . ."

Kitty stopped herself as she saw a tear trickle beneath Storm's sunglasses.

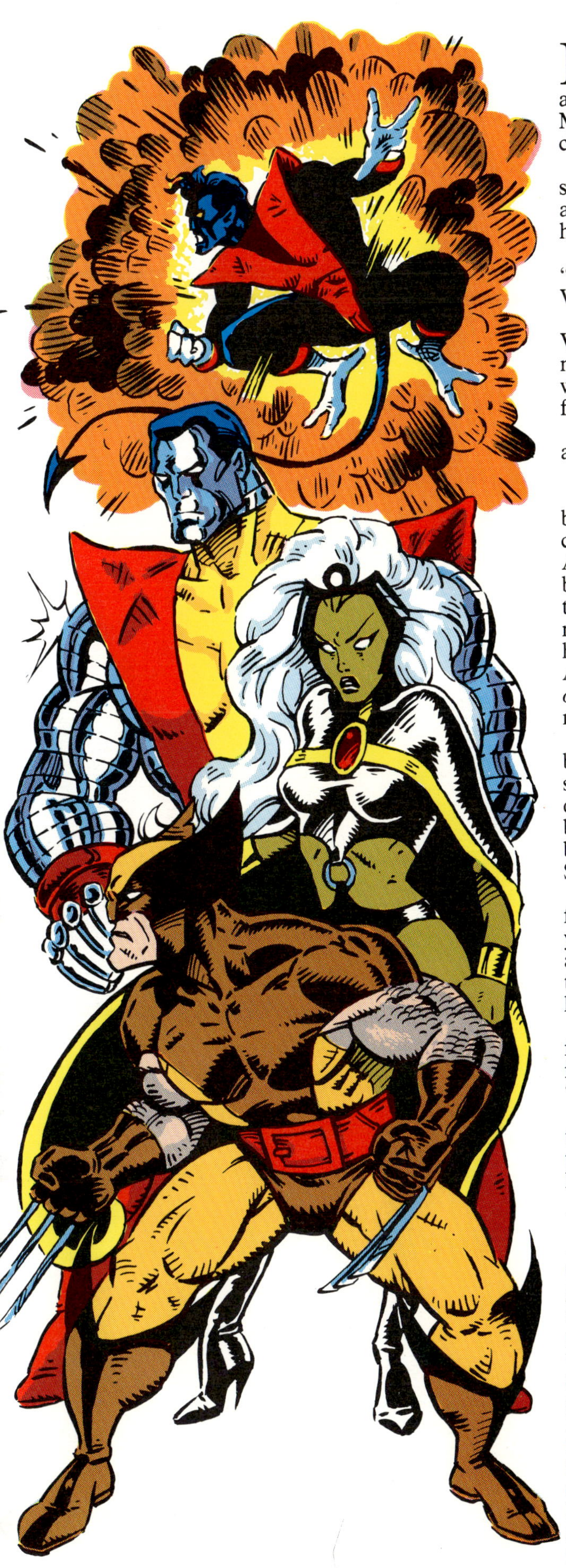

Kitty and Ororo were greeted by the wheelchair bound Professor Charles Xavier as their chauffeur pulled up at the entrance to X-Men mansion. Behind him, pushing the wheelchair, was Colossus, still in his human form.

"Children," Xavier began as soon as they stepped from the car, as though what he was about to say had gone past its sell-by date, "Scott has returned with some . . . old friends."

Storm was the first to question the Professor: "Cyclops? Here? Why the long face, Professor? Where's Warren?"

As if to answer Storms' question, Warren Worthington III, better known as the high flying mutant, Angel, stepped from the mansion wearing a familiar blue and gold outfit. Three figures followed him.

"Hello, Storm. Why so shocked?" Angel asked, his wing feathers rippling in the breeze.

"That costume . . . you're. . ."

"Going back to our roots, Storm," Cyclops butted in. "You new X-Men have had your chance to prove yourselves and you've blown it. All of you have acted like amateurs in the field of battle and it cost Marvel Girl her life. This new team are destroying the dream that Xavier and myself worked towards. The dream of global harmony between the human and mutant races. And so I have taken it upon myself to re-form the *original* X-Men to try to save the X-Men's good name."

Storm looked slowly at her comrades as the blue-furred beast and the frost-covered Iceman stepped from the shadows. Kitty's face had dropped in disbelief. Colossus stood silently behind the Professor's wheelchair with a look of bewilderment across his strong features. Xavier, Storm noted, was as unemotional as ever.

It was the Beast who finally brought Storm from her thoughts. "Face it, Storm – you had your chance. Now it's time to stop the horseplay and let the *real* X-Men take over. You can leave the mansion at your leisure. But don't take too long or you might get cold feet!"

A snowball slapped across the Beast's furry features. "And what's wrong with having cold feet, Hank?" laughed Bobby Drake, the Iceman. "I spend half my life with froze' toes!"

How the X-Men could lark about at a time like this was beyond Ororo – but then she was too busy thinking about the ramifications this twist would have on her and her team-mates.

Kitty Pryde lay on her bed crying to no-one in particular when she heard the knock at her door. Peter Rasputin stood in her doorway gazing into space for long moments before he spoke. Peter Rasputin, whose name was on every page of Kitty's diary since they had first met. He was a hunk. He was amazing. He was also the mutant X-Man known as Colossus, with the ability to transform his body into organic steel. Kitty cursed her stupid teenage shyness every time she looked at him. She wiped the tears from her eyes as Colossus spoke, but she knew she couldn't wipe away the red nose-and-cheeks they had left. Perhaps she was glad of the red cheeks, at least they would disguise her embarrassment from him.

"Kitty," Colossus began, in his soft, friendly voice. Despite his formidable appearance Peter Rasputin was one of the gentlest souls one is ever likely to meet. "I heard you sobbing as I passed and thought . . . thought you might need a friend."

Kitty wrapped her arms around his enormous shoulders as she began to wail once more. "Oh, Peter – I'm never going to be an X-Man now. I know it must sound stupid but I really wanted to fit in and now . . .now I'll never get the chance."

"Look at you, Kitten – crying over something you've never even had. Being an X-Man is never as easy as it looks. There has been a lot of heartache in this team already and I think that one of your tender years might be better off never having to suffer such things."

Kitty almost throttled Rasputin: "Just because I'm younger than the rest of you doesn't mean th. . ." she stopped herself. What had she been thinking of? If she was really so mature she'd have to start acting like it. And that meant taking this like an adult.

Storm was watering her plants in her attic room. When Storm watered her plants she simply flicked her wrist and created, as her name suggested, a tiny rain shower. "I can't believe it, little ones," she told her houseplants. "All of us have done our best to be good X-Men, all of us believed in the dream, but now, by the Goddess, we have all been cast away like . . ."

Storm clenched her fists in an attempt to contain her rage. As the leader of this team, she thought, it was her duty to do as she saw fit. Even if that meant fighting her would-be friends to regain her place in the team.

"I hope it doesn't come to that," she said quietly. "But I fear that it will."

"Dem's fightin' words!!" cried the Beast as Professor Xavier threw the switch that brought the Danger Room to life.

Iceman had already created an ice shield to protect his team-mates against an armada of tiny robots. Each was armed with a minute laser cannon stocking enough power to knock any of the mutant heroes in the room for six. Angel took to the air as Cyclops barked commands at his three comrades. The Angel had never seen Scott so eager for battle. Sweat was already visible on Cyclops' face (where his mask and ruby quartz visor didn't hide it) and he didn't seem to be holding back with his optic blasts – bolts of pure energy powerful enough to level a building. The Angel always remembered Scott as the cautious member of the team, the one who always kept his power in check, the one who would never let his own emotions control his actions on the battle field. Now, however, Cyclops was attacking these robots as though his very life depended on it, as though it would bring back the woman he loved. . . Angel stopped himself in mid-thought; to think that Scott should have changed so much since Jean (Marvel Girl) Grey's death was impossible. He told himself several times during their session in the Danger Room that Scott was just trying to prove how good the original X-Men were, or that he himself had hung around with these amateur X-Men for too long and forgotten

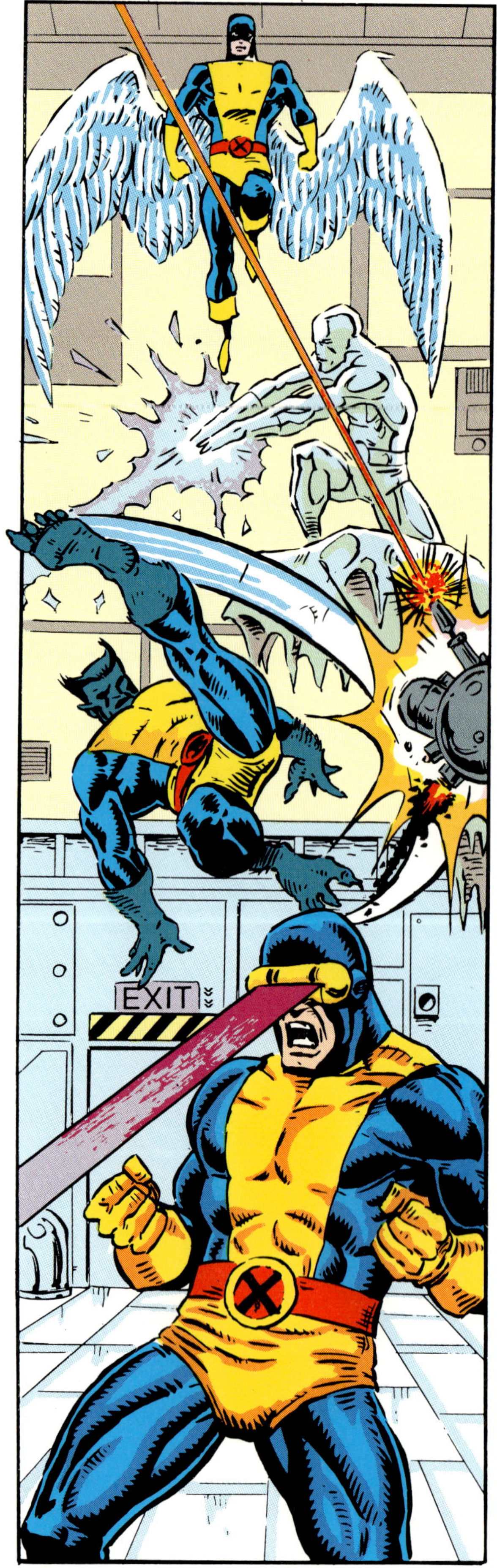

what a real hero fights like, or that Scott had always fought this hard and that the Angel had simply forgotten or not noticed before now. But whatever the Angel told himself he knew, in his heart-of-hearts, that this was not the same Scott Summers whom he had grown up with. This was a stronger, surer and far more angry young man. And, the Angel pondered as he destroyed another robot by swooping past its visual sensors at high speed and setting it into a state of computerised confusion, his other friends – Hank (Beast) McCoy and Bobby (Iceman) Drake – seemed to be playing a little harder than he remembered.

"Perhaps you're just getting old, Warren," he told himself as he dive-bombed another of the computerised attackers.

Professor Charles Xavier was confused. Xavier, the greatest living telepath known and the leader and founder of the X-Men, was rarely a confused man. When you can read any individual's mind as easily as you can read the daily newspaper, it is a very rare day indeed that the world can truly surprise you. But, for some reason, Professor X could not read the mind waves of these newcomers to X-Men mansion. It was even more surprising since he had known this trio since they were teenagers no older than Kitty Pryde. Yet, for some reason, Xavier was having a lot of difficulty making out anything from the garbled mind messages he was receiving from Cyclops, Iceman and the Beast. He toyed with a pencil for a moment as he stared out at the Danger Room. When he put down the pencil he had reached an answer: the trio of Original X-Men had been trained by Xavier himself to resist mind control and it was only natural that their own mental training left mechanisms which could resist any attempt to infiltrate their minds. Xavier picked up the pencil and scribbled down two words idly for later reference in his journal.

It was an uncomfortable situation but none of them really expected it to be anything but. Eight mutants sat around the massive dinner table finishing dessert. Cyclops, Iceman, the Beast and the Angel still wore their yellow and indigo costumes – the Beast looking somewhat cramped to be wearing a full-body outfit over his recently acquired shaggy blue fur. The four of them had just left their training session for this meal and sat opposite Storm, Colossus, the Professor and Kitty. The meal had been deadly silent except for the slurping of the soup as the Beast tried to get his fangs around the spoon. But now it was Kitty's turn to break the ice:

"You smell!"

The table turned to face the young would-be hero, collectively confused at her awkward statement.

"You heard me. I said you smell. Real bad," she stood with her palms on the table top and looked at the four mutants opposite her. "In fact," she said as the table sat with bated breath, "you guys really stink!"

"Gee, Katherine, we didn't get time for a shower before the meal. . .I'm sorry if it put you off your food," the Iceman tried in his best diplomatic voice. He was met with a blob of ice cream from Kitty's spoon full in the eye closely followed by the spoon itself.

Professor Xavier reached for Kitty's arm to make her sit at the table again but his own mental powers warned him that this was a girl who needed to vent some anger.

"Why did you have to come along now – when I'd just gained my place as a trainee X-Man? You come along here like you own the place and act like the X-Men are the worst thing since. . ."

"Hush, child," Cyclops stared Kitty in the eye for an excruciatingly long second, or at least she thought he was staring at her beneath his ruby visor. "You know nothing of what it is to be an X-Man so I would advise that you sit down before you make anymore a fool of yourself than you already have!" Scott was unusually cold.

Kitty stood there for a moment, looking at Peter and Ororo and, finally, the Professor. Her eyes begged for some support, some back-up, something.

Storm eventually joined the argument: "She does have a point, Scott – the new X-Men have proven a formidable force in the field of combat. We are hardly the amateurs you make us out to be. Why, Wolverine is more seasoned in combat than any of us, including yourself."

Cyclops' mouth dropped. "Wolverine," he said slowly, taking a breath between each word as if playing for time, "is primarily a loner. His team spirit is hardly evident from his current behaviour – running off to Canada to fight his own little wars as though his commitment to the X-Men is just an afterthought."

"That's hardly fair, Scott," the Professor added in Storm's defence, "Wolverine is in Canada tying up some loose ends that have dangled since I first recruited his services from the Canadian government. He's doing it to keep us all *out* of his personal wars. . ."

"And 'wars' just about sums up Wolverines' position in this team. He's dangerous, in fact he's a psychopath and he can't be controlled. I think we'd all be better off if he didn't come back at all, don't you?" Scott Summers gritted his teeth as he sat back in his chair, glaring at the others across the table.

Colossus began in his soft masculine voice, tinged with the accent of his Russian homeland, "I can't say that I am opposed to your argument that you X-Men have had more experience than us, Scott, but I do object to you defaming Wolverine's character. He has proven both a valuable asset and a faithful friend to me and my colleagues and, whatever your personal grudges against the man, I think it is very unfair of you to speak of him with such malice."

"He's right, Scott. You and Wolvie may never have seen eye-to-eye on tactics and principles but the man has shown himself to be trustworthy," the Angel said without looking up from the table. It was clearly hard for the Angel to say anything against his long-time friend – Cyclops – but he would not stand for this schoolgirlish bitching about a fellow X-Man. The Angel was very confused as to who his friends were right now and this petty arguing did not help matters. He had felt out of place with the new X-Men, joining their ranks only recently and discovering that he had to put in a lot of long hours in the Danger

Room to come up to their high calibre and hold his head proudly as he fought beside them. He had hoped for a return of the halcyon days when the originals fought and played together. But now that Scott and the others had returned he found them different somehow, colder. His loyalties most assuredly lay with the X-Men but the question he kept asking himself was 'who are the X-Men, now?'. And so he found himself arguing for both teams, old and new, and yet he had sided with his old team-mates. Perhaps it was his lot to always be an outcast. From humanity because of his sixteen feet wings, and from the mutants because of his confused principles.

"Cripes – listen to yourselves," Kitty butted in, "talking about Wolverine as though he were dead!"

"With the tactics he employs to fight I'm surprised that he isn't!" Bobby muttered, still wiping ice cream from his eyes.

"Whatever you may think of us, Scott Summers, we have all learnt one thing from being X-Men . . . and that is never to give up on what you believe in," the passion in Storm's voice was vibrant.

"Make your point, Storm," said the Beast, smiling to himself.

"Well, 'X-Men'," Storm emphasised the word as though it were derogatory, "I refuse to give up on this team. Whatever you say about our abilities we have all pledged allegiance to the Professor's dream and I, for one, will fight for my position in this team in every way available to me."

Ironically, Ororo *stormed* off, slamming the door to the dining room as she went.

Early the next morning, as Peter Rasputin packed his stuff and prepared to leave the American mansion he had called home these past months, he heard the warning signal of the X-Mens' vid-phone. He rushed to answer it, questioning as he went whether it was his place to receive their messages since he was no longer an official X-Man.

Switching to his Colossus mode of organic steel as he pressed the 'receive call' button (to protect his identity) he told the caller that they had reached X-Men mansion. On the other end of the line, dressed in red, white and blue was the star spangled Captain America:

"Hi, Colossus – this is Captain America at Avengers Mansion," his legendary smile filled the screen. The sort of smile that grandparents are supposed to have, the sort of smile that could bring you out of your worst depression. In fact, Captain America's smiling face on war bonds had helped many through the Great Depression more than forty years ago. Colossus had never understood how young the Captain still looked. "We've just received a message from our liaison in the Canadian Government to say that our counterparts there – Alpha Flight – are finding some evidence on their current mission and hope to have it all wrapped up in the next few hours. Details are top secret, but I gather Wolverine and Nightcrawler, two of your own members, have met with the team and are safe and sound. Just thought I'd pass the message along in case you were worried about their safety."

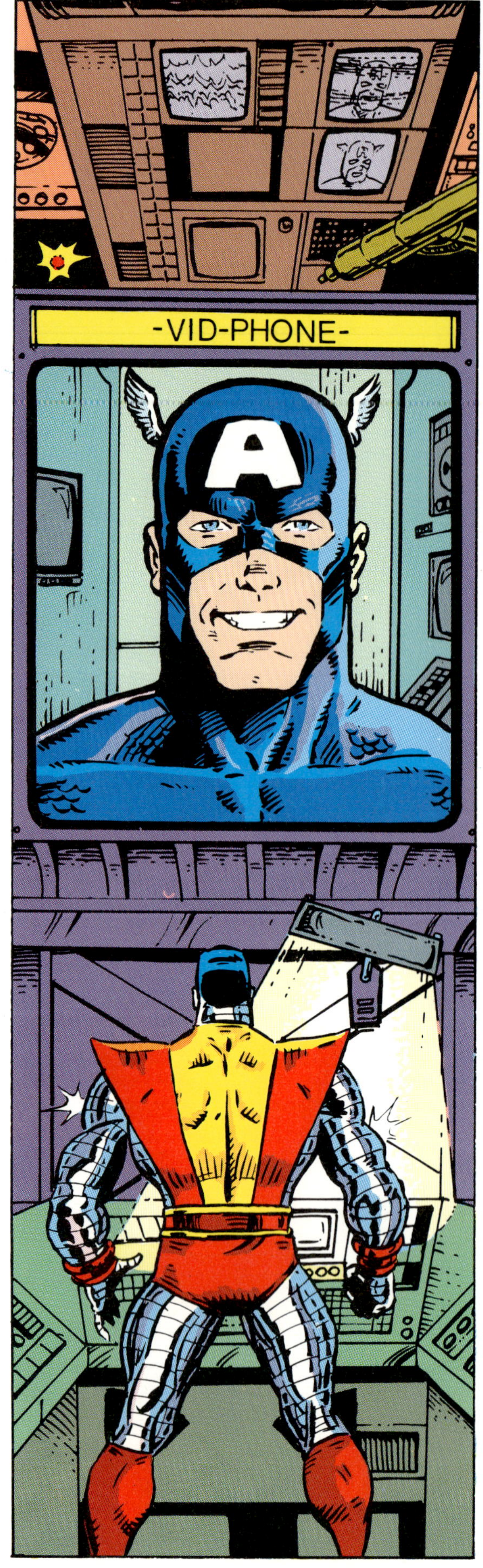

"We learned long ago never to worry for Wolverine's safety, Captain, but thank you for keeping us informed."

The link broke and Colossus went back to his packing, something nagging him in the back of his mind. He went through the message in his mind again: The Captain with his smile and his kind manner and tone as though he had known you all your life and more; the other Avengers passing by behind, doubtless heading towards another Earth-threatening disaster; the mention that the case was top secret. Yes, he thought, it must be that. Peter Rasputin hated things that were 'Top Secret'. It always lead to a mistrust between the State and its people. That must be it. He put the event to the back of his mind and continued to pack his clothes. "Wait 'til you see what I got, Ma," he chuckled to himself as he packed his 'Rolling Stones on Tour' t-shirt. Had they heard of the Rolling Stones in Russia, he wondered?

Xavier read through the message left by Colossus on his desk. It told him of the conversation with Captain America and that he was sorry if he'd missed the Professor when he left. "Such a good hearted lad," he said to himself.

Xavier linked himself up with the Cerebro headset and computer attachment. Cerebro enhanced Xavier's already formidable psi-powers so that he could look at the World Scope. It enabled him to track down and list all the mutants in the world as and when their powers manifested themselves. That was how he had discovered Kitty. A little blip on his skull's interior had told him where to locate her. Of course, it was a dangerous process, enhancing one's powers to read minds so that he could touch everyone in the nation, at least, but Xavier had pledged himself to catalogue the growing mutant population. Latest figures suggested that as many as one in every five children born had the possibility to generate some mutant power, however trivial, although thankfully most would never exhibit any signs of their potential. Those that did, of course, could prove to be dangerous to humanity unless Xavier could reach them in time to show them how to use their powers. That was one of the reasons Xavier had taken in Kitty at such a young age. Her power to phase through walls could prove destructive if it got into the wrong hands. The wrong hands were, unfortunately, all too often those who pledge to do us good, thought Xavier.

Now, call it luck or call it coincidence, but whatever it was it would prove drastically important to the X-Men's future that Xavier decided to use his enhancing machine, Cerebro, to scan his own pupils. It was the last time they would all be here, thought Xavier, and there would be no harm done in taking a quick peek at their inner cogs.

Colossus was still packing with thoughts of his motherland – Russia, which he missed very much. Xavier was always amazed at the simplicity of Peter's thoughts. They were always of a happier future, of a determination to better himself. They were beautiful thoughts that Peter reflected in his sketches.

Then he moved on to the smooth contours of Storm's mind. Her thoughts were no longer as serene as they had been in the past. Xavier had often felt he could wallow in a foam bath of her thoughts and never want to escape, but such things, he knew from experience, were dangerous.

Kitty's thoughts were full of the anger and vitality and naivety of youth. They were the sort of thoughts we can only hold onto during our brief teenage years – where everything is a crisis against us but it's all forgotten in the morning.

The Angel's thoughts were more ugly than the others. He was filled with fear of his own future with the team. Every day, it seemed, the Angel looked for a better tomorrow.

And what of the older X-Men?

Cyclops?

Beast?

Iceman?

Xavier was shocked to see they had no understandable thought patterns. It was as though their sea of thought waves had reached low tide and never come back. Xavier checked Cerebro's display once more. There were five mutants in the house including himself. Storm, Colossus, Kitty, Angel and himself. No other mutants.

Xavier continued checking and double checking his conclusions for almost an hour before he realised that the so-called Original X-Men *weren't*.

CONTINUED ON PAGE 56

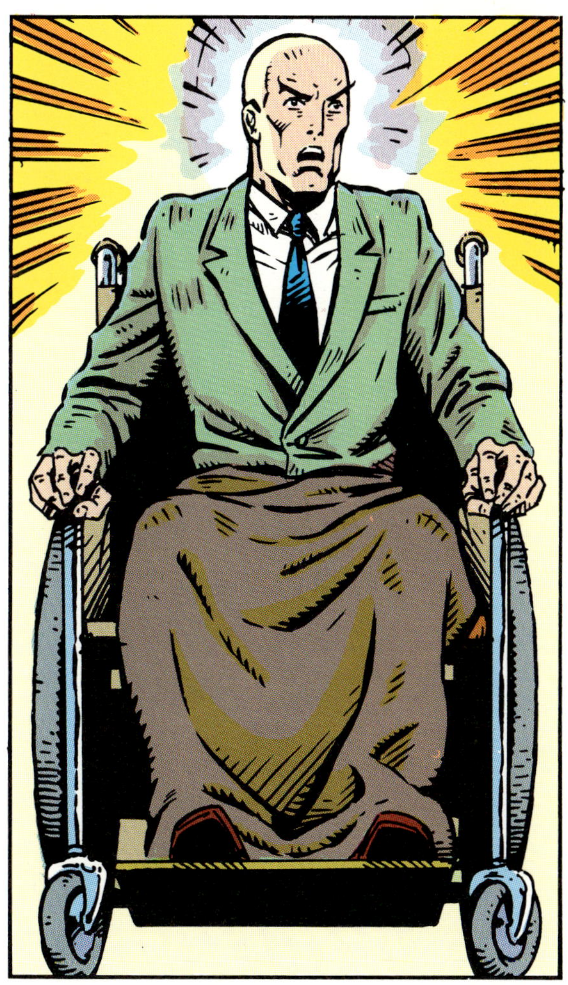

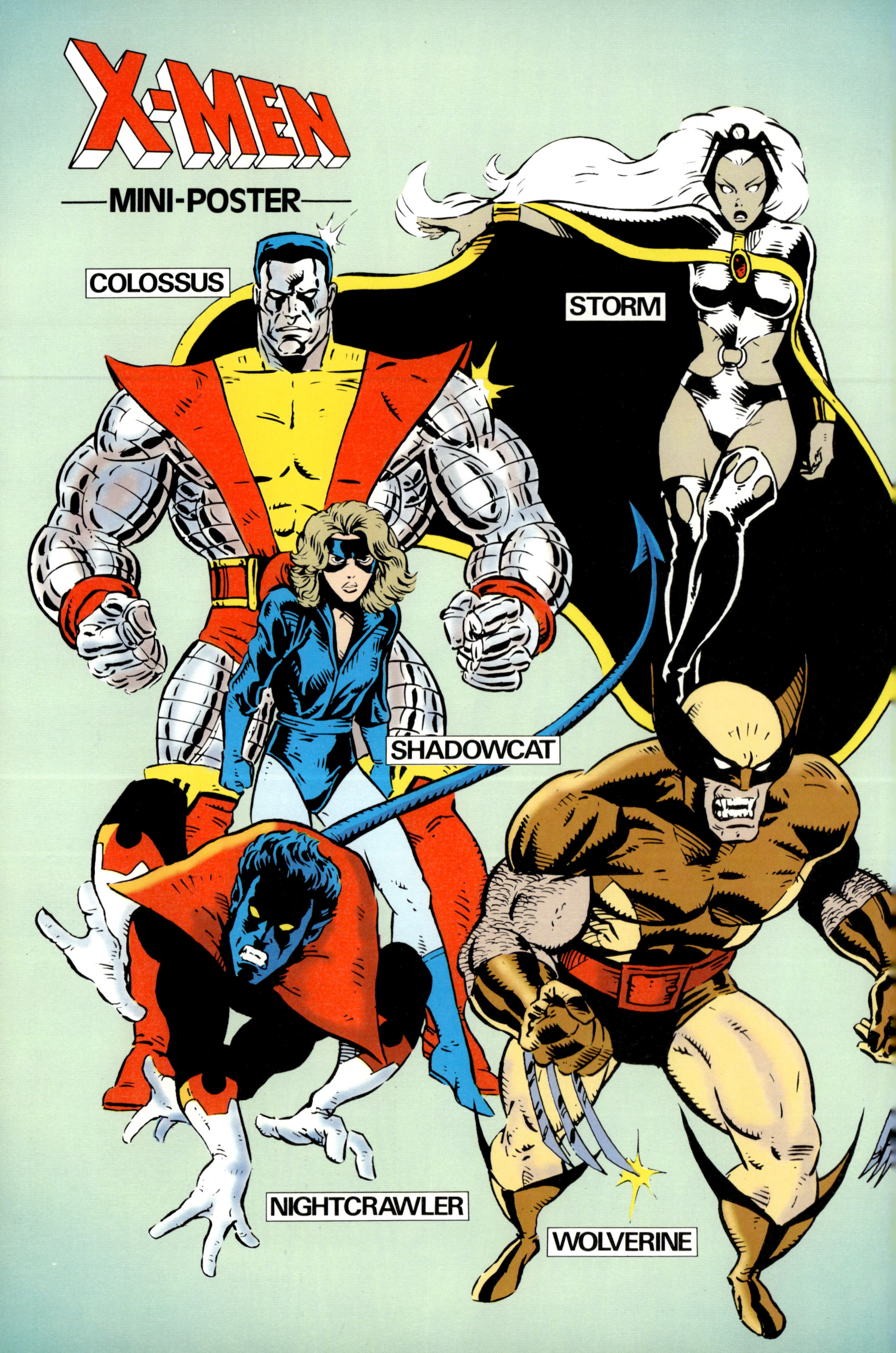
X-MEN
MINI-POSTER
COLOSSUS
STORM
SHADOWCAT
NIGHTCRAWLER
WOLVERINE

Cyclops. Storm. Nightcrawler. Wolverine. Colossus. Children of the atom, students of Charles Xavier, MUTANTS — feared and hated by the world they have sworn to protect. These are the STRANGEST heroes of all!

Stan Lee PRESENTS: THE UNCANNY X-MEN!™

CHRIS CLAREMONT WRITER | JOHN BYRNE PLOT-PENCILS | TERRY AUSTIN INKER | TOM ORZECHOWSKI, letterer GLYNIS WEIN, colourist | LOUISE JONES EDITOR | PART 2

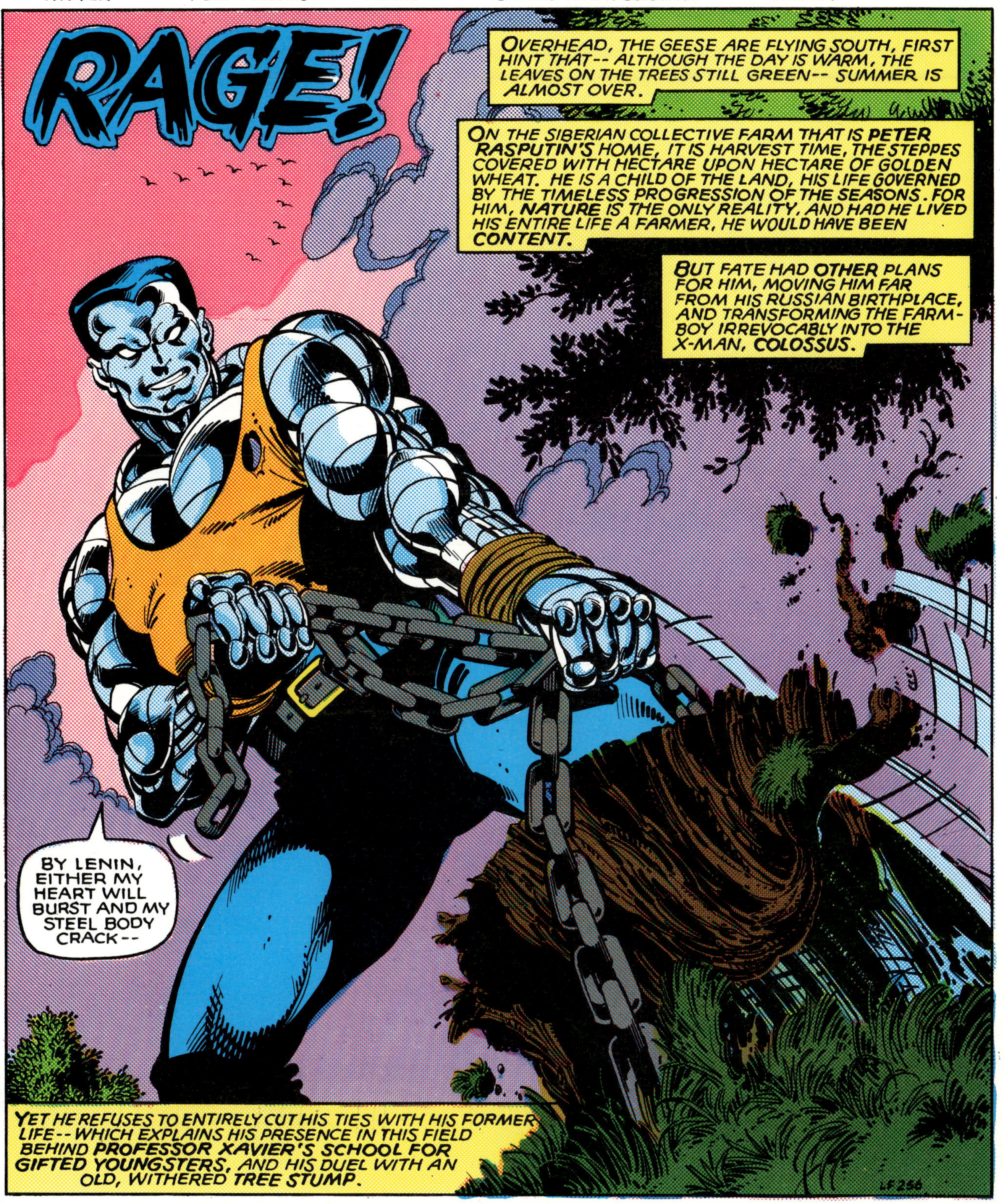

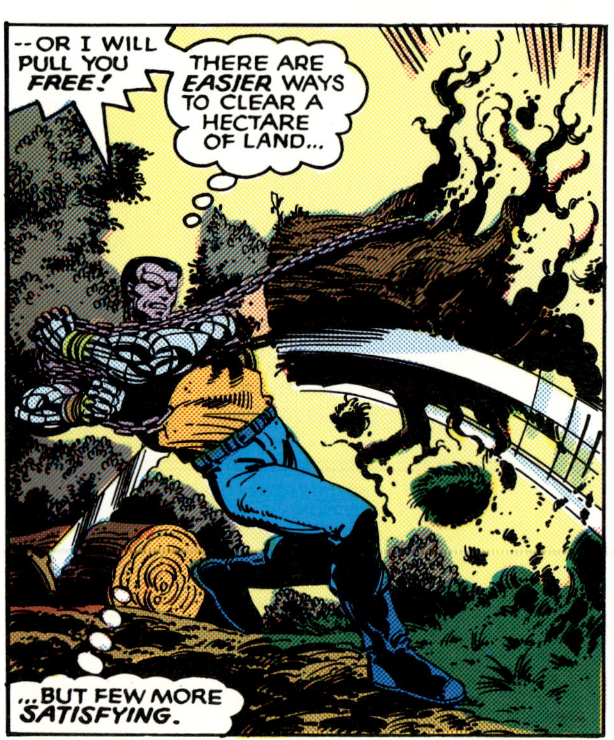
--OR I WILL PULL YOU FREE!
THERE ARE EASIER WAYS TO CLEAR A HECTARE OF LAND...
...BUT FEW MORE SATISFYING.

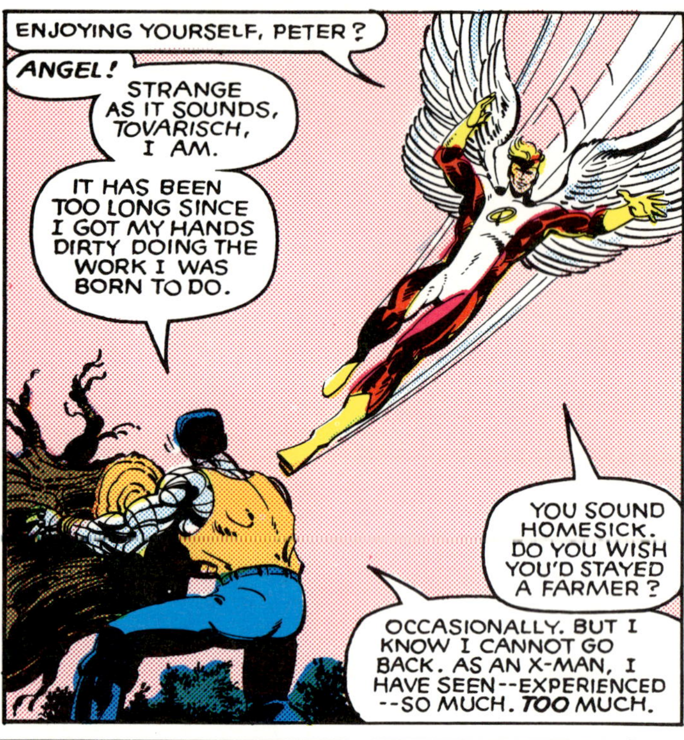
ENJOYING YOURSELF, PETER?
ANGEL!
STRANGE AS IT SOUNDS, TOVARISCH, I AM.
IT HAS BEEN TOO LONG SINCE I GOT MY HANDS DIRTY DOING THE WORK I WAS BORN TO DO.
YOU SOUND HOMESICK. DO YOU WISH YOU'D STAYED A FARMER?
OCCASIONALLY. BUT I KNOW I CANNOT GO BACK. AS AN X-MAN, I HAVE SEEN--EXPERIENCED --SO MUCH. TOO MUCH.

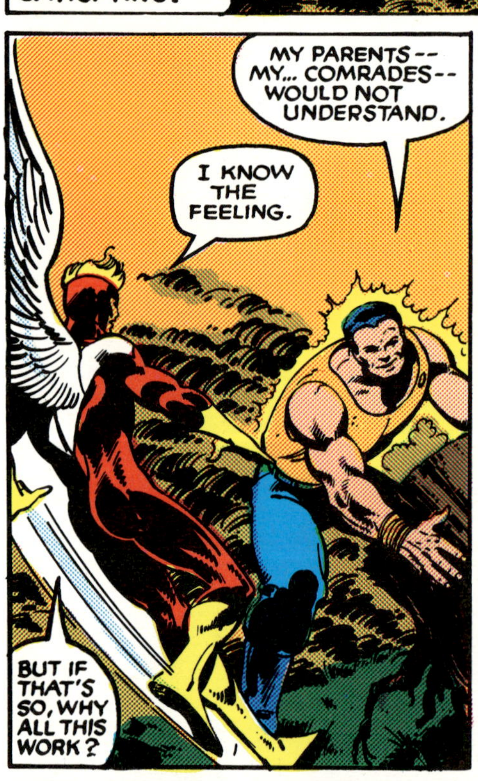
MY PARENTS--MY... COMRADES--WOULD NOT UNDERSTAND.
I KNOW THE FEELING.
BUT IF THAT'S SO, WHY ALL THIS WORK?

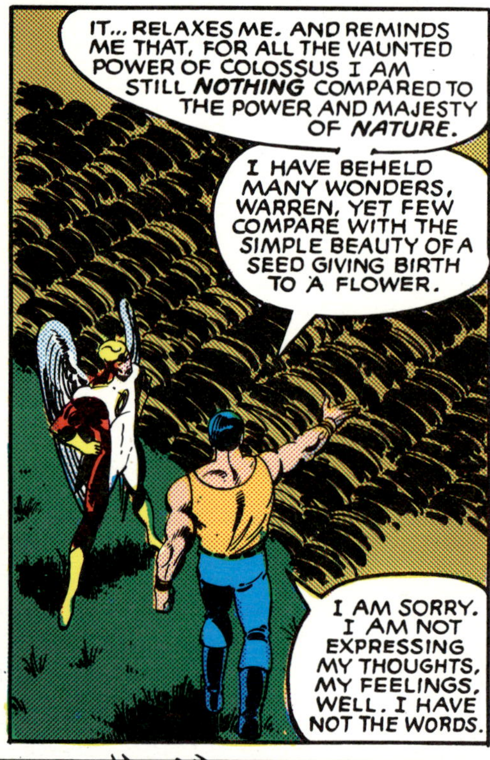
IT... RELAXES ME. AND REMINDS ME THAT, FOR ALL THE VAUNTED POWER OF COLOSSUS I AM STILL NOTHING COMPARED TO THE POWER AND MAJESTY OF NATURE.
I HAVE BEHELD MANY WONDERS, WARREN, YET FEW COMPARE WITH THE SIMPLE BEAUTY OF A SEED GIVING BIRTH TO A FLOWER.
I AM SORRY. I AM NOT EXPRESSING MY THOUGHTS, MY FEELINGS, WELL. I HAVE NOT THE WORDS.

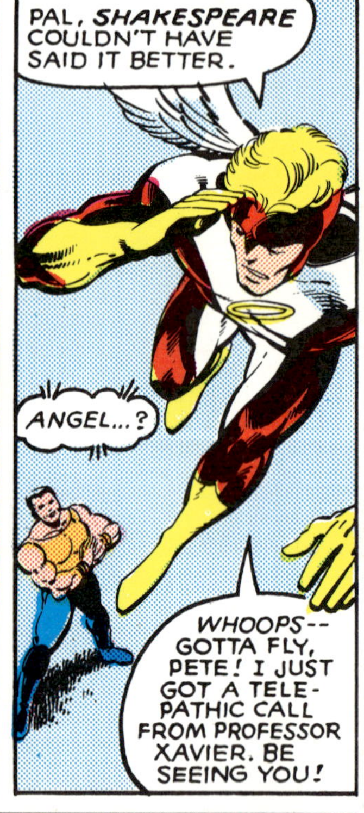
PAL, SHAKESPEARE COULDN'T HAVE SAID IT BETTER.
ANGEL...?
WHOOPS--GOTTA FLY, PETE! I JUST GOT A TELE-PATHIC CALL FROM PROFESSOR XAVIER. BE SEEING YOU!

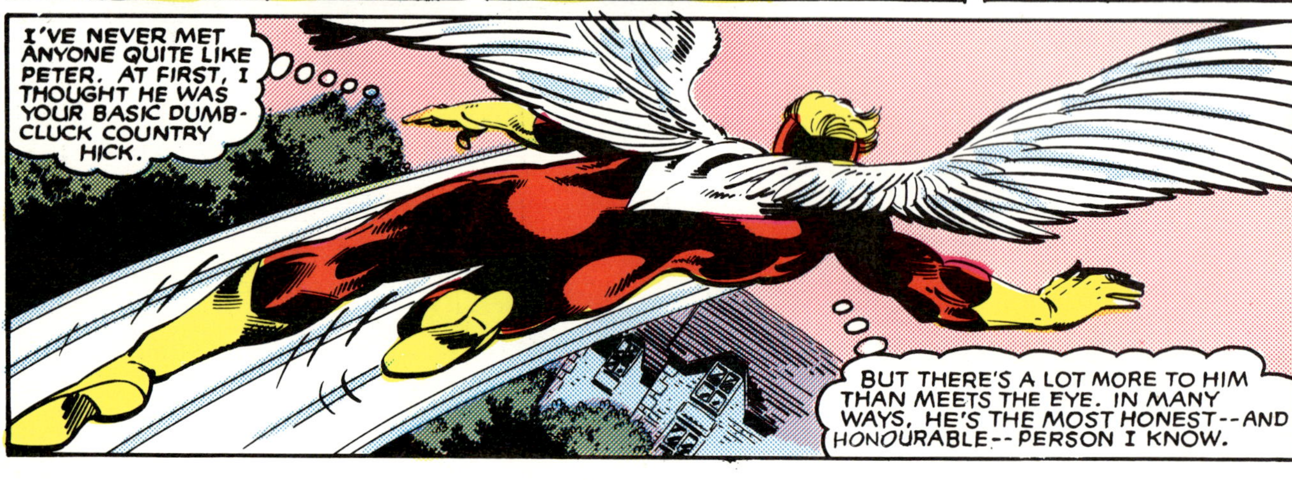
I'VE NEVER MET ANYONE QUITE LIKE PETER. AT FIRST, I THOUGHT HE WAS YOUR BASIC DUMB-CLUCK COUNTRY HICK.
BUT THERE'S A LOT MORE TO HIM THAN MEETS THE EYE. IN MANY WAYS, HE'S THE MOST HONEST--AND HONOURABLE--PERSON I KNOW.

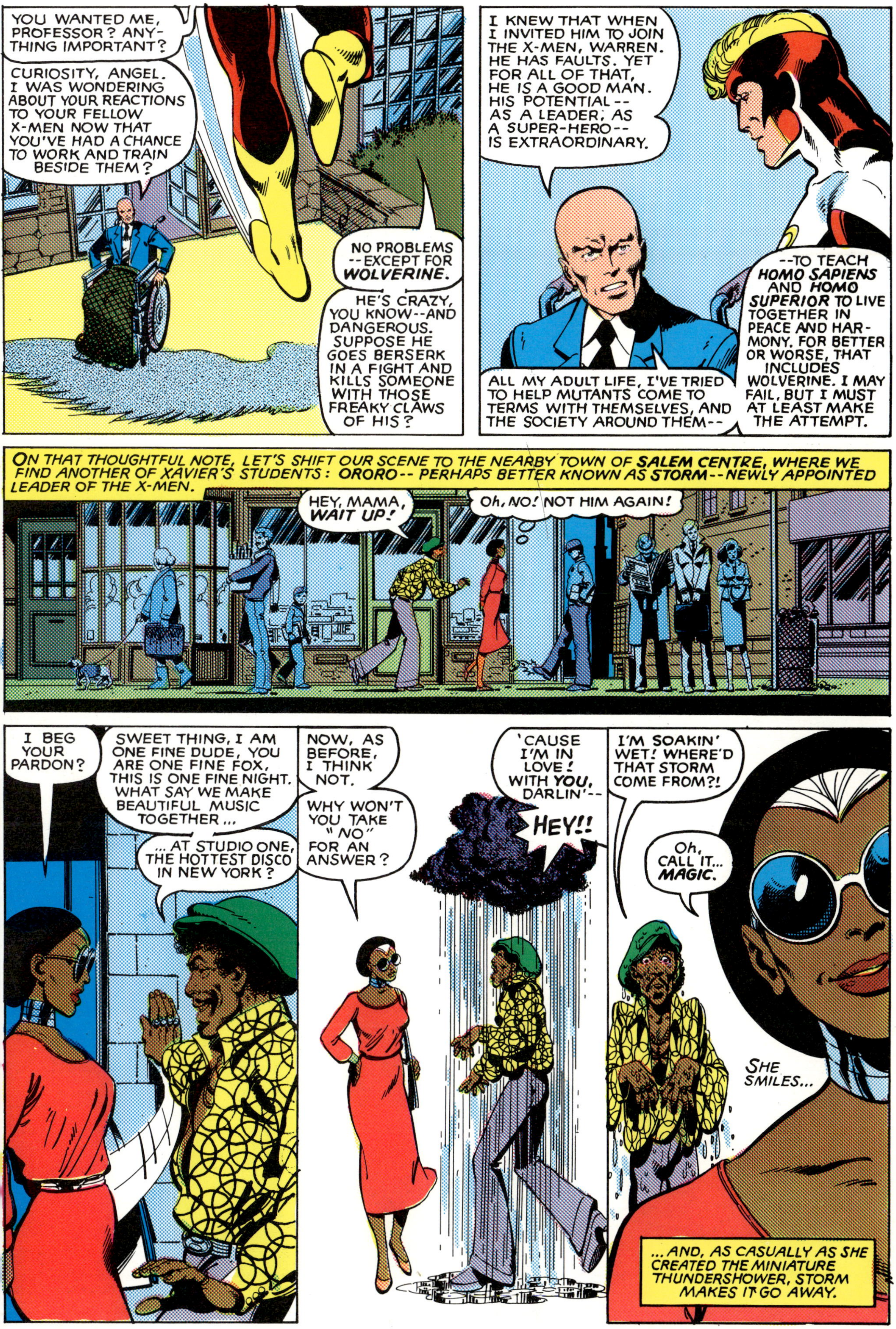

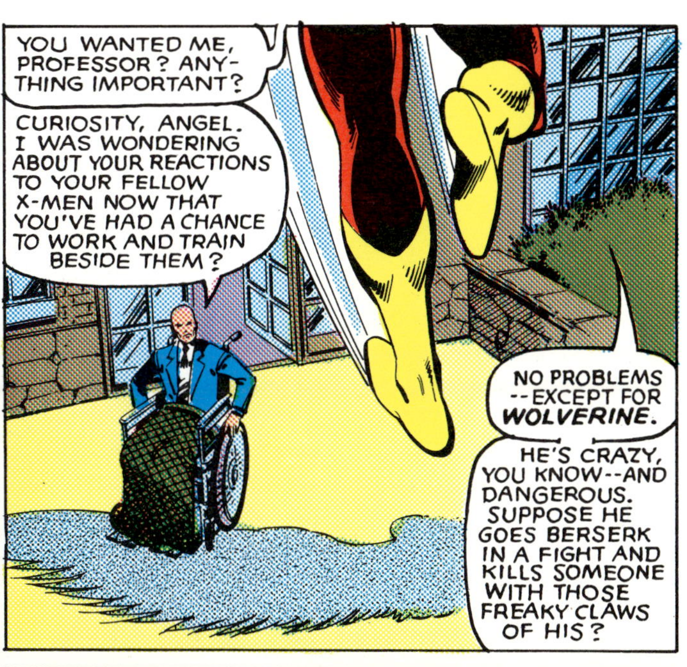

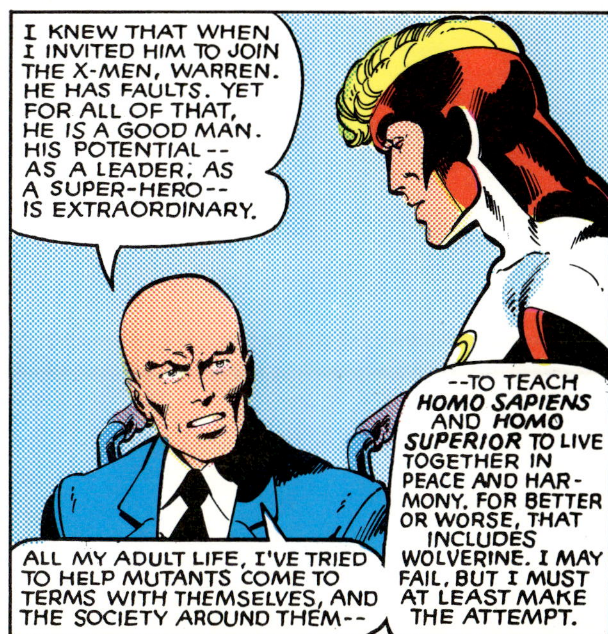

*ON THAT THOUGHTFUL NOTE, LET'S SHIFT OUR SCENE TO THE NEARBY TOWN OF **SALEM CENTRE**, WHERE WE FIND ANOTHER OF XAVIER'S STUDENTS: **ORORO**-- PERHAPS BETTER KNOWN AS **STORM**--NEWLY APPOINTED LEADER OF THE X-MEN.*

HEY, MAMA, ***WAIT UP!***

Oh, NO! NOT HIM AGAIN!

I BEG YOUR PARDON?

SWEET THING, I AM ONE FINE DUDE, YOU ARE ONE FINE FOX, THIS IS ONE FINE NIGHT. WHAT SAY WE MAKE BEAUTIFUL MUSIC TOGETHER...

...AT STUDIO ONE, THE HOTTEST DISCO IN NEW YORK?

NOW, AS BEFORE, I THINK NOT.

WHY WON'T YOU TAKE "NO" FOR AN ANSWER?

'CAUSE I'M IN LOVE! WITH **YOU**, DARLIN'--

HEY!!

I'M SOAKIN' WET! WHERE'D THAT STORM COME FROM?!

Oh, CALL IT... ***MAGIC.***

SHE SMILES...

...AND, AS CASUALLY AS SHE CREATED THE MINIATURE THUNDERSHOWER, STORM MAKES IT GO AWAY.

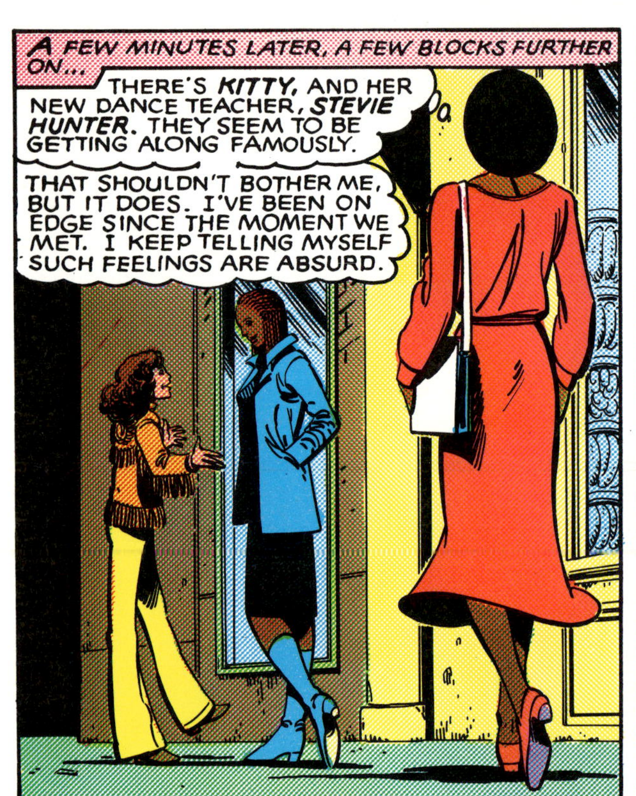
A FEW MINUTES LATER, A FEW BLOCKS FURTHER ON...
THERE'S KITTY, AND HER NEW DANCE TEACHER, STEVIE HUNTER. THEY SEEM TO BE GETTING ALONG FAMOUSLY.
THAT SHOULDN'T BOTHER ME, BUT IT DOES. I'VE BEEN ON EDGE SINCE THE MOMENT WE MET. I KEEP TELLING MYSELF SUCH FEELINGS ARE ABSURD.

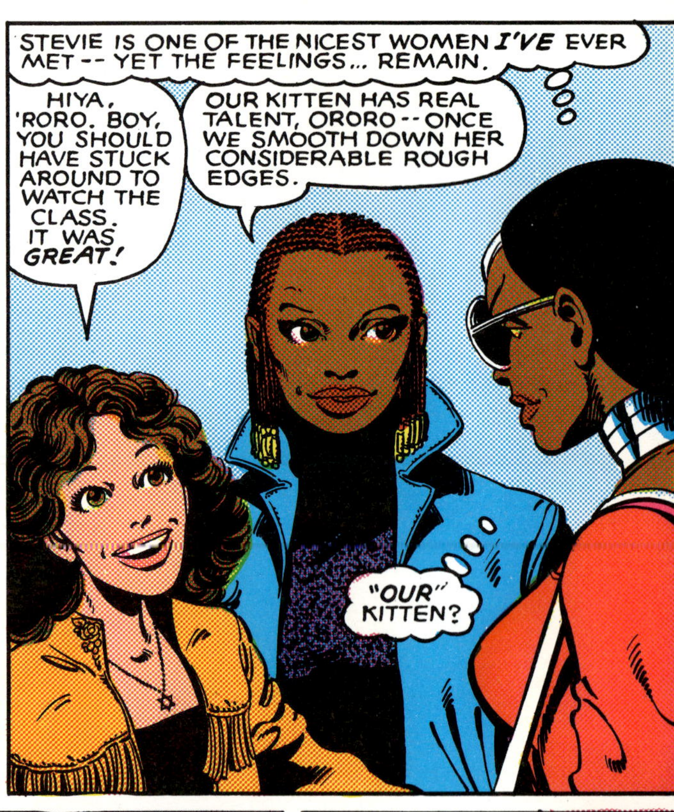
STEVIE IS ONE OF THE NICEST WOMEN I'VE EVER MET -- YET THE FEELINGS... REMAIN.
HIYA, 'RORO. BOY, YOU SHOULD HAVE STUCK AROUND TO WATCH THE CLASS. IT WAS GREAT!
OUR KITTEN HAS REAL TALENT, ORORO -- ONCE WE SMOOTH DOWN HER CONSIDERABLE ROUGH EDGES.
"OUR" KITTEN?

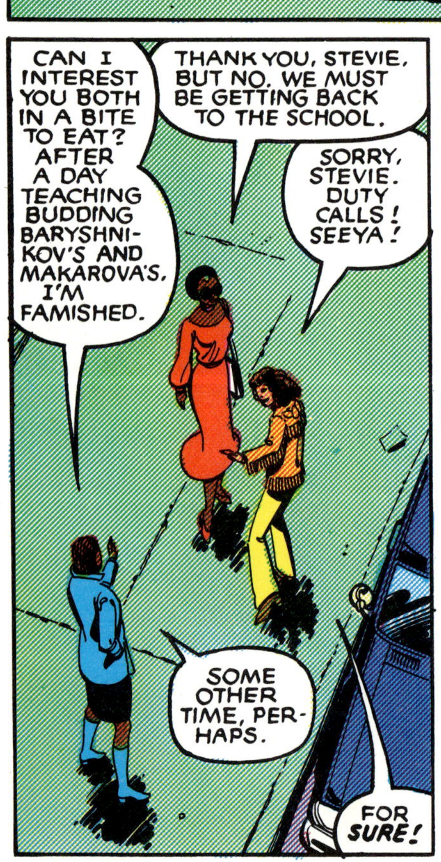
CAN I INTEREST YOU BOTH IN A BITE TO EAT? AFTER A DAY TEACHING BUDDING BARYSHNIKOV'S AND MAKAROVA'S, I'M FAMISHED.
THANK YOU, STEVIE, BUT NO. WE MUST BE GETTING BACK TO THE SCHOOL.
SORRY, STEVIE. DUTY CALLS! SEEYA!
SOME OTHER TIME, PERHAPS.
FOR SURE!

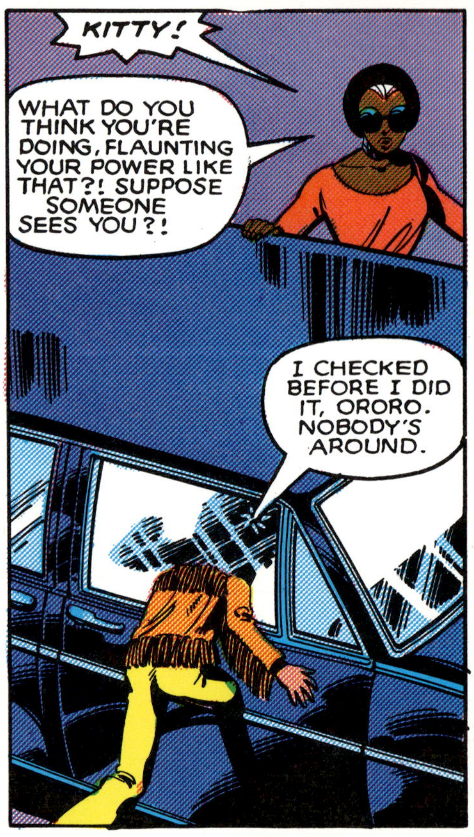
KITTY!
WHAT DO YOU THINK YOU'RE DOING, FLAUNTING YOUR POWER LIKE THAT?! SUPPOSE SOMEONE SEES YOU?!
I CHECKED BEFORE I DID IT, ORORO. NOBODY'S AROUND.

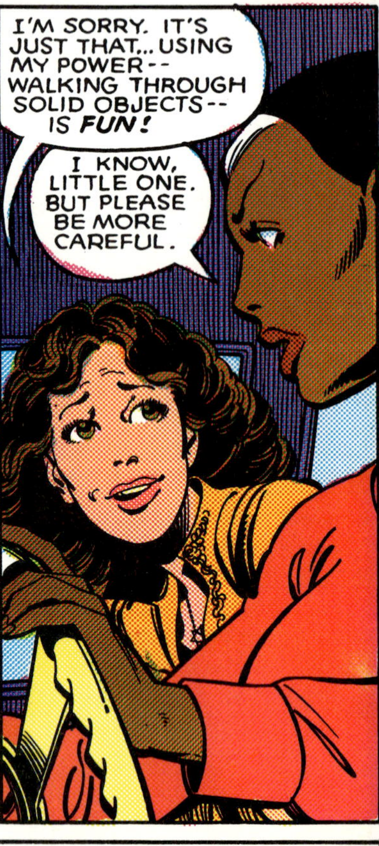
I'M SORRY. IT'S JUST THAT... USING MY POWER -- WALKING THROUGH SOLID OBJECTS -- IS FUN!
I KNOW, LITTLE ONE. BUT PLEASE BE MORE CAREFUL.

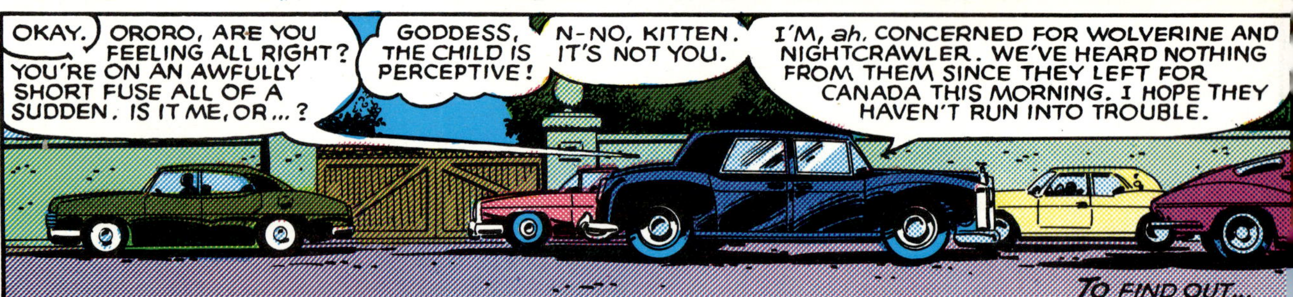
OKAY.
ORORO, ARE YOU FEELING ALL RIGHT? YOU'RE ON AN AWFULLY SHORT FUSE ALL OF A SUDDEN. IS IT ME, OR...?
GODDESS, THE CHILD IS PERCEPTIVE!
N-NO, KITTEN. IT'S NOT YOU.
I'M, ah, CONCERNED FOR WOLVERINE AND NIGHTCRAWLER. WE'VE HEARD NOTHING FROM THEM SINCE THEY LEFT FOR CANADA THIS MORNING. I HOPE THEY HAVEN'T RUN INTO TROUBLE.
TO FIND OUT...

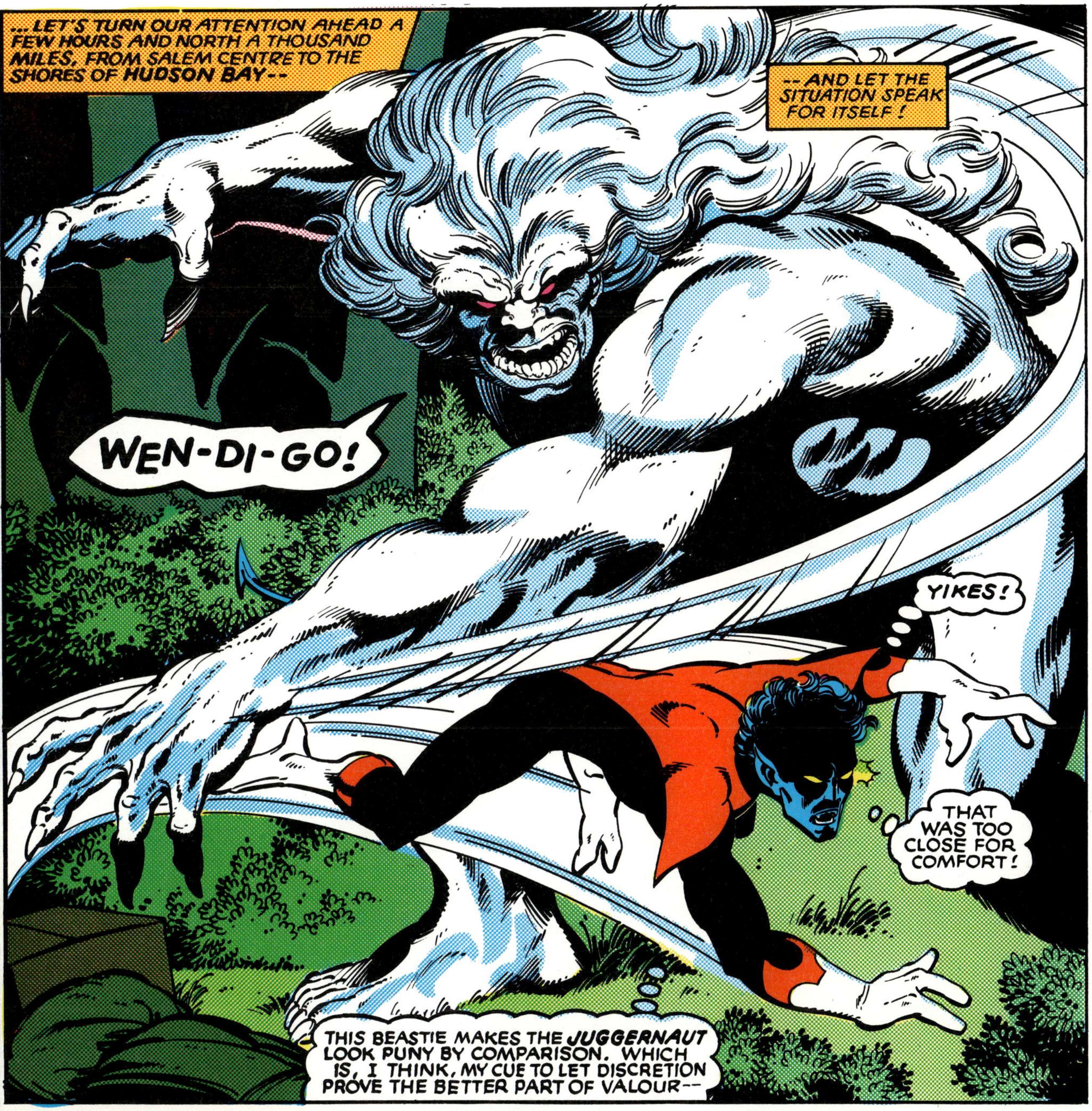

...LET'S TURN OUR ATTENTION AHEAD A FEW HOURS AND NORTH A THOUSAND MILES, FROM SALEM CENTRE TO THE SHORES OF HUDSON BAY--

--AND LET THE SITUATION SPEAK FOR ITSELF!

WEN-DI-GO!

YIKES!

THAT WAS TOO CLOSE FOR COMFORT!

THIS BEASTIE MAKES THE JUGGERNAUT LOOK PUNY BY COMPARISON. WHICH IS, I THINK, MY CUE TO LET DISCRETION PROVE THE BETTER PART OF VALOUR--

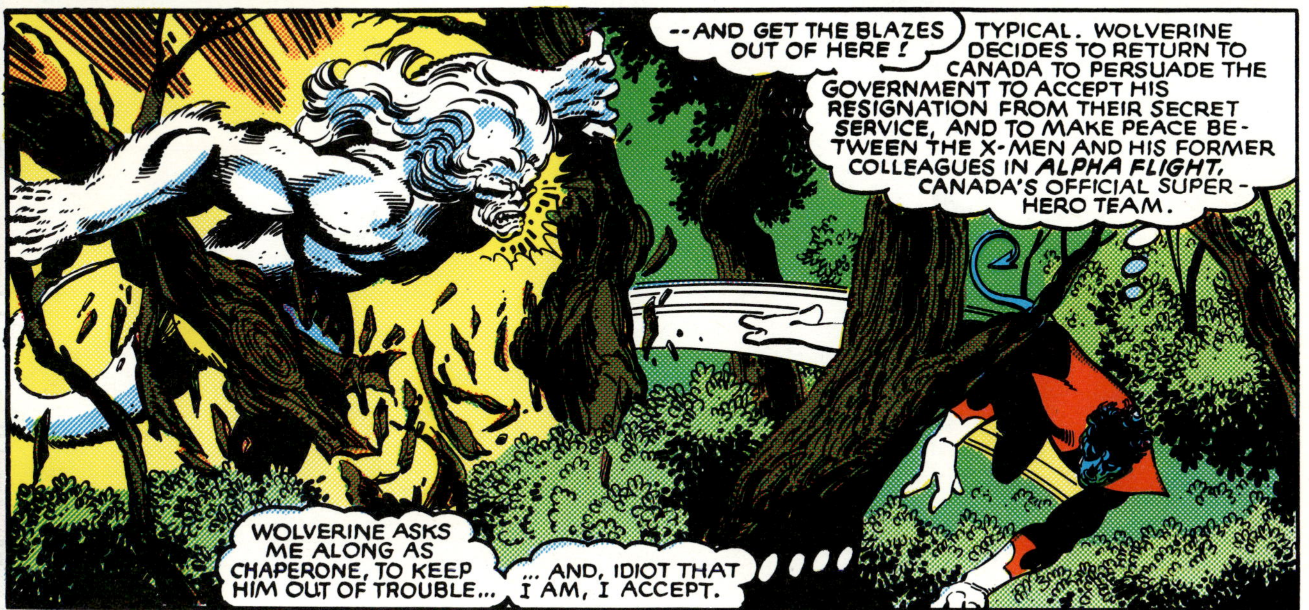

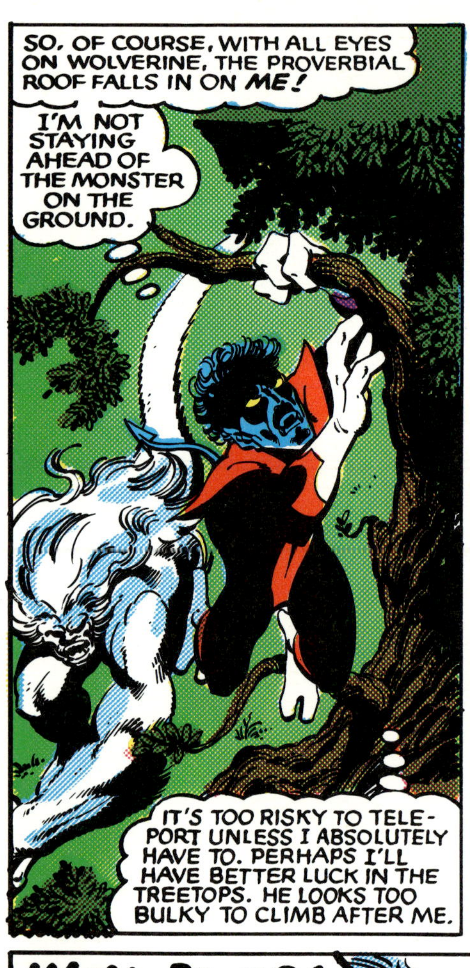
SO, OF COURSE, WITH ALL EYES ON WOLVERINE, THE PROVERBIAL ROOF FALLS IN ON ME!
I'M NOT STAYING AHEAD OF THE MONSTER ON THE GROUND.
IT'S TOO RISKY TO TELE-PORT UNLESS I ABSOLUTELY HAVE TO. PERHAPS I'LL HAVE BETTER LUCK IN THE TREETOPS. HE LOOKS TOO BULKY TO CLIMB AFTER ME.

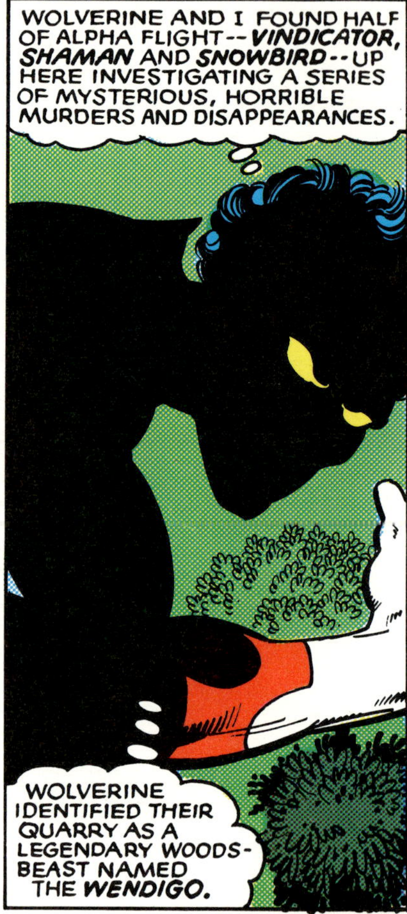
WOLVERINE AND I FOUND HALF OF ALPHA FLIGHT--VINDICATOR, SHAMAN AND SNOWBIRD--UP HERE INVESTIGATING A SERIES OF MYSTERIOUS, HORRIBLE MURDERS AND DISAPPEARANCES.
WOLVERINE IDENTIFIED THEIR QUARRY AS A LEGENDARY WOODS-BEAST NAMED THE WENDIGO.

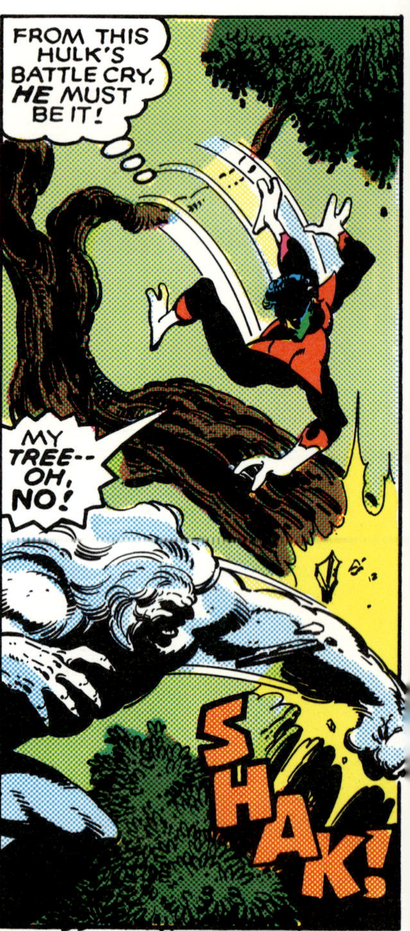
FROM THIS HULK'S BATTLE CRY, HE MUST BE IT!
MY TREE-- OH, NO!
SHAK!

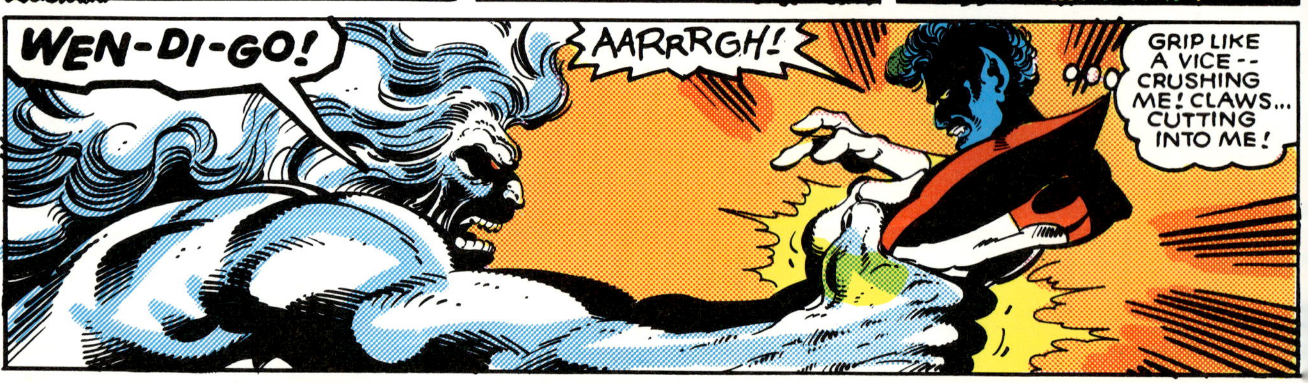
WEN-DI-GO!
AARRRGH!
GRIP LIKE A VICE-- CRUSHING ME! CLAWS... CUTTING INTO ME!

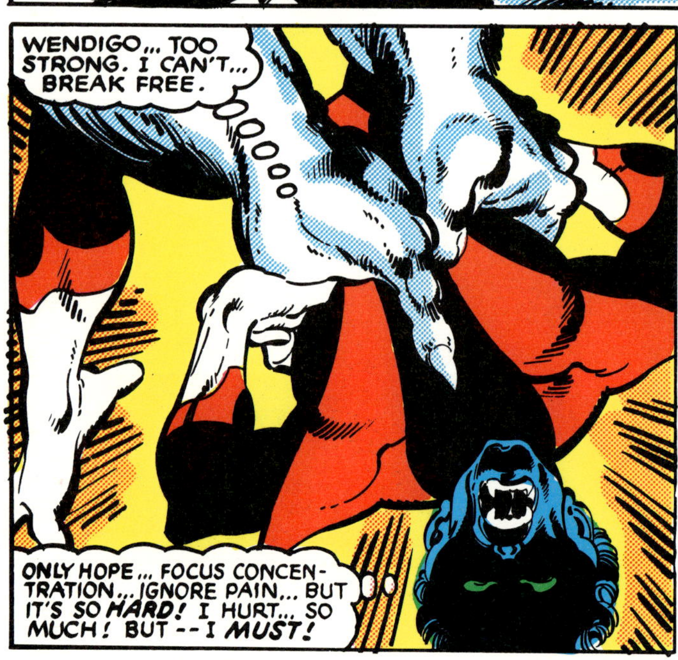
WENDIGO... TOO STRONG. I CAN'T... BREAK FREE.
ONLY HOPE... FOCUS CONCEN-TRATION... IGNORE PAIN... BUT IT'S SO HARD! I HURT... SO MUCH! BUT--I MUST!

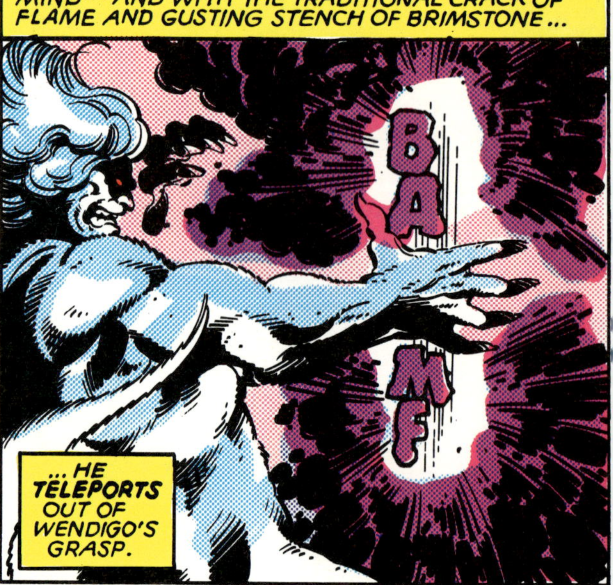
A PSYCHIC SWITCH CLOSES IN NIGHTCRAWLER'S MIND--AND WITH THE TRADITIONAL CRACK OF FLAME AND GUSTING STENCH OF BRIMSTONE...
BAMF
...HE TELEPORTS OUT OF WENDIGO'S GRASP.

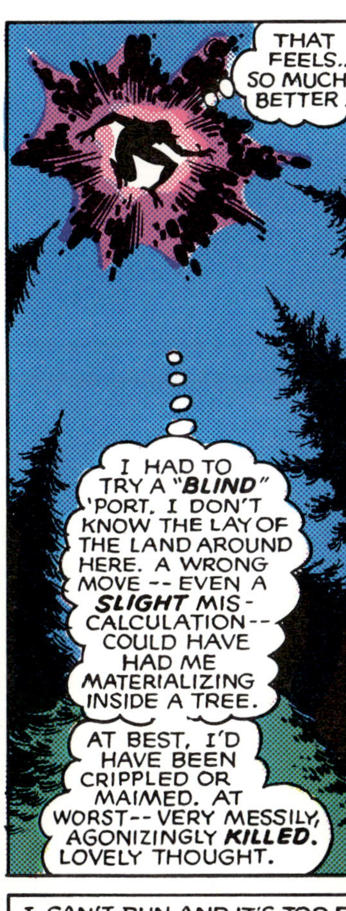
THAT FEELS... SO MUCH BETTER!
I HAD TO TRY A "BLIND" 'PORT. I DON'T KNOW THE LAY OF THE LAND AROUND HERE. A WRONG MOVE -- EVEN A SLIGHT MIS-CALCULATION -- COULD HAVE HAD ME MATERIALIZING INSIDE A TREE.
AT BEST, I'D HAVE BEEN CRIPPLED OR MAIMED. AT WORST -- VERY MESSILY, AGONIZINGLY KILLED. LOVELY THOUGHT.

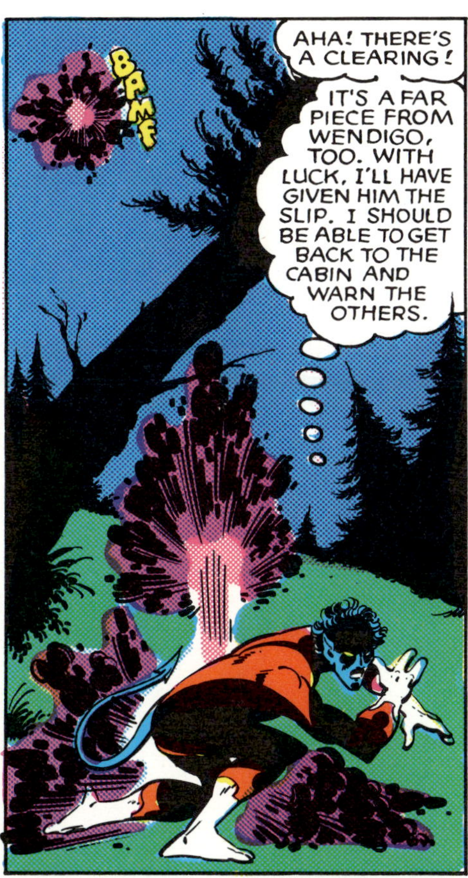
BAMF
AHA! THERE'S A CLEARING!
IT'S A FAR PIECE FROM WENDIGO, TOO. WITH LUCK, I'LL HAVE GIVEN HIM THE SLIP. I SHOULD BE ABLE TO GET BACK TO THE CABIN AND WARN THE OTHERS.

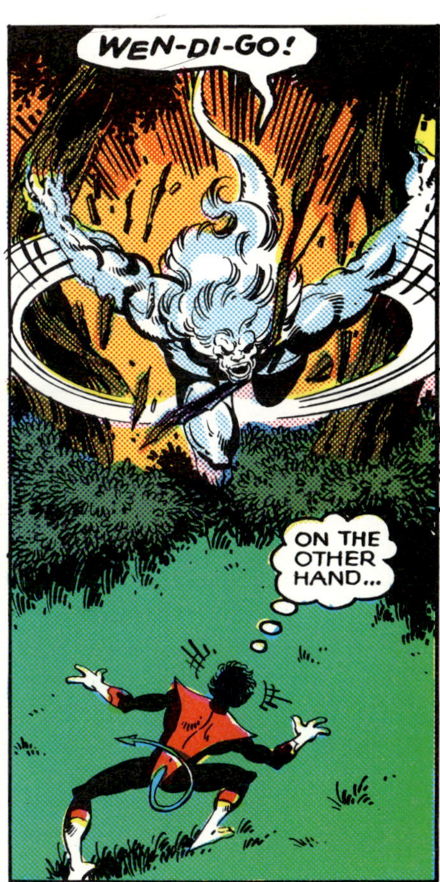
WEN-DI-GO!
ON THE OTHER HAND...

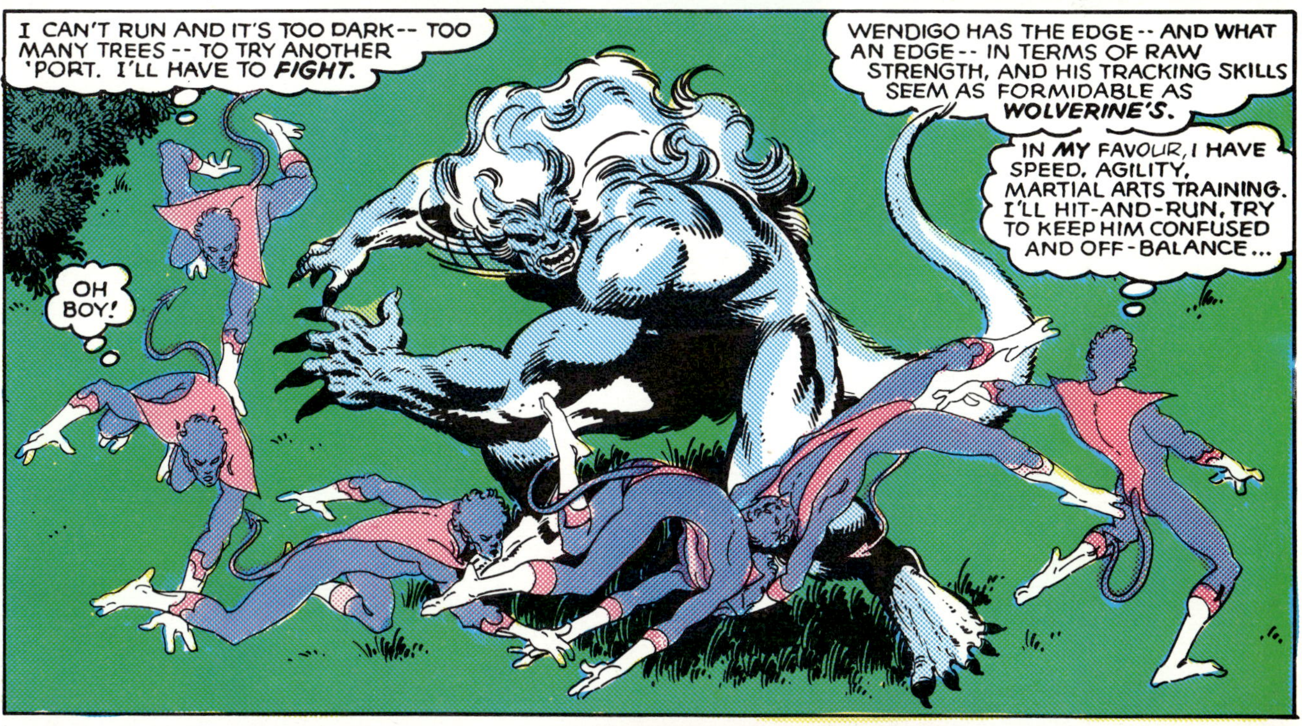
I CAN'T RUN AND IT'S TOO DARK -- TOO MANY TREES -- TO TRY ANOTHER 'PORT. I'LL HAVE TO FIGHT.
WENDIGO HAS THE EDGE -- AND WHAT AN EDGE -- IN TERMS OF RAW STRENGTH, AND HIS TRACKING SKILLS SEEM AS FORMIDABLE AS WOLVERINE'S.
IN MY FAVOUR, I HAVE SPEED, AGILITY, MARTIAL ARTS TRAINING. I'LL HIT-AND-RUN, TRY TO KEEP HIM CONFUSED AND OFF-BALANCE...
OH BOY!

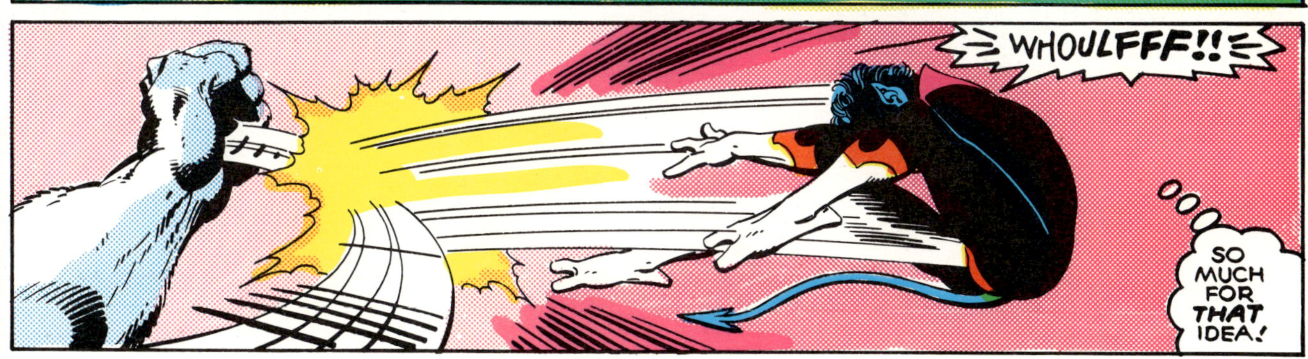
WHOULFFF!!
SO MUCH FOR THAT IDEA!

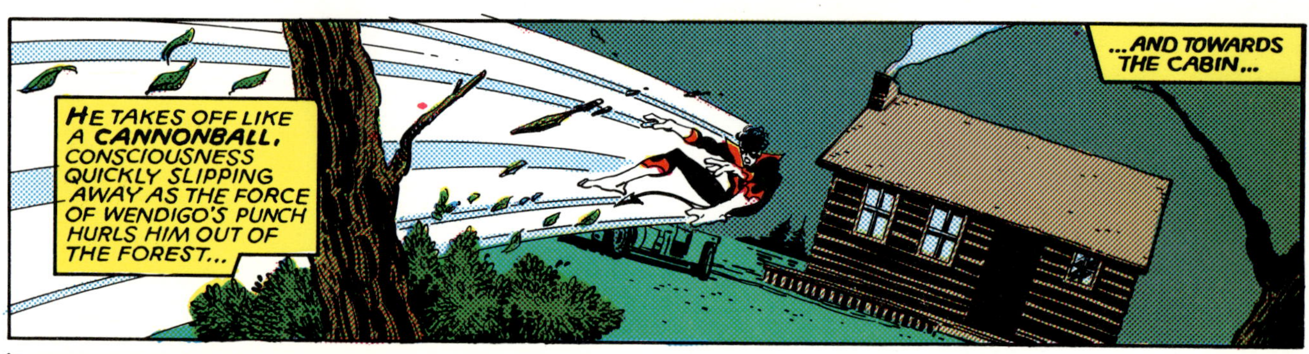
HE TAKES OFF LIKE A CANNONBALL, CONSCIOUSNESS QUICKLY SLIPPING AWAY AS THE FORCE OF WENDIGO'S PUNCH HURLS HIM OUT OF THE FOREST...
...AND TOWARDS THE CABIN...

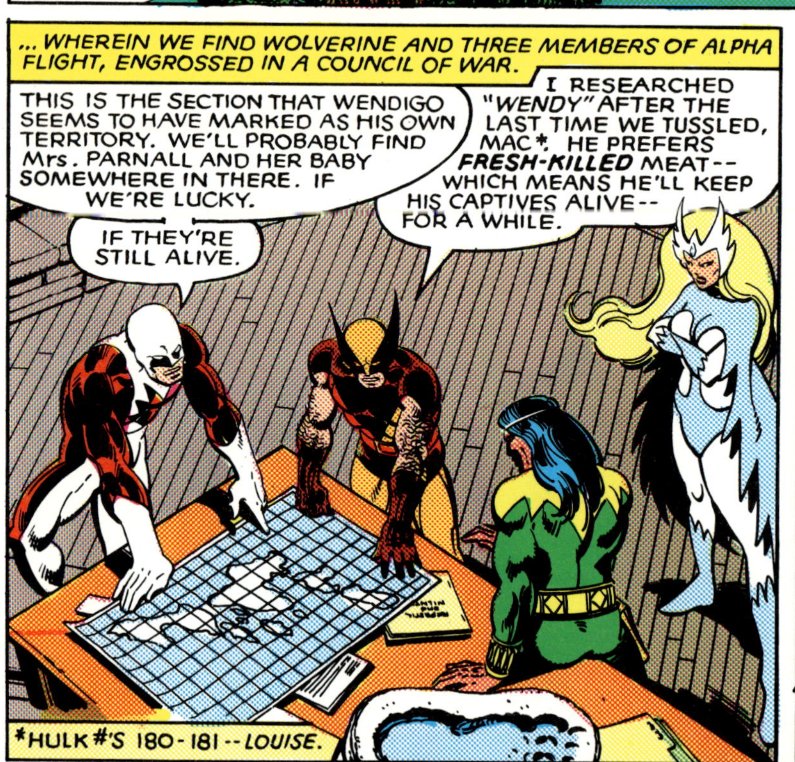
...WHEREIN WE FIND WOLVERINE AND THREE MEMBERS OF ALPHA FLIGHT, ENGROSSED IN A COUNCIL OF WAR.
THIS IS THE SECTION THAT WENDIGO SEEMS TO HAVE MARKED AS HIS OWN TERRITORY. WE'LL PROBABLY FIND Mrs. PARNALL AND HER BABY SOMEWHERE IN THERE. IF WE'RE LUCKY.
IF THEY'RE STILL ALIVE.
I RESEARCHED "WENDY" AFTER THE LAST TIME WE TUSSLED, MAC*. HE PREFERS FRESH-KILLED MEAT-- WHICH MEANS HE'LL KEEP HIS CAPTIVES ALIVE-- FOR A WHILE.
*HULK #'S 180-181 --LOUISE.

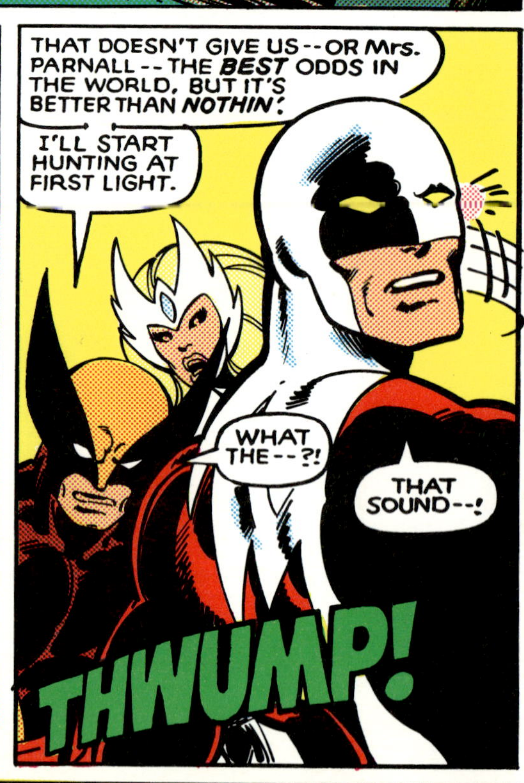
THAT DOESN'T GIVE US--OR Mrs. PARNALL--THE BEST ODDS IN THE WORLD, BUT IT'S BETTER THAN NOTHIN'.
I'LL START HUNTING AT FIRST LIGHT.
WHAT THE--?!
THAT SOUND--!
THWUMP!

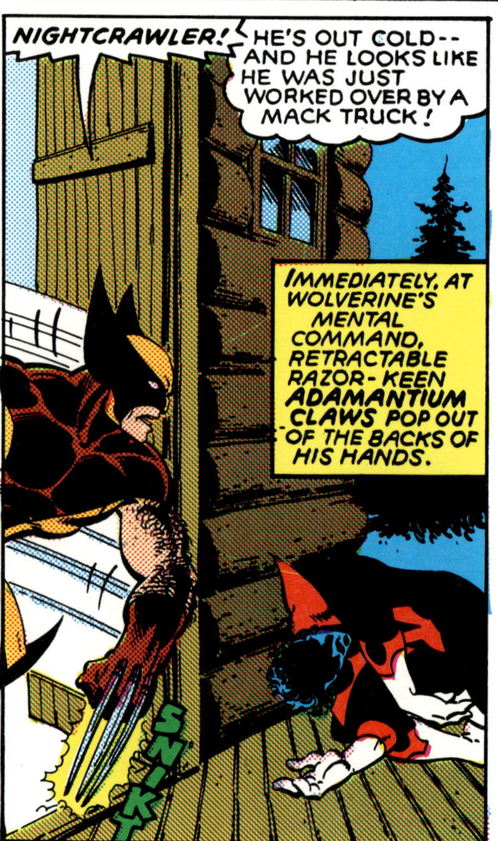
NIGHTCRAWLER!
HE'S OUT COLD-- AND HE LOOKS LIKE HE WAS JUST WORKED OVER BY A MACK TRUCK!
IMMEDIATELY, AT WOLVERINE'S MENTAL COMMAND, RETRACTABLE RAZOR-KEEN ADAMANTIUM CLAWS POP OUT OF THE BACKS OF HIS HANDS.
SNIKT

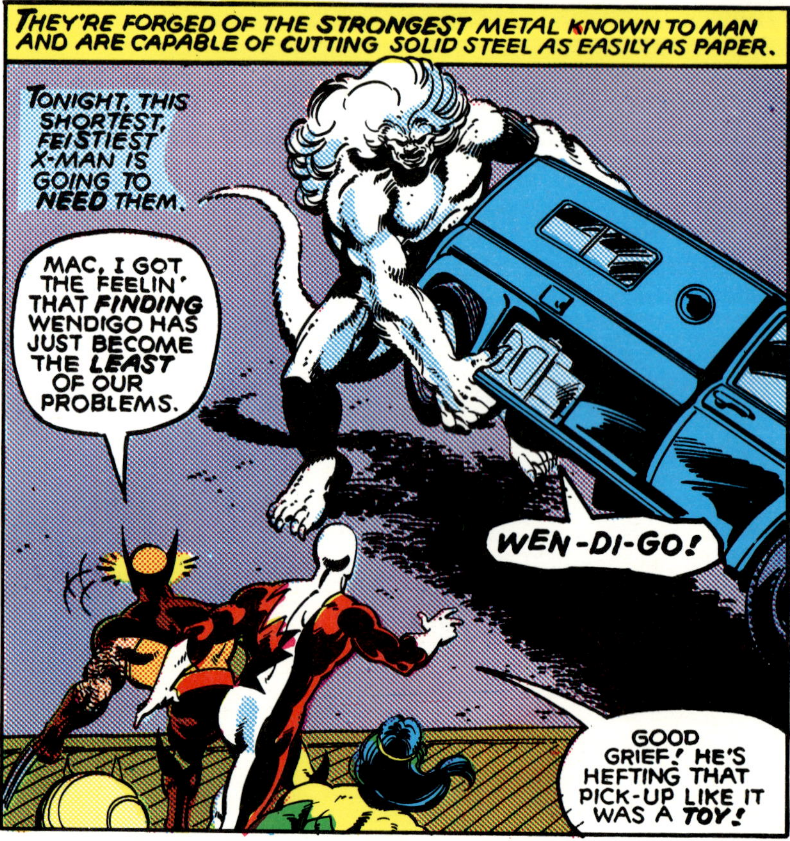
THEY'RE FORGED OF THE STRONGEST METAL KNOWN TO MAN AND ARE CAPABLE OF CUTTING SOLID STEEL AS EASILY AS PAPER.
TONIGHT, THIS SHORTEST, FEISTIEST X-MAN IS GOING TO NEED THEM.
MAC, I GOT THE FEELIN' THAT FINDING WENDIGO HAS JUST BECOME THE LEAST OF OUR PROBLEMS.
WEN-DI-GO!
GOOD GRIEF! HE'S HEFTING THAT PICK-UP LIKE IT WAS A TOY!

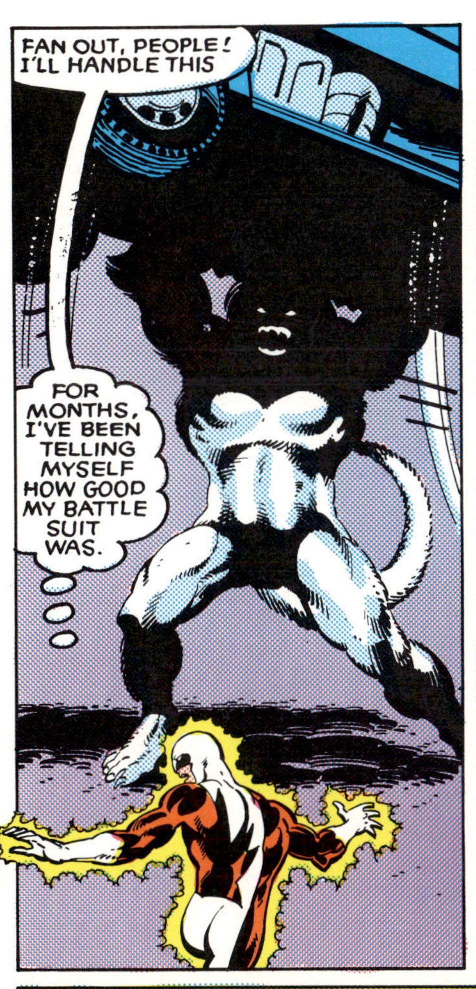
FAN OUT, PEOPLE! I'LL HANDLE THIS
FOR MONTHS, I'VE BEEN TELLING MYSELF HOW GOOD MY BATTLE SUIT WAS.

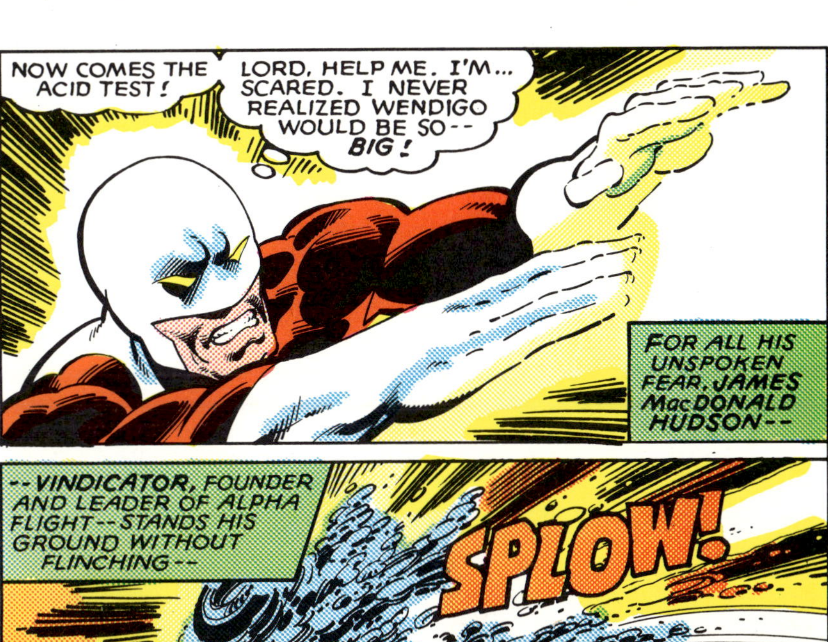
NOW COMES THE ACID TEST!
LORD, HELP ME. I'M... SCARED. I NEVER REALIZED WENDIGO WOULD BE SO-- BIG!
FOR ALL HIS UNSPOKEN FEAR, JAMES MacDONALD HUDSON--

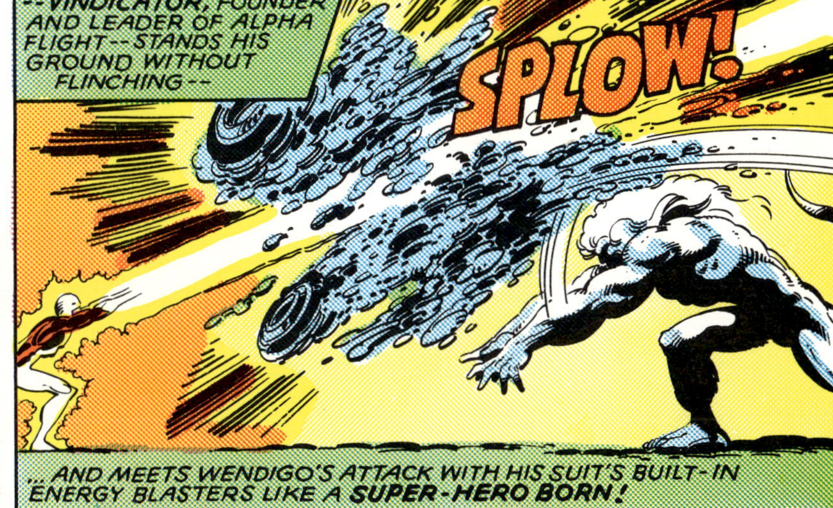
--VINDICATOR, FOUNDER AND LEADER OF ALPHA FLIGHT--STANDS HIS GROUND WITHOUT FLINCHING--
SPLOW!
...AND MEETS WENDIGO'S ATTACK WITH HIS SUIT'S BUILT-IN ENERGY BLASTERS LIKE A SUPER-HERO BORN!

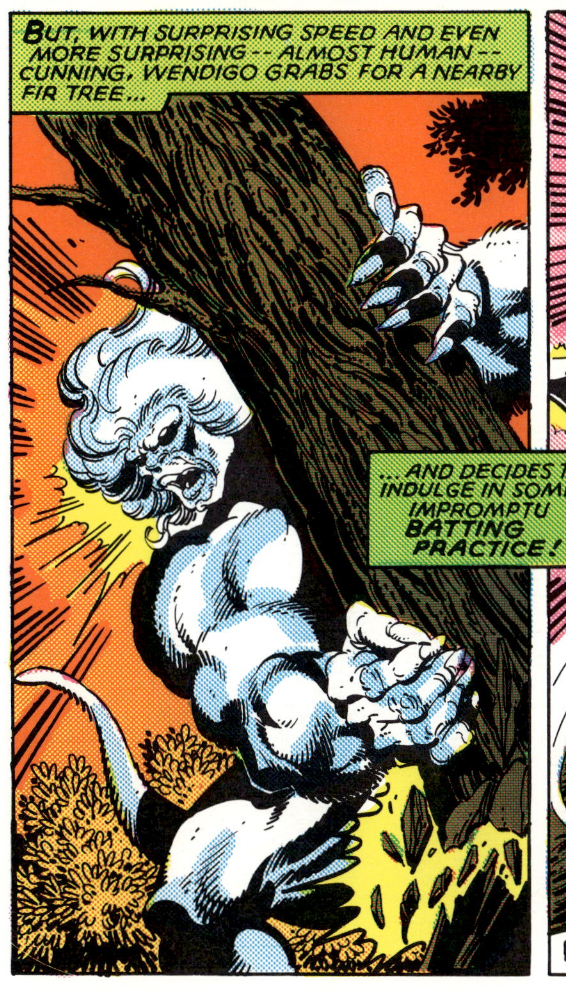
BUT, WITH SURPRISING SPEED AND EVEN MORE SURPRISING--ALMOST HUMAN--CUNNING, WENDIGO GRABS FOR A NEARBY FIR TREE...
...AND DECIDES TO INDULGE IN SOME IMPROMPTU BATTING PRACTICE!

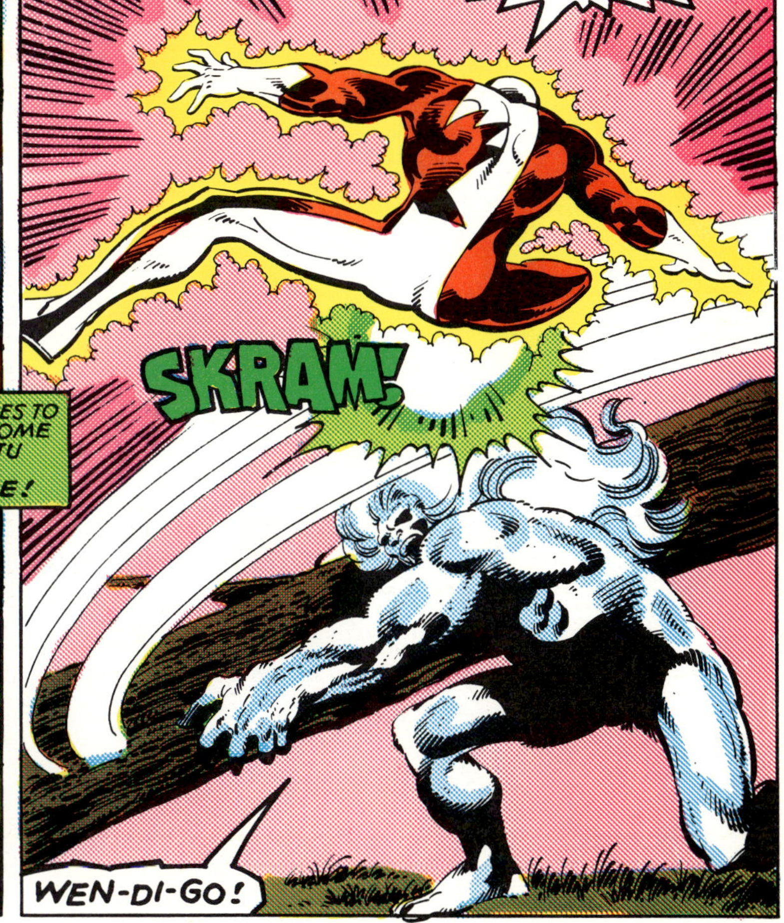
UNNNFFF!
SKRAM!
WEN-DI-GO!

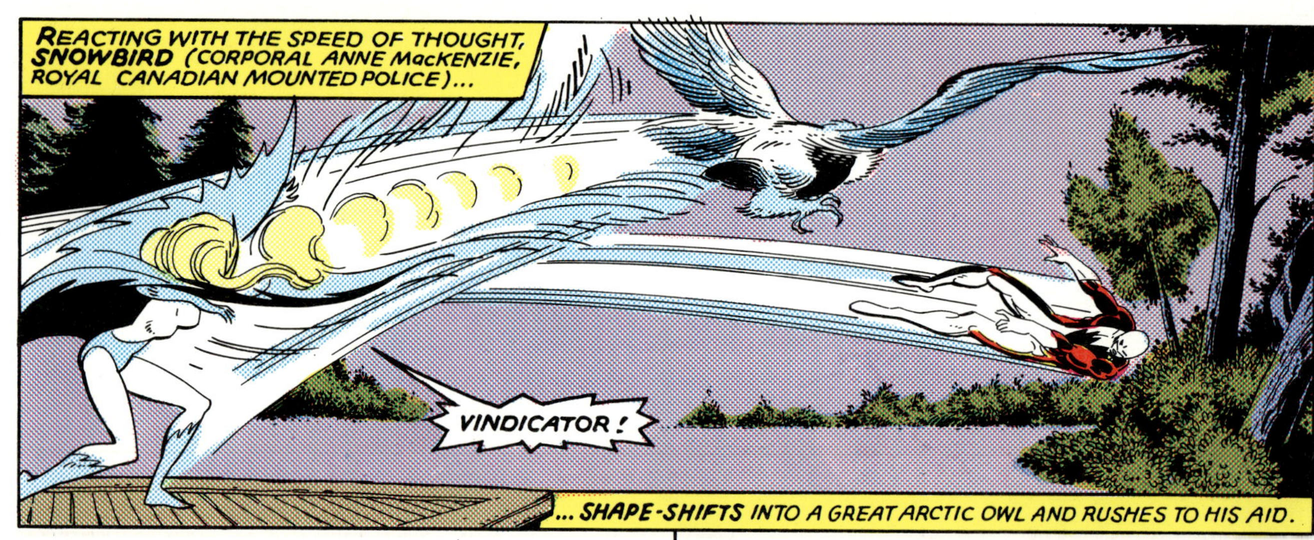
REACTING WITH THE SPEED OF THOUGHT, SNOWBIRD (CORPORAL ANNE MacKENZIE, ROYAL CANADIAN MOUNTED POLICE)...
VINDICATOR!
... SHAPE-SHIFTS INTO A GREAT ARCTIC OWL AND RUSHES TO HIS AID.

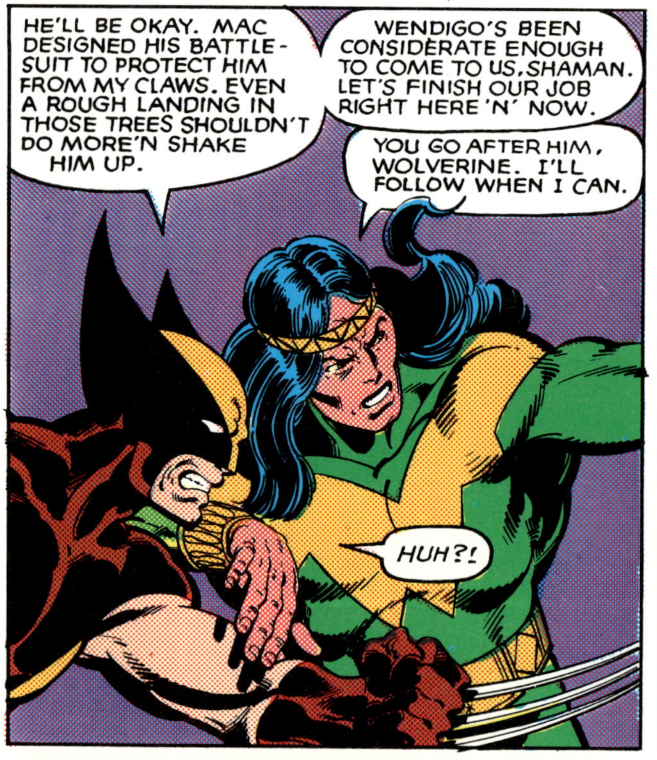
HE'LL BE OKAY. MAC DESIGNED HIS BATTLE-SUIT TO PROTECT HIM FROM MY CLAWS. EVEN A ROUGH LANDING IN THOSE TREES SHOULDN'T DO MORE'N SHAKE HIM UP.
WENDIGO'S BEEN CONSIDERATE ENOUGH TO COME TO US, SHAMAN. LET'S FINISH OUR JOB RIGHT HERE 'N' NOW.
YOU GO AFTER HIM, WOLVERINE. I'LL FOLLOW WHEN I CAN.
HUH?!

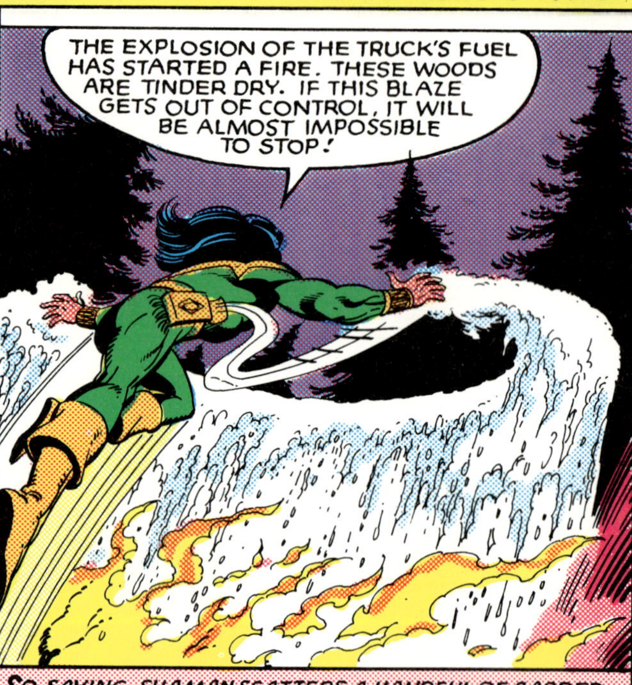
THE EXPLOSION OF THE TRUCK'S FUEL HAS STARTED A FIRE. THESE WOODS ARE TINDER DRY. IF THIS BLAZE GETS OUT OF CONTROL, IT WILL BE ALMOST IMPOSSIBLE TO STOP!
SO SAYING, SHAMAN SCATTERS A HANDFUL OF SACRED POWDER ACROSS THE FACE OF THE FIRE, CREATING A WALL OF ICE TO SMOTHER IT. AND WHILE HE ACTS, HE LAUGHS INSIDE AT THE IRONY OF THE SITUATION --

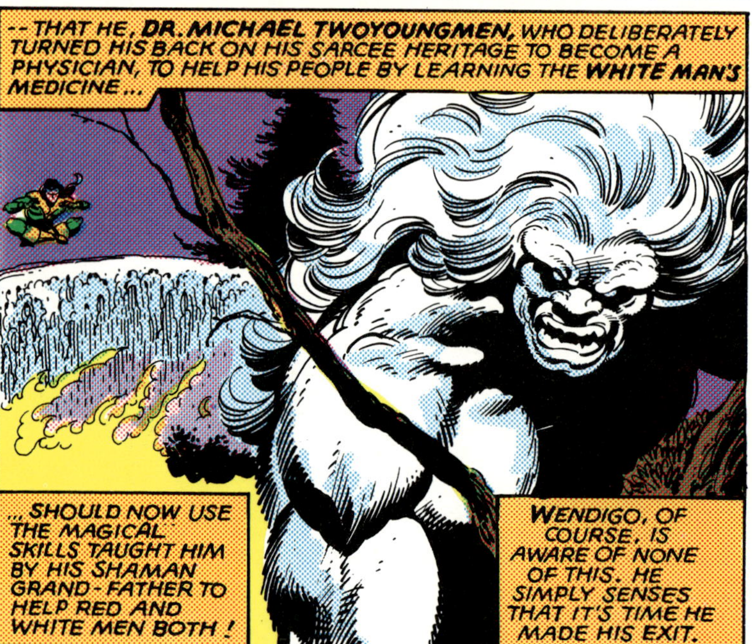
-- THAT HE, DR. MICHAEL TWOYOUNGMEN, WHO DELIBERATELY TURNED HIS BACK ON HIS SARCEE HERITAGE TO BECOME A PHYSICIAN, TO HELP HIS PEOPLE BY LEARNING THE WHITE MAN'S MEDICINE...
... SHOULD NOW USE THE MAGICAL SKILLS TAUGHT HIM BY HIS SHAMAN GRAND-FATHER TO HELP RED AND WHITE MEN BOTH!
WENDIGO, OF COURSE, IS AWARE OF NONE OF THIS. HE SIMPLY SENSES THAT IT'S TIME HE MADE HIS EXIT.

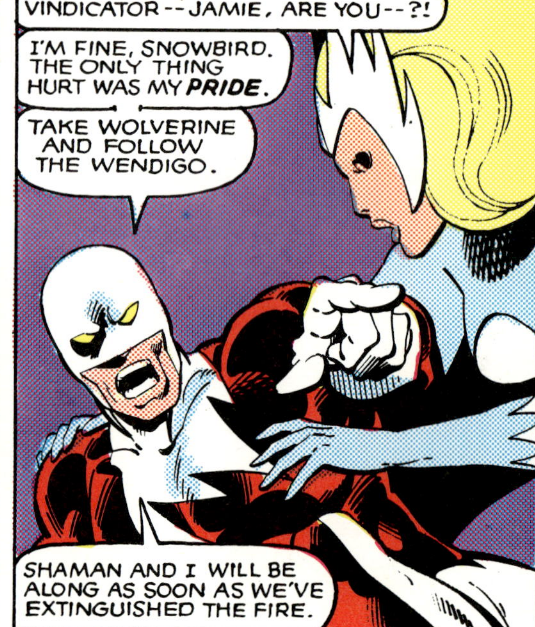
VINDICATOR -- JAMIE, ARE YOU --?!
I'M FINE, SNOWBIRD. THE ONLY THING HURT WAS MY PRIDE.
TAKE WOLVERINE AND FOLLOW THE WENDIGO.
SHAMAN AND I WILL BE ALONG AS SOON AS WE'VE EXTINGUISHED THE FIRE.

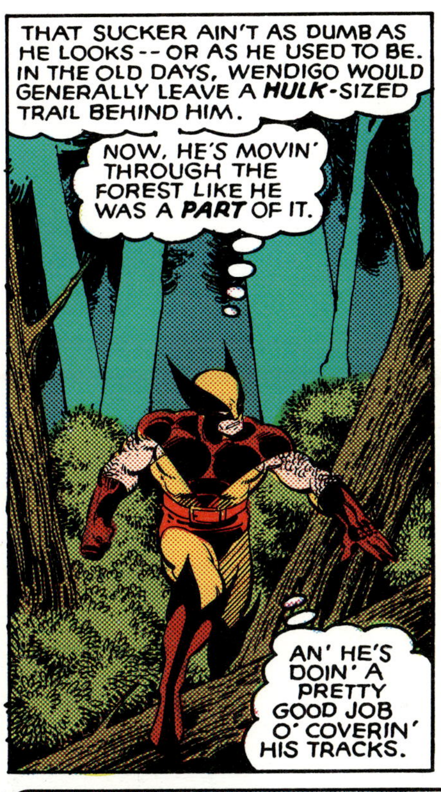
THAT SUCKER AIN'T AS DUMB AS HE LOOKS -- OR AS HE USED TO BE. IN THE OLD DAYS, WENDIGO WOULD GENERALLY LEAVE A **HULK**-SIZED TRAIL BEHIND HIM.
NOW, HE'S MOVIN' THROUGH THE FOREST LIKE HE WAS A **PART** OF IT.
AN' HE'S DOIN' A PRETTY GOOD JOB O' COVERIN' HIS TRACKS.

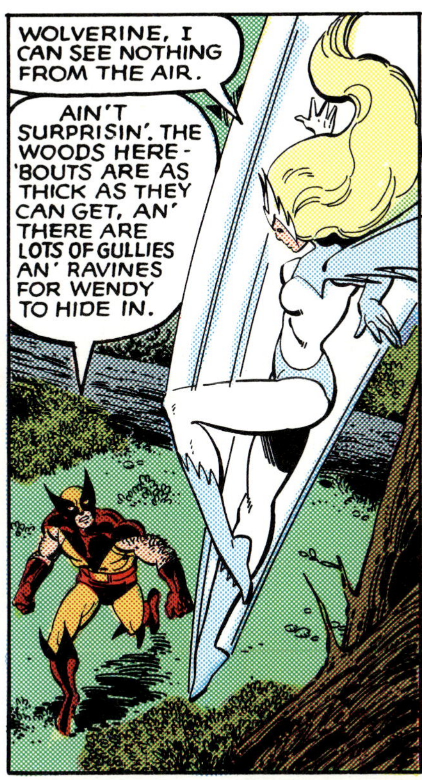
WOLVERINE, I CAN SEE NOTHING FROM THE AIR.
AIN'T SURPRISIN'. THE WOODS HERE-'BOUTS ARE AS THICK AS THEY CAN GET, AN' THERE ARE LOTS OF GULLIES AN' RAVINES FOR WENDY TO HIDE IN.

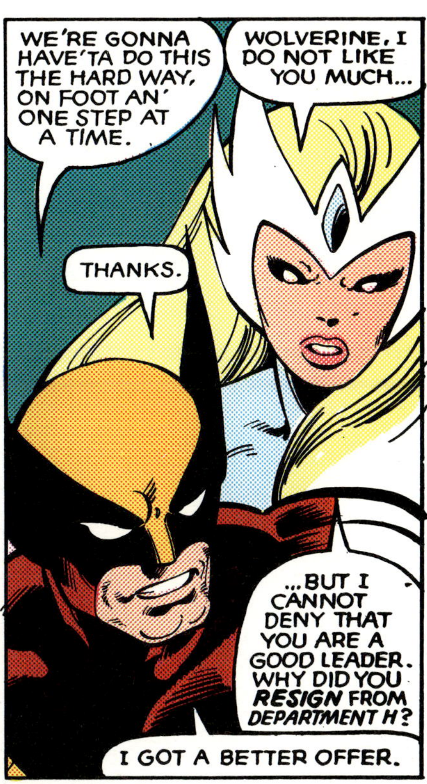
WE'RE GONNA HAVE'TA DO THIS THE HARD WAY, ON FOOT AN' ONE STEP AT A TIME.
WOLVERINE, I DO NOT LIKE YOU MUCH...
THANKS.
...BUT I CANNOT DENY THAT YOU ARE A GOOD LEADER. WHY DID YOU **RESIGN** FROM *DEPARTMENT H*?
I GOT A BETTER OFFER.

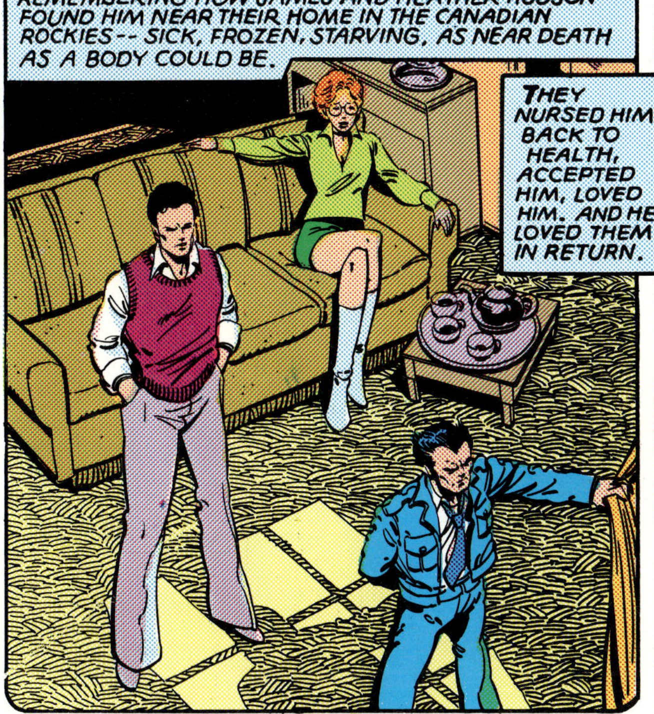
UNBIDDEN, HIS MIND FLASHES BACK ACROSS THE YEARS, REMEMBERING HOW JAMES AND HEATHER HUDSON FOUND HIM NEAR THEIR HOME IN THE CANADIAN ROCKIES -- SICK, FROZEN, STARVING, AS NEAR DEATH AS A BODY COULD BE.
THEY NURSED HIM BACK TO HEALTH, ACCEPTED HIM, LOVED HIM. AND HE LOVED THEM IN RETURN.

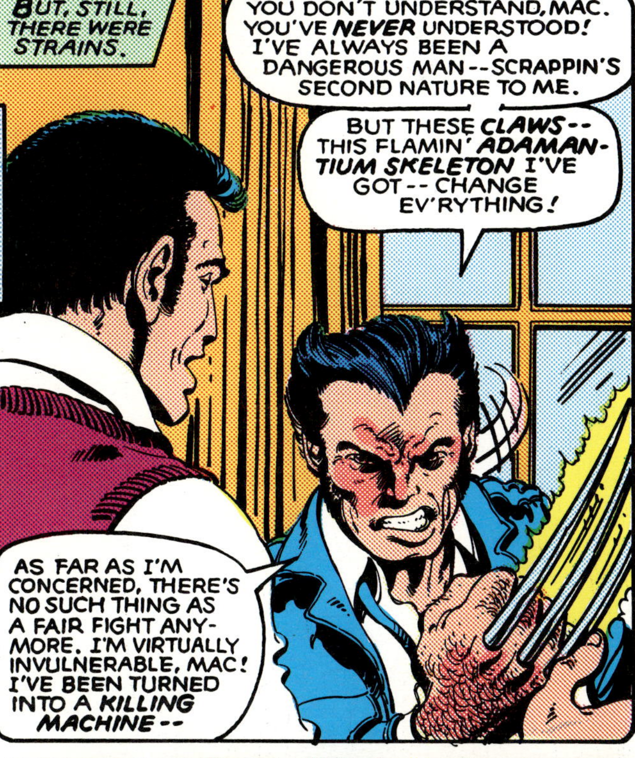
BUT, STILL, THERE WERE STRAINS.
YOU DON'T UNDERSTAND, MAC. YOU'VE **NEVER** UNDERSTOOD! I'VE ALWAYS BEEN A DANGEROUS MAN -- SCRAPPIN'S SECOND NATURE TO ME.
BUT THESE **CLAWS** -- THIS FLAMIN' **ADAMANTIUM SKELETON** I'VE GOT -- CHANGE EV'RYTHING!
AS FAR AS I'M CONCERNED, THERE'S NO SUCH THING AS A FAIR FIGHT ANYMORE. I'M VIRTUALLY INVULNERABLE, MAC! I'VE BEEN TURNED INTO A **KILLING MACHINE** --

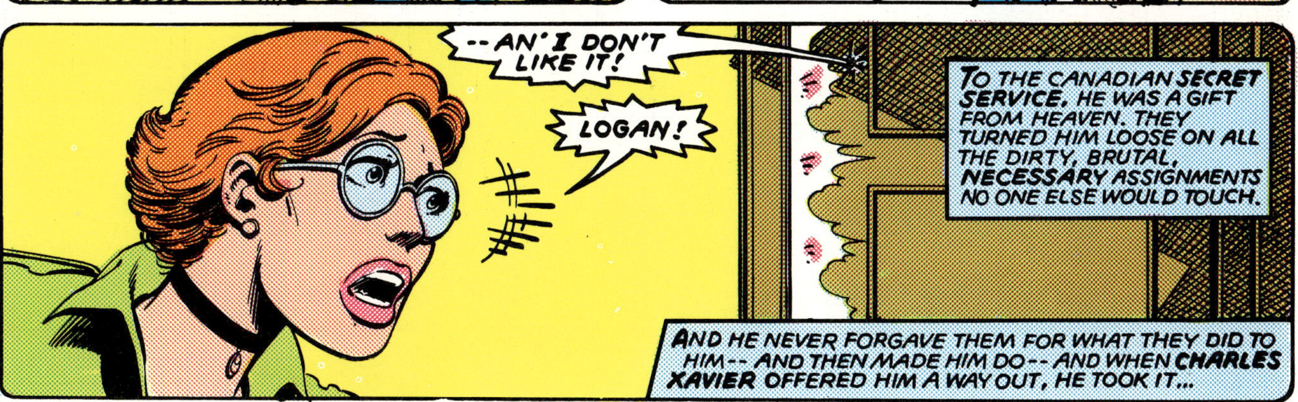
-- AN' I DON'T LIKE IT!
LOGAN!
*TO THE CANADIAN **SECRET SERVICE**, HE WAS A GIFT FROM HEAVEN. THEY TURNED HIM LOOSE ON ALL THE DIRTY, BRUTAL, **NECESSARY** ASSIGNMENTS NO ONE ELSE WOULD TOUCH.*
*AND HE NEVER FORGAVE THEM FOR WHAT THEY DID TO HIM -- AND THEN MADE HIM DO -- AND WHEN **CHARLES XAVIER** OFFERED HIM A WAY OUT, HE TOOK IT...*

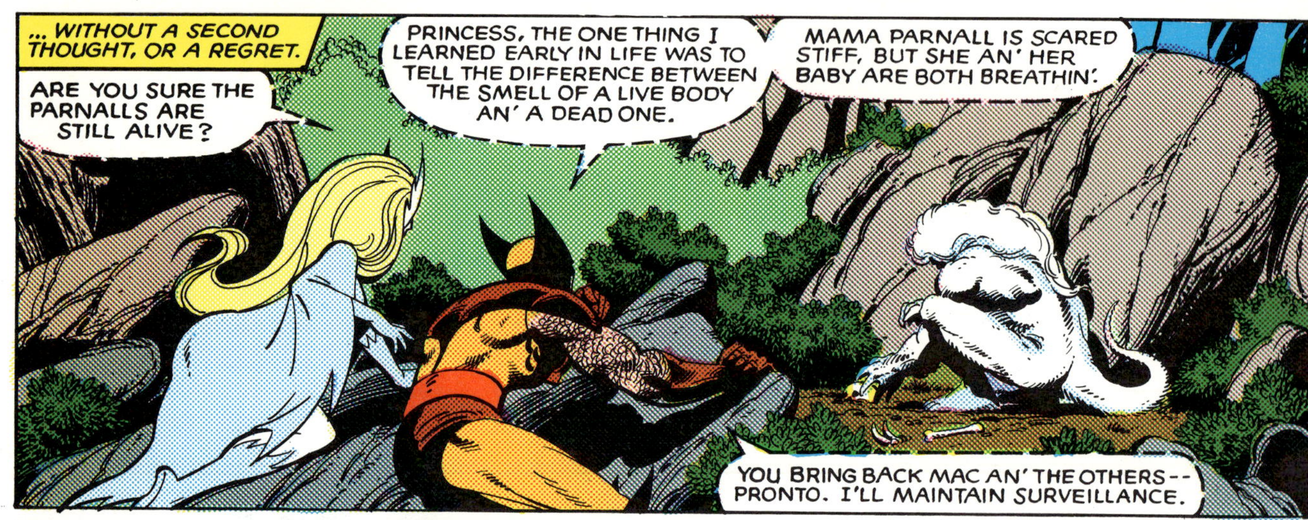
...WITHOUT A SECOND THOUGHT, OR A REGRET.
ARE YOU SURE THE PARNALLS ARE STILL ALIVE?
PRINCESS, THE ONE THING I LEARNED EARLY IN LIFE WAS TO TELL THE DIFFERENCE BETWEEN THE SMELL OF A LIVE BODY AN' A DEAD ONE.
MAMA PARNALL IS SCARED STIFF, BUT SHE AN' HER BABY ARE BOTH BREATHIN'.
YOU BRING BACK MAC AN' THE OTHERS-- PRONTO. I'LL MAINTAIN SURVEILLANCE.

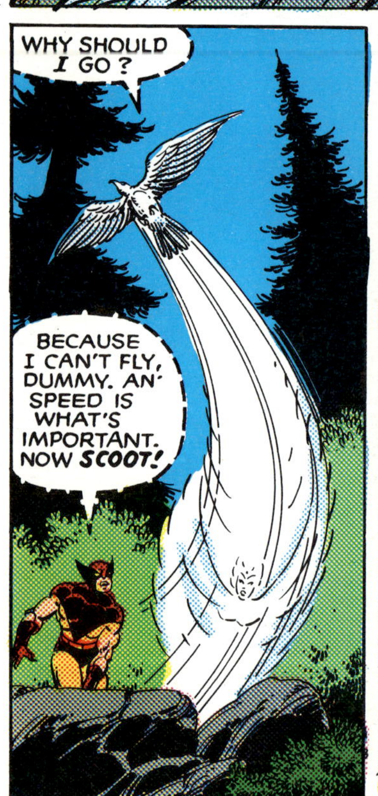
WHY SHOULD I GO?
BECAUSE I CAN'T FLY, DUMMY. AN' SPEED IS WHAT'S IMPORTANT. NOW SCOOT!

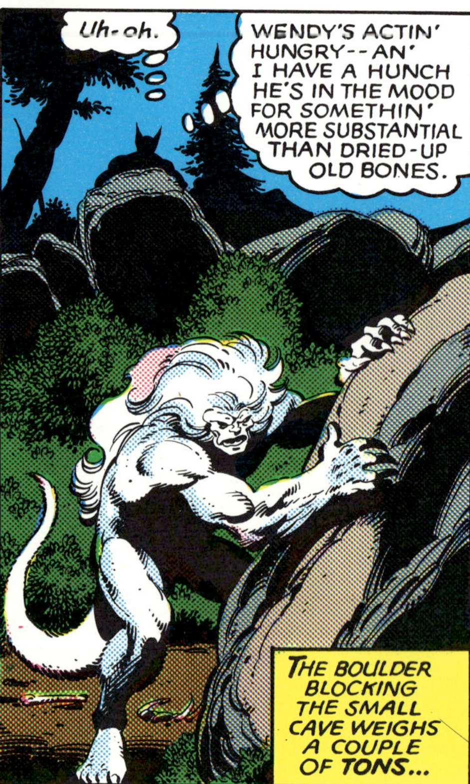
Uh-oh.
WENDY'S ACTIN' HUNGRY--AN' I HAVE A HUNCH HE'S IN THE MOOD FOR SOMETHIN' MORE SUBSTANTIAL THAN DRIED-UP OLD BONES.
THE BOULDER BLOCKING THE SMALL CAVE WEIGHS A COUPLE OF TONS...

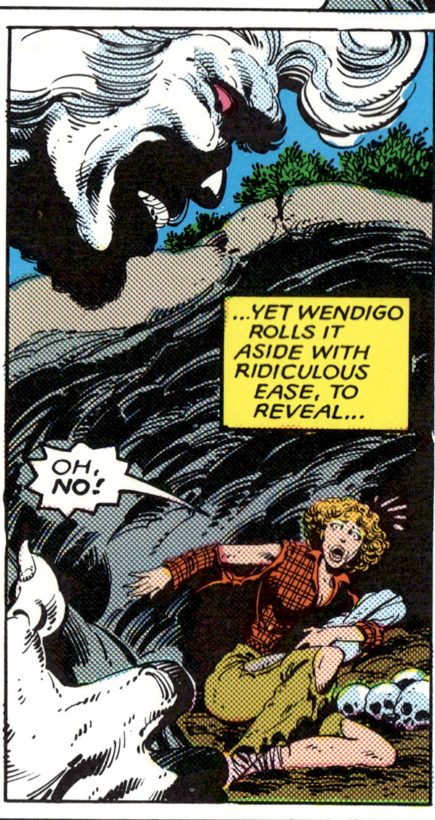
...YET WENDIGO ROLLS IT ASIDE WITH RIDICULOUS EASE, TO REVEAL...
OH, NO!

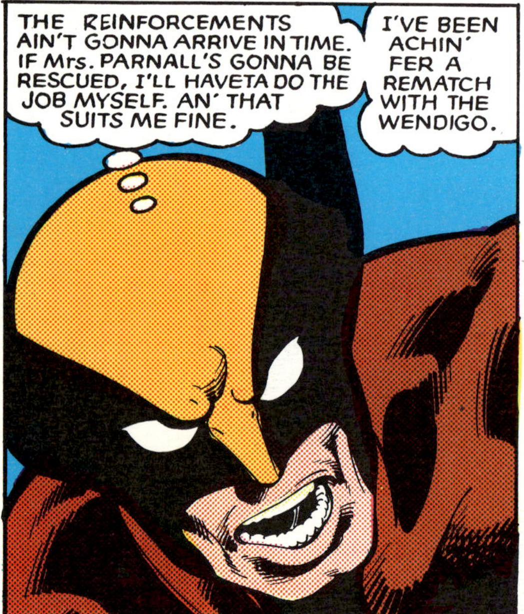
THE REINFORCEMENTS AIN'T GONNA ARRIVE IN TIME. IF Mrs. PARNALL'S GONNA BE RESCUED, I'LL HAVETA DO THE JOB MYSELF. AN' THAT SUITS ME FINE.
I'VE BEEN ACHIN' FER A REMATCH WITH THE WENDIGO.

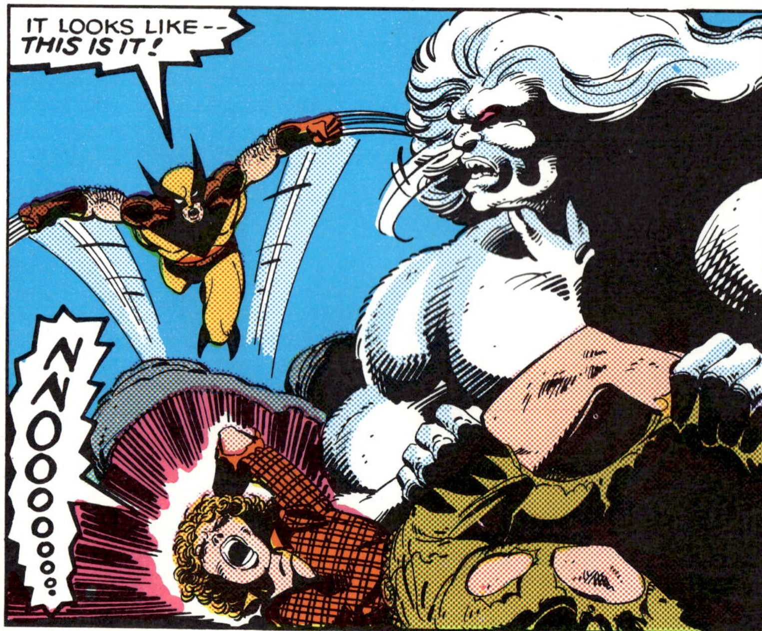
IT LOOKS LIKE-- THIS IS IT!
NNOOOOooo

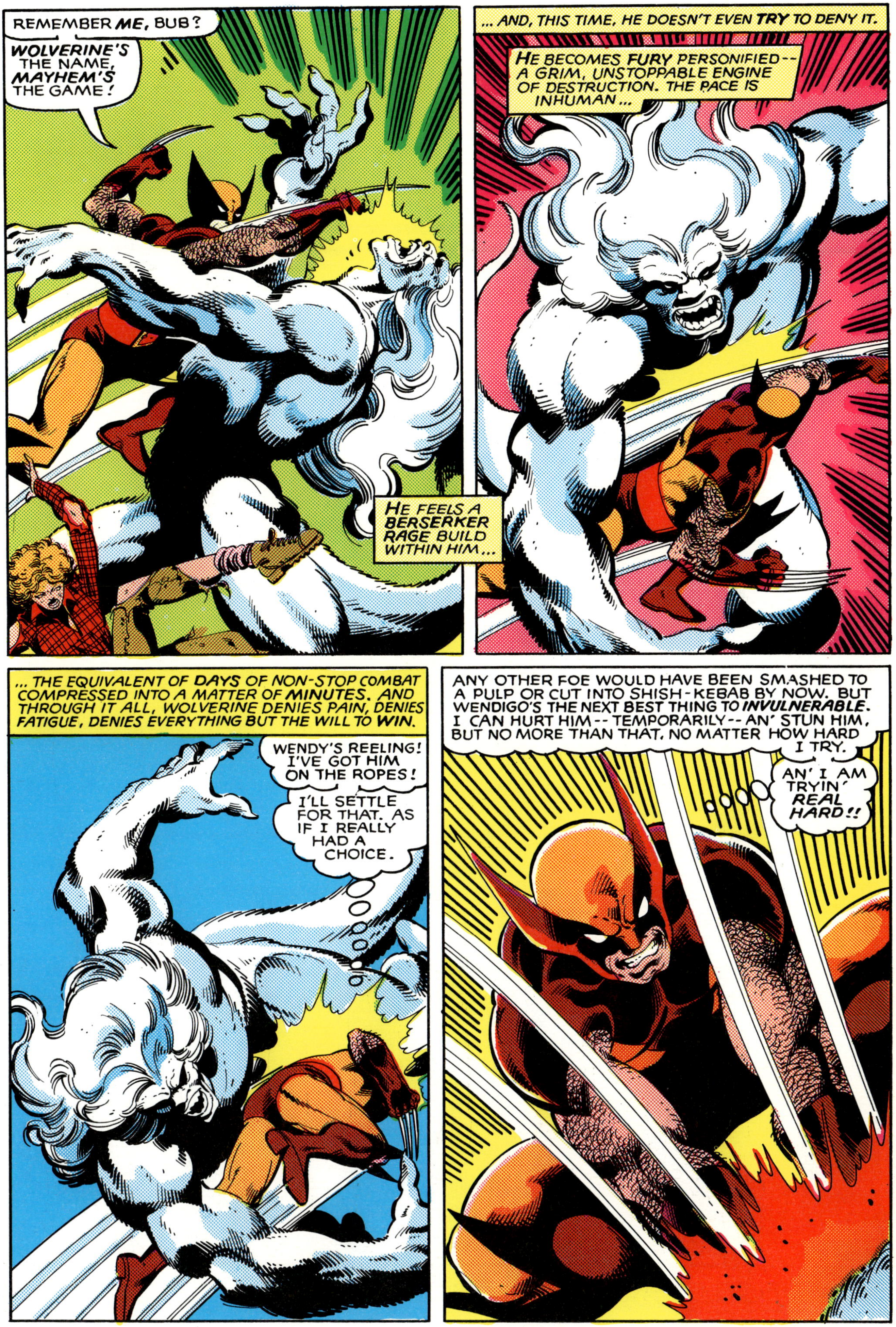

REMEMBER **ME**, BUB? **WOLVERINE'S** THE NAME, **MAYHEM'S** THE GAME!

HE FEELS A **BERSERKER RAGE** BUILD WITHIN HIM...

... AND, THIS TIME, HE DOESN'T EVEN **TRY** TO DENY IT.

HE BECOMES **FURY** PERSONIFIED-- A GRIM, UNSTOPPABLE ENGINE OF DESTRUCTION. THE PACE IS INHUMAN...

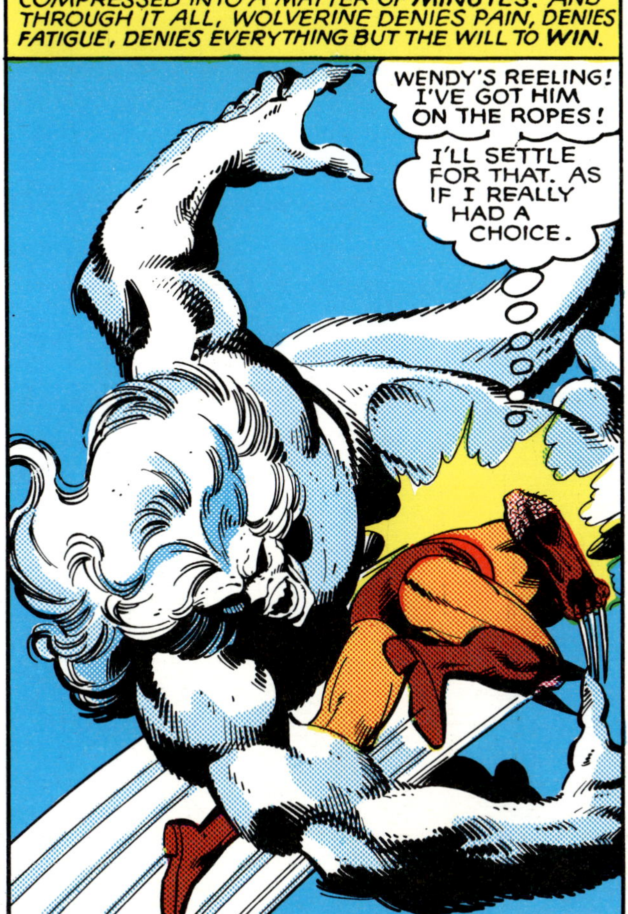

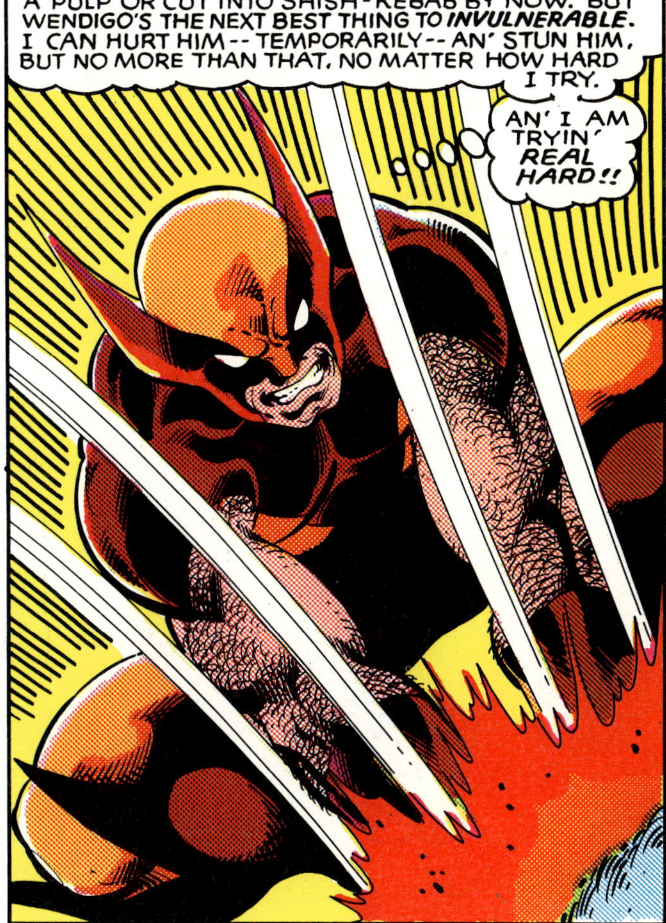

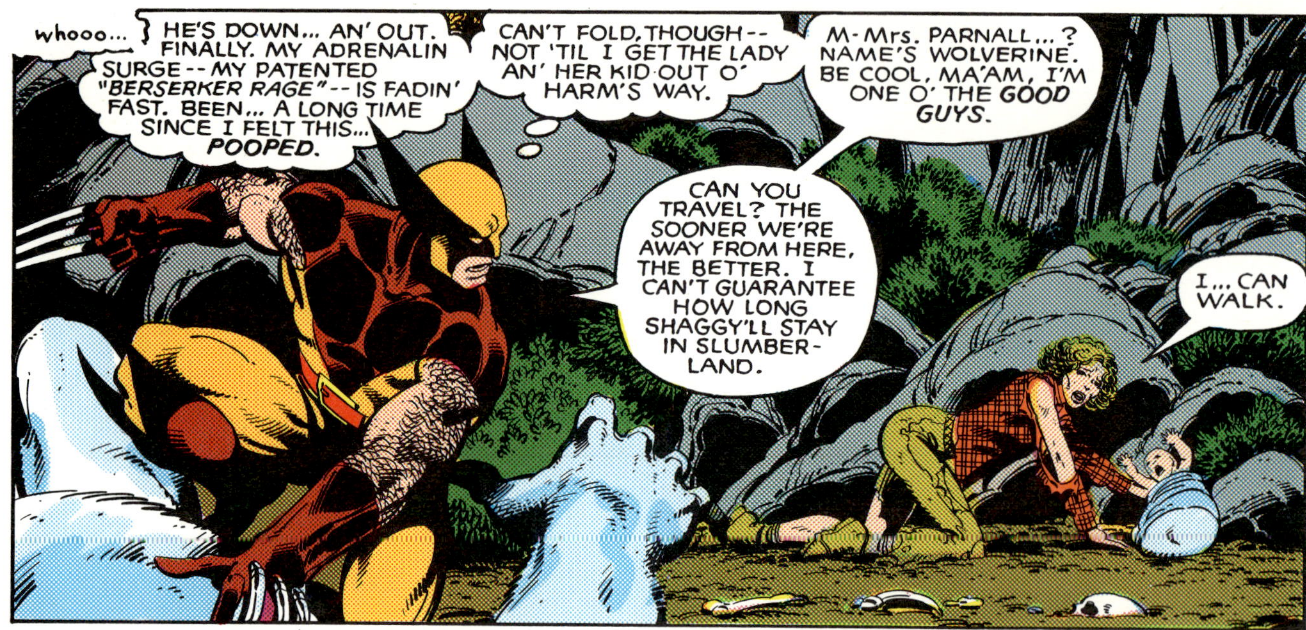
whooo...
HE'S DOWN... AN' OUT. FINALLY. MY ADRENALIN SURGE -- MY PATENTED "BERSERKER RAGE" -- IS FADIN' FAST. BEEN... A LONG TIME SINCE I FELT THIS... POOPED.
CAN'T FOLD, THOUGH -- NOT 'TIL I GET THE LADY AN' HER KID OUT O' HARM'S WAY.
M-Mrs. PARNALL...? NAME'S WOLVERINE. BE COOL, MA'AM, I'M ONE O' THE GOOD GUYS.
CAN YOU TRAVEL? THE SOONER WE'RE AWAY FROM HERE, THE BETTER. I CAN'T GUARANTEE HOW LONG SHAGGY'LL STAY IN SLUMBER-LAND.
I... CAN WALK.

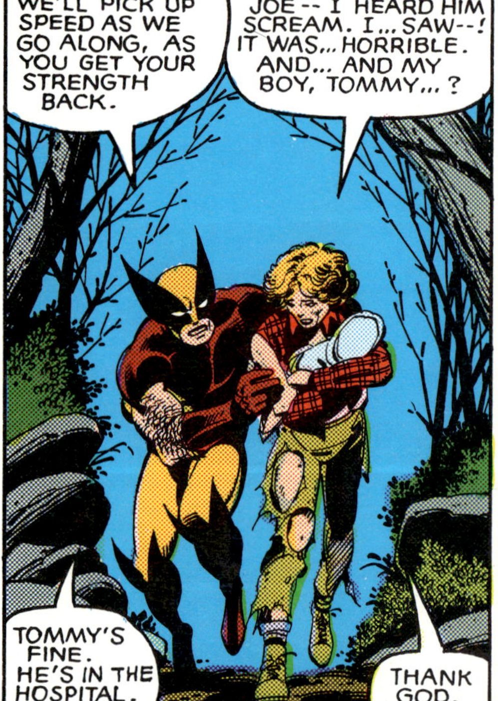
THAT'S A START. WE'LL PICK UP SPEED AS WE GO ALONG, AS YOU GET YOUR STRENGTH BACK.
M-MY HUSBAND, JOE -- I HEARD HIM SCREAM. I... SAW--! IT WAS... HORRIBLE. AND... AND MY BOY, TOMMY...?
TOMMY'S FINE. HE'S IN THE HOSPITAL.
THANK GOD.

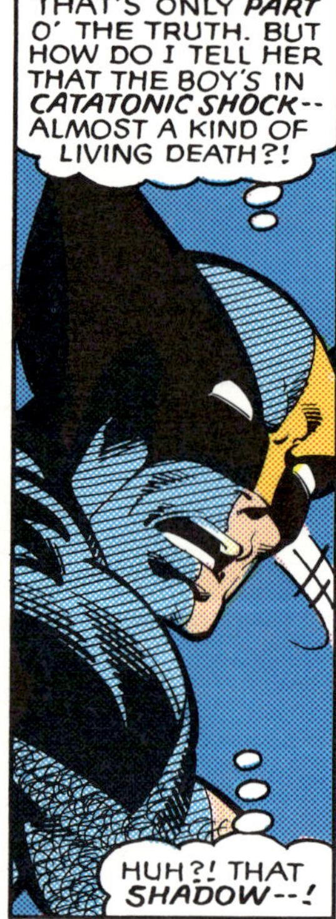
THAT'S ONLY PART O' THE TRUTH. BUT HOW DO I TELL HER THAT THE BOY'S IN CATATONIC SHOCK -- ALMOST A KIND OF LIVING DEATH?!
HUH?! THAT SHADOW--!

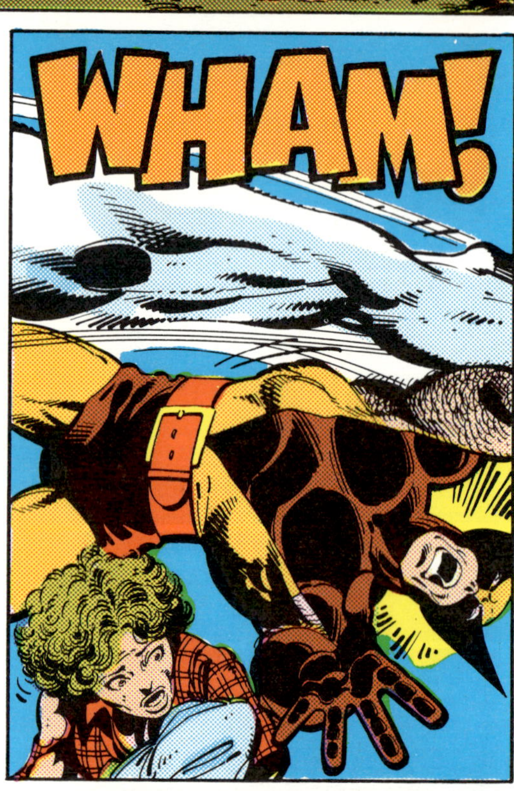
WHAM!

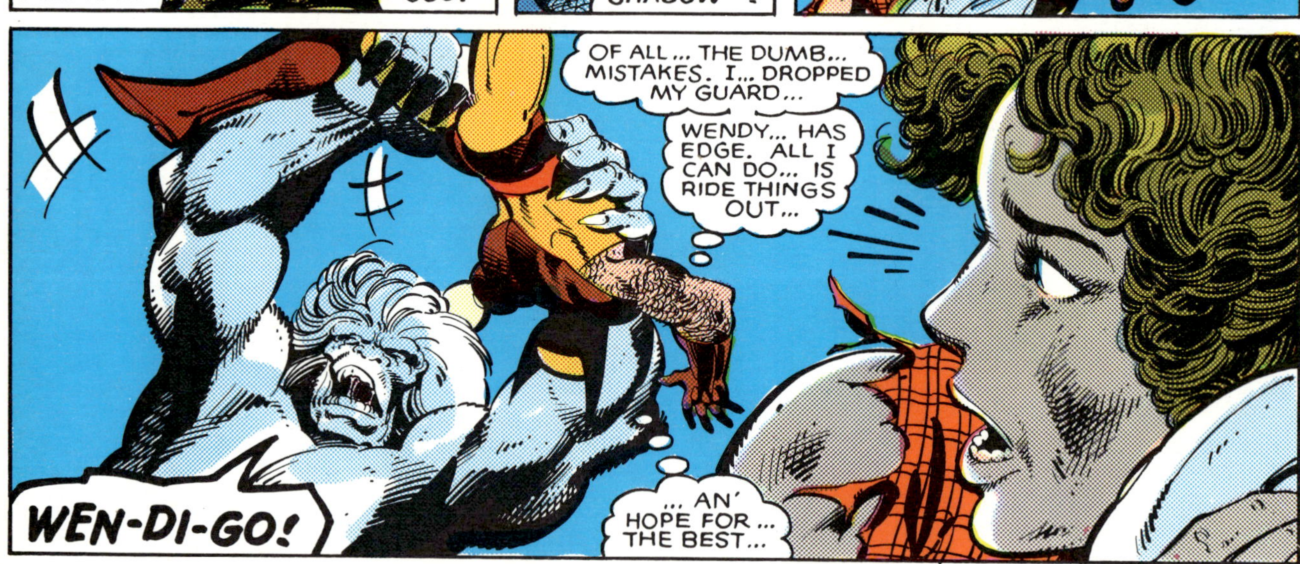
OF ALL... THE DUMB... MISTAKES. I... DROPPED MY GUARD...
WENDY... HAS EDGE. ALL I CAN DO... IS RIDE THINGS OUT...
WEN-DI-GO!
... AN' HOPE FOR... THE BEST...

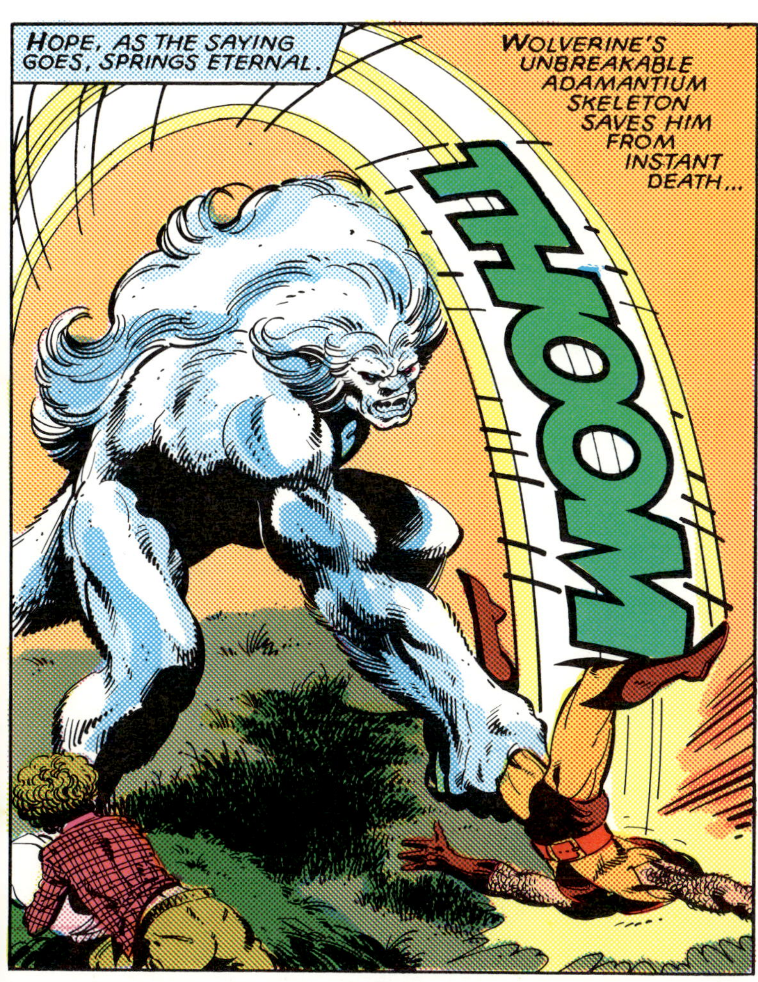
HOPE, AS THE SAYING GOES, SPRINGS ETERNAL.
WOLVERINE'S UNBREAKABLE ADAMANTIUM SKELETON SAVES HIM FROM INSTANT DEATH...
THOOOM

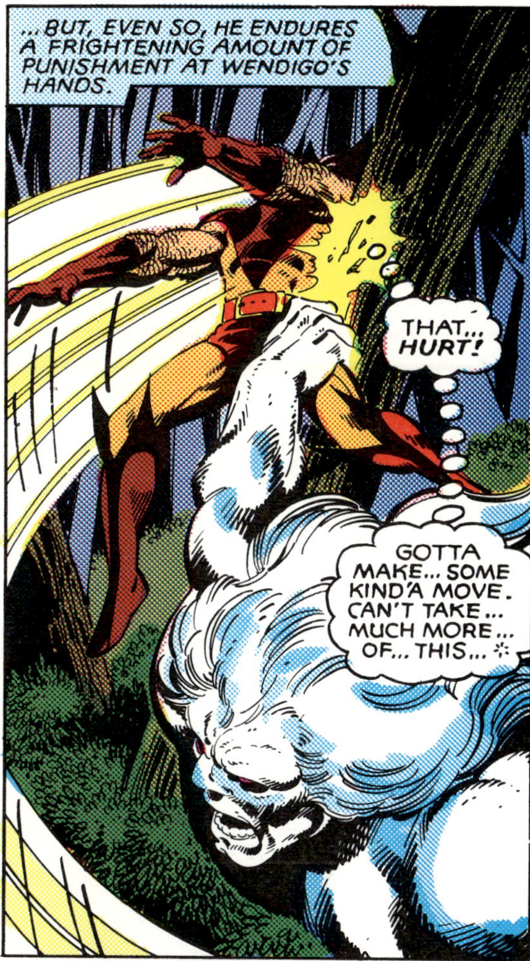
...BUT, EVEN SO, HE ENDURES A FRIGHTENING AMOUNT OF PUNISHMENT AT WENDIGO'S HANDS.
THAT... HURT!
GOTTA MAKE... SOME KIND'A MOVE. CAN'T TAKE... MUCH MORE... OF... THIS...

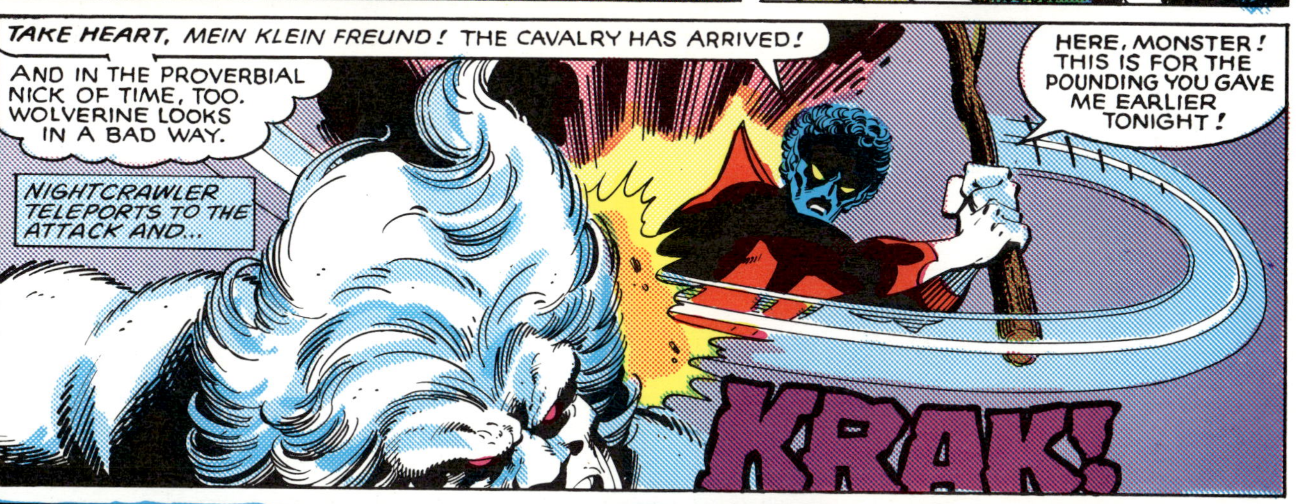
TAKE HEART, MEIN KLEIN FREUND! THE CAVALRY HAS ARRIVED!
AND IN THE PROVERBIAL NICK OF TIME, TOO. WOLVERINE LOOKS IN A BAD WAY.
NIGHTCRAWLER TELEPORTS TO THE ATTACK AND...
HERE, MONSTER! THIS IS FOR THE POUNDING YOU GAVE ME EARLIER TONIGHT!
KRAK!

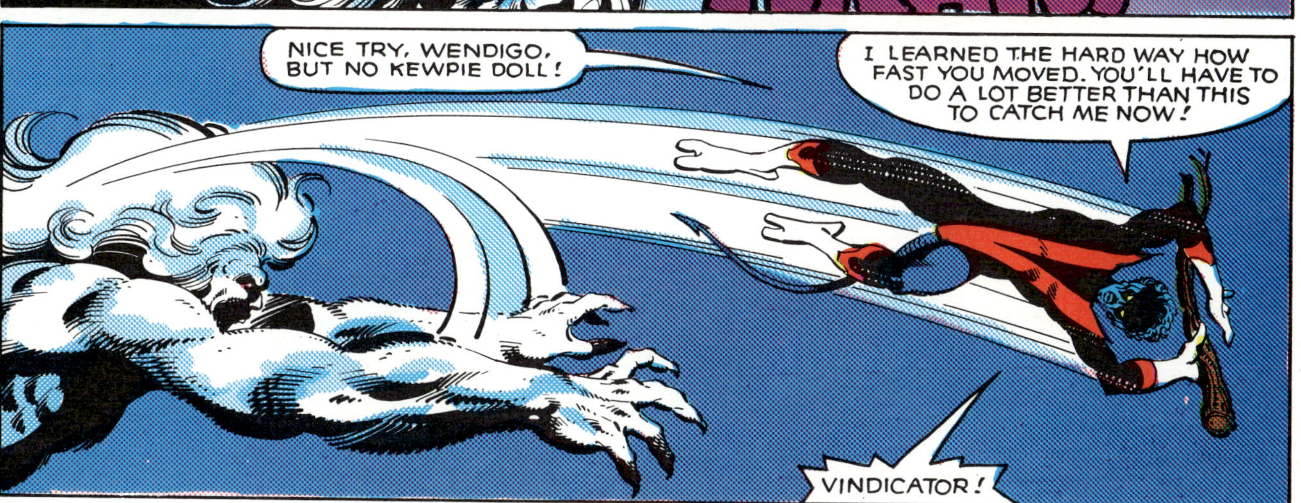
NICE TRY, WENDIGO, BUT NO KEWPIE DOLL!
I LEARNED THE HARD WAY HOW FAST YOU MOVED. YOU'LL HAVE TO DO A LOT BETTER THAN THIS TO CATCH ME NOW!
VINDICATOR!

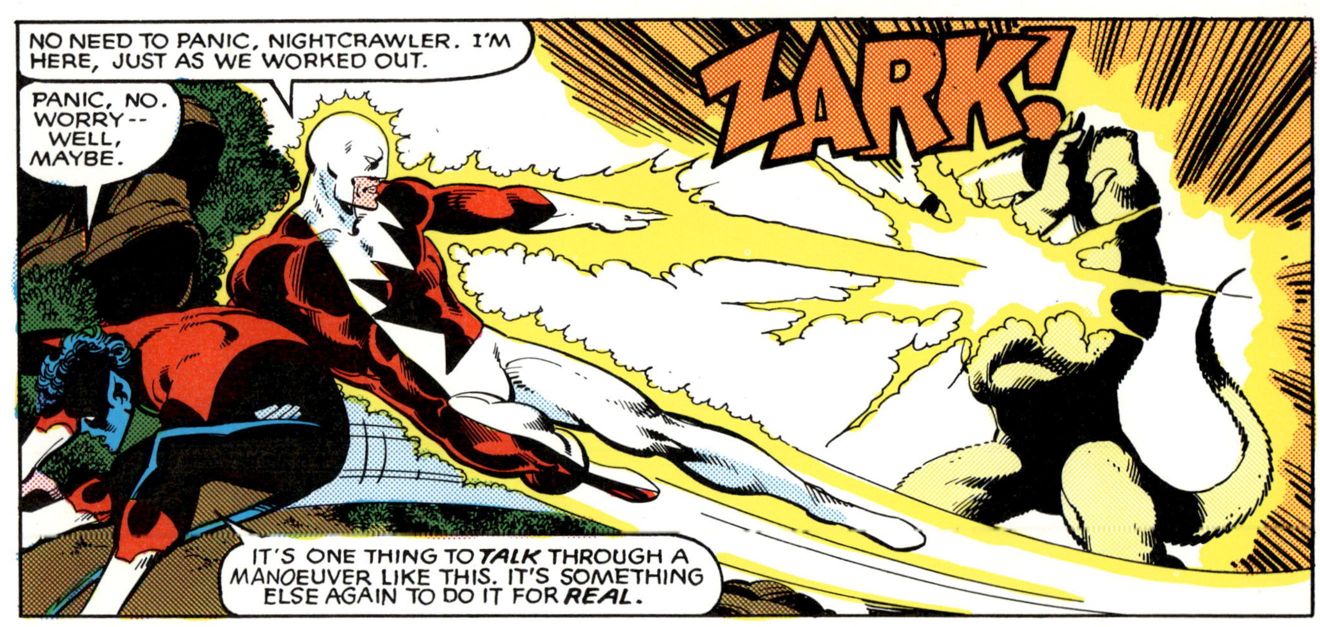
NO NEED TO PANIC, NIGHTCRAWLER. I'M HERE, JUST AS WE WORKED OUT.
PANIC, NO. WORRY-- WELL, MAYBE.
ZARK!
IT'S ONE THING TO TALK THROUGH A MANOEUVER LIKE THIS. IT'S SOMETHING ELSE AGAIN TO DO IT FOR REAL.

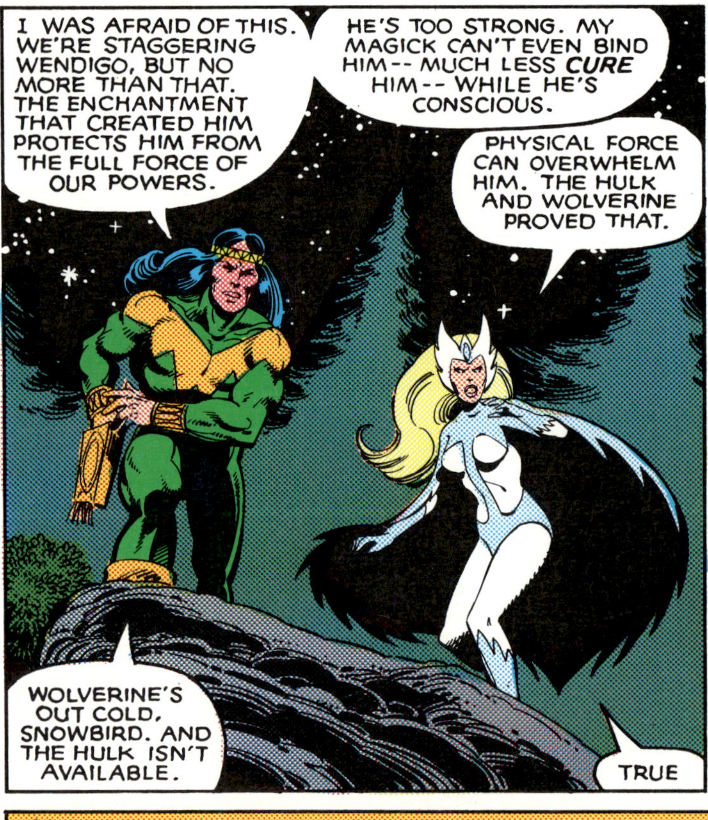
I WAS AFRAID OF THIS. WE'RE STAGGERING WENDIGO, BUT NO MORE THAN THAT. THE ENCHANTMENT THAT CREATED HIM PROTECTS HIM FROM THE FULL FORCE OF OUR POWERS.
HE'S TOO STRONG. MY MAGICK CAN'T EVEN BIND HIM-- MUCH LESS CURE HIM-- WHILE HE'S CONSCIOUS.
PHYSICAL FORCE CAN OVERWHELM HIM. THE HULK AND WOLVERINE PROVED THAT.
WOLVERINE'S OUT COLD, SNOWBIRD. AND THE HULK ISN'T AVAILABLE.
TRUE

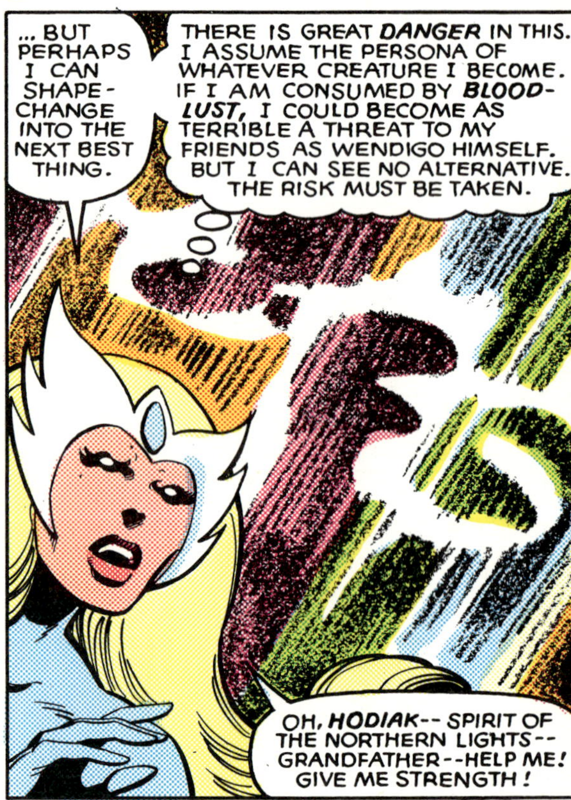
... BUT PERHAPS I CAN SHAPE-CHANGE INTO THE NEXT BEST THING.
THERE IS GREAT DANGER IN THIS. I ASSUME THE PERSONA OF WHATEVER CREATURE I BECOME. IF I AM CONSUMED BY BLOOD-LUST, I COULD BECOME AS TERRIBLE A THREAT TO MY FRIENDS AS WENDIGO HIMSELF. BUT I CAN SEE NO ALTERNATIVE. THE RISK MUST BE TAKEN.
OH, HODIAK-- SPIRIT OF THE NORTHERN LIGHTS-- GRANDFATHER--HELP ME! GIVE ME STRENGTH!

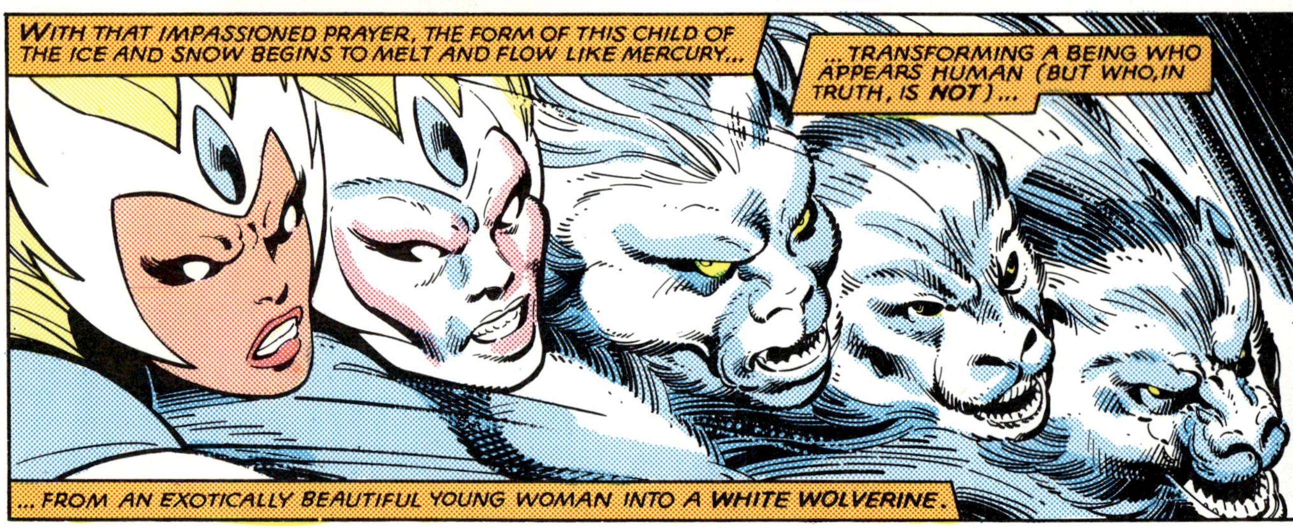
WITH THAT IMPASSIONED PRAYER, THE FORM OF THIS CHILD OF THE ICE AND SNOW BEGINS TO MELT AND FLOW LIKE MERCURY...
...TRANSFORMING A BEING WHO APPEARS HUMAN (BUT WHO, IN TRUTH, IS NOT)...
...FROM AN EXOTICALLY BEAUTIFUL YOUNG WOMAN INTO A WHITE WOLVERINE.

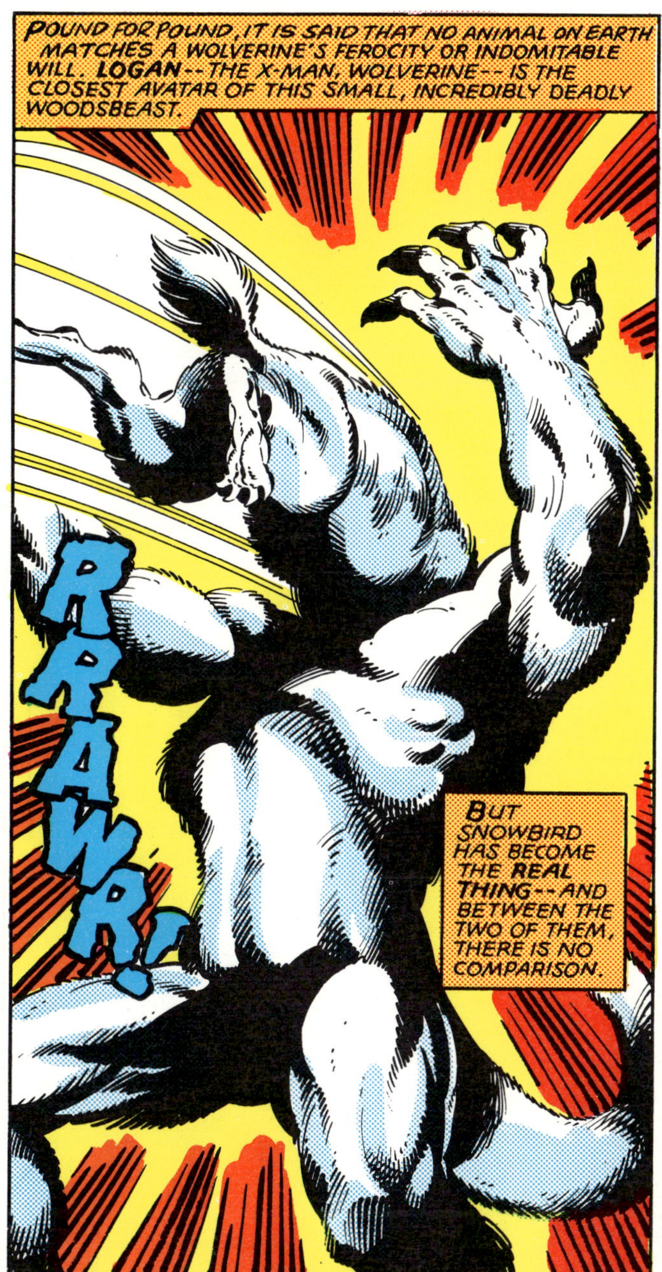
POUND FOR POUND, IT IS SAID THAT NO ANIMAL ON EARTH MATCHES A WOLVERINE'S FEROCITY OR INDOMITABLE WILL. LOGAN--THE X-MAN, WOLVERINE--IS THE CLOSEST AVATAR OF THIS SMALL, INCREDIBLY DEADLY WOODSBEAST.
RRAWR!
BUT SNOWBIRD HAS BECOME THE REAL THING--AND BETWEEN THE TWO OF THEM, THERE IS NO COMPARISON.

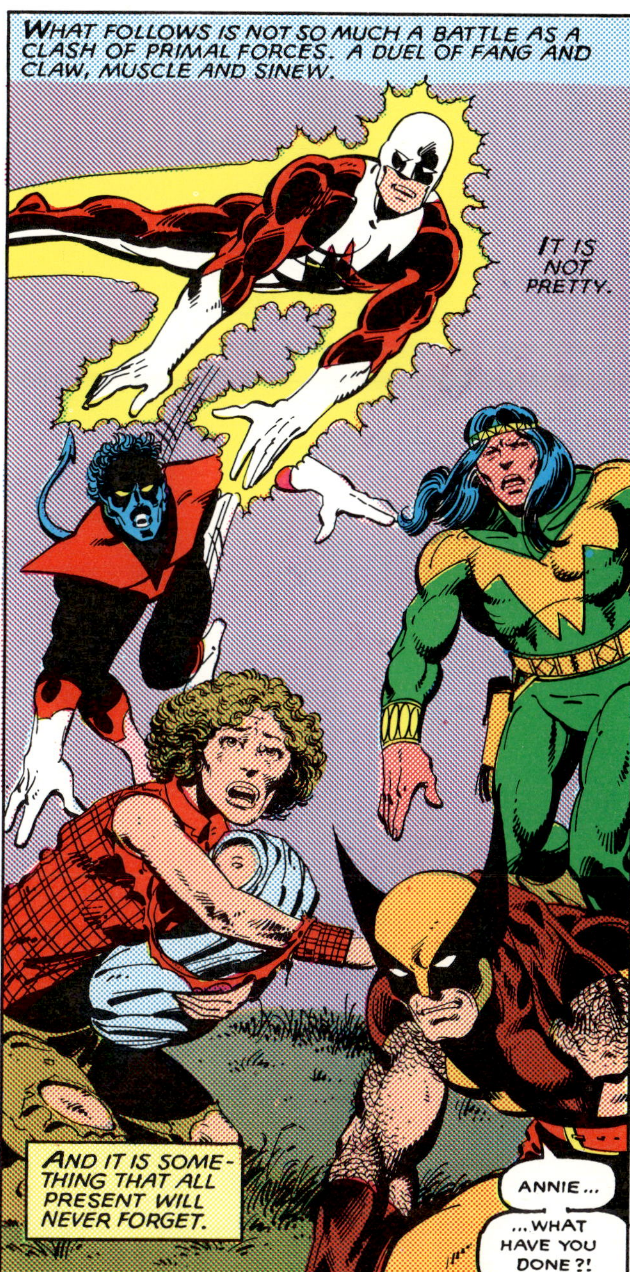
WHAT FOLLOWS IS NOT SO MUCH A BATTLE AS A CLASH OF PRIMAL FORCES. A DUEL OF FANG AND CLAW, MUSCLE AND SINEW.
IT IS NOT PRETTY.
AND IT IS SOMETHING THAT ALL PRESENT WILL NEVER FORGET.
ANNIE...
...WHAT HAVE YOU DONE?!

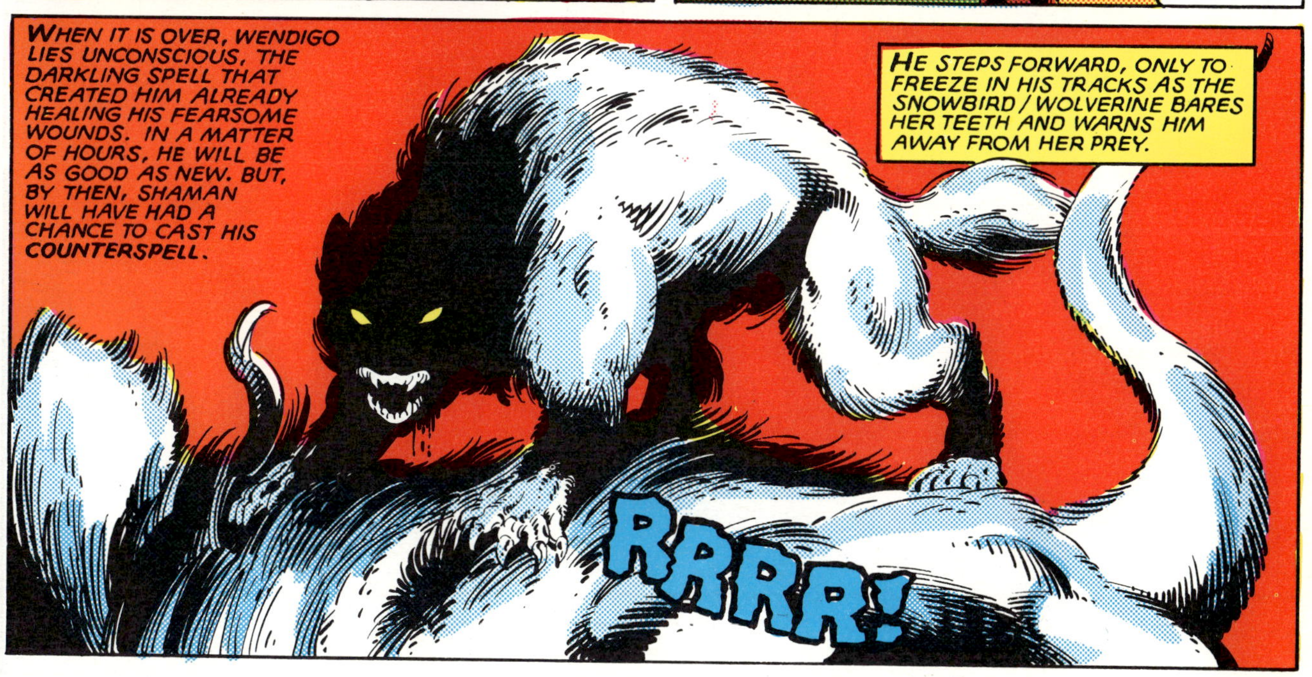
WHEN IT IS OVER, WENDIGO LIES UNCONSCIOUS, THE DARKLING SPELL THAT CREATED HIM ALREADY HEALING HIS FEARSOME WOUNDS. IN A MATTER OF HOURS, HE WILL BE AS GOOD AS NEW. BUT, BY THEN, SHAMAN WILL HAVE HAD A CHANCE TO CAST HIS COUNTERSPELL.
HE STEPS FORWARD, ONLY TO FREEZE IN HIS TRACKS AS THE SNOWBIRD / WOLVERINE BARES HER TEETH AND WARNS HIM AWAY FROM HER PREY.
RRRR!

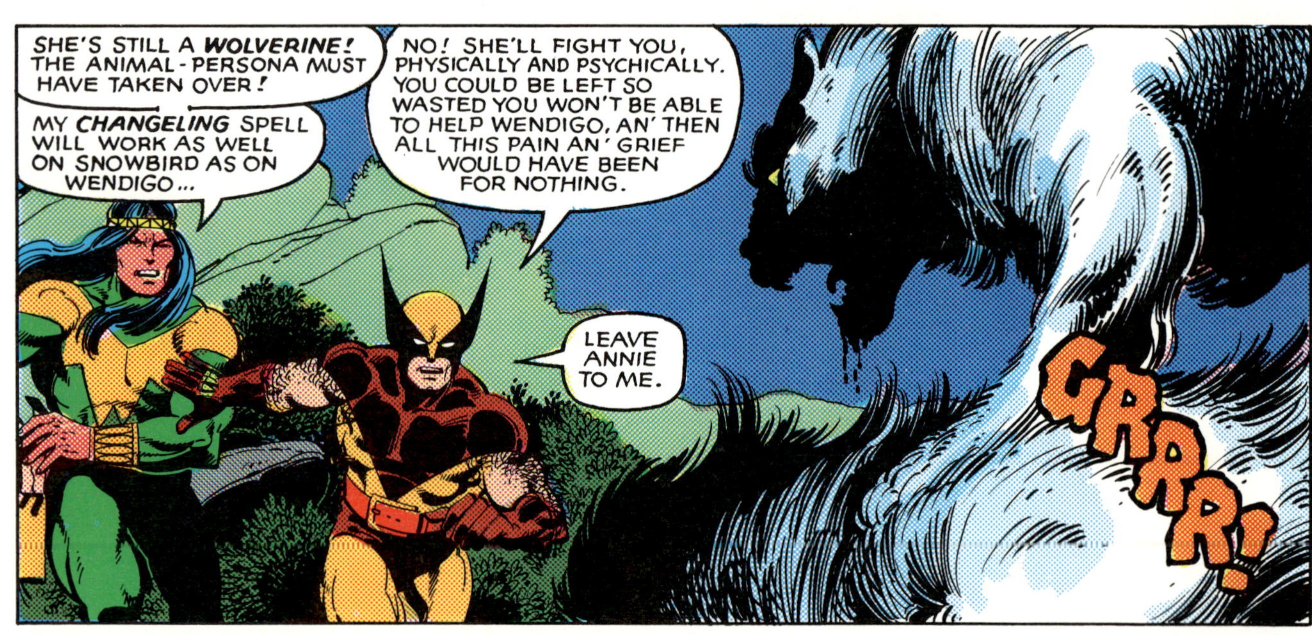
SHE'S STILL A **WOLVERINE!** THE ANIMAL-PERSONA MUST HAVE TAKEN OVER!
MY **CHANGELING** SPELL WILL WORK AS WELL ON SNOWBIRD AS ON WENDIGO...
NO! SHE'LL FIGHT YOU, PHYSICALLY AND PSYCHICALLY. YOU COULD BE LEFT SO WASTED YOU WON'T BE ABLE TO HELP WENDIGO, AN' THEN ALL THIS PAIN AN' GRIEF WOULD HAVE BEEN FOR NOTHING.
LEAVE ANNIE TO ME.
GRRR!

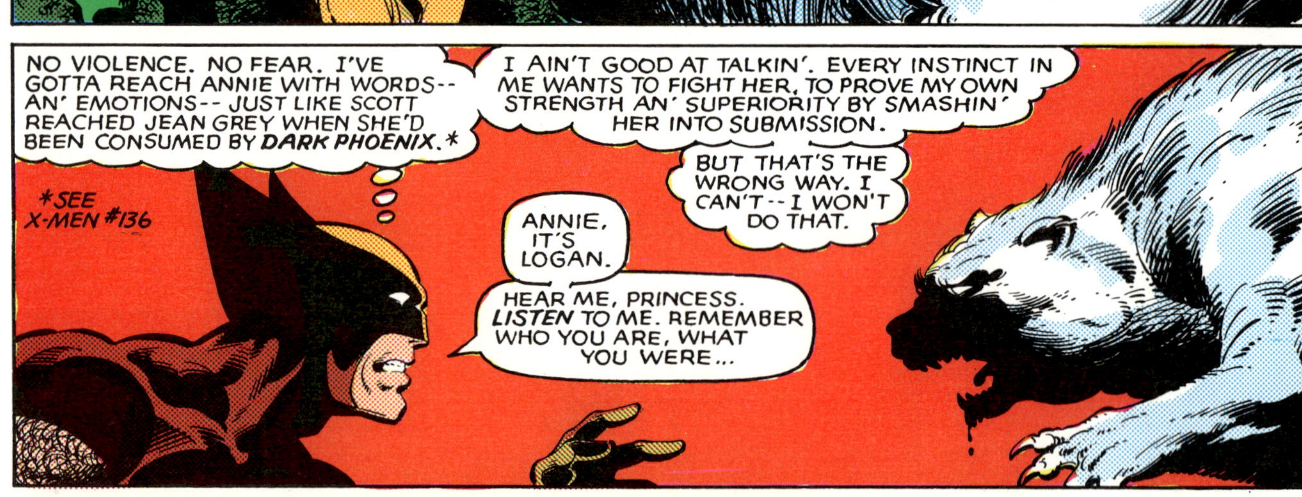
NO VIOLENCE. NO FEAR. I'VE GOTTA REACH ANNIE WITH WORDS-- AN' EMOTIONS-- JUST LIKE SCOTT REACHED JEAN GREY WHEN SHE'D BEEN CONSUMED BY **DARK PHOENIX**.*
I AIN'T GOOD AT TALKIN'. EVERY INSTINCT IN ME WANTS TO FIGHT HER, TO PROVE MY OWN STRENGTH AN' SUPERIORITY BY SMASHIN' HER INTO SUBMISSION.
BUT THAT'S THE WRONG WAY. I CAN'T -- I WON'T DO THAT.
*SEE X-MEN #136
ANNIE, IT'S LOGAN.
HEAR ME, PRINCESS. **LISTEN** TO ME. REMEMBER WHO YOU ARE, WHAT YOU WERE...

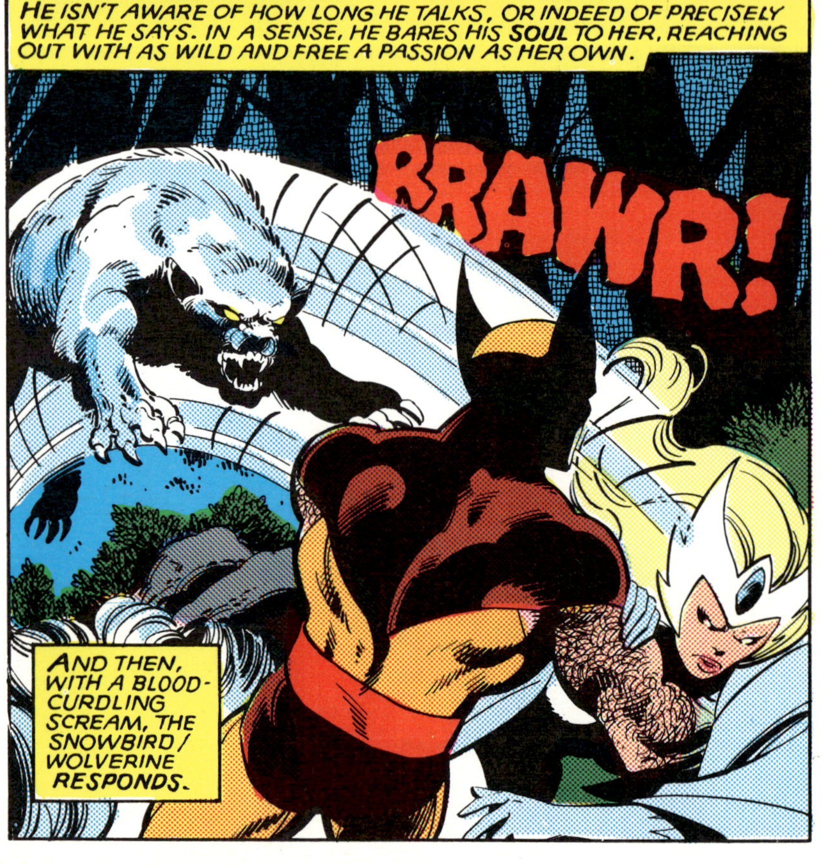
HE ISN'T AWARE OF HOW LONG HE TALKS, OR INDEED OF PRECISELY WHAT HE SAYS. IN A SENSE, HE BARES HIS **SOUL** TO HER, REACHING OUT WITH AS WILD AND FREE A PASSION AS HER OWN.
BRAWR!
AND THEN, WITH A BLOOD-CURDLING SCREAM, THE SNOWBIRD/ WOLVERINE **RESPONDS**.

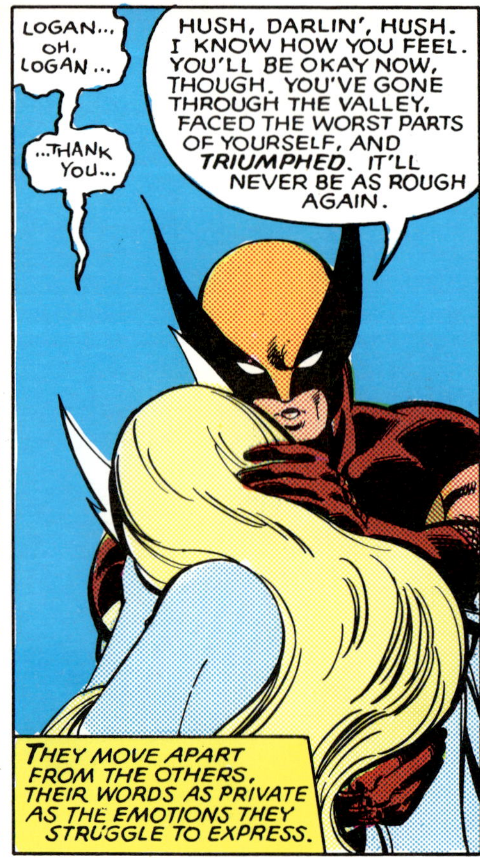
LOGAN... OH, LOGAN...
...THANK YOU...
HUSH, DARLIN', HUSH. I KNOW HOW YOU FEEL. YOU'LL BE OKAY NOW, THOUGH. YOU'VE GONE THROUGH THE VALLEY, FACED THE WORST PARTS OF YOURSELF, AND **TRIUMPHED**. IT'LL NEVER BE AS ROUGH AGAIN.
THEY MOVE APART FROM THE OTHERS, THEIR WORDS AS PRIVATE AS THE EMOTIONS THEY STRUGGLE TO EXPRESS.

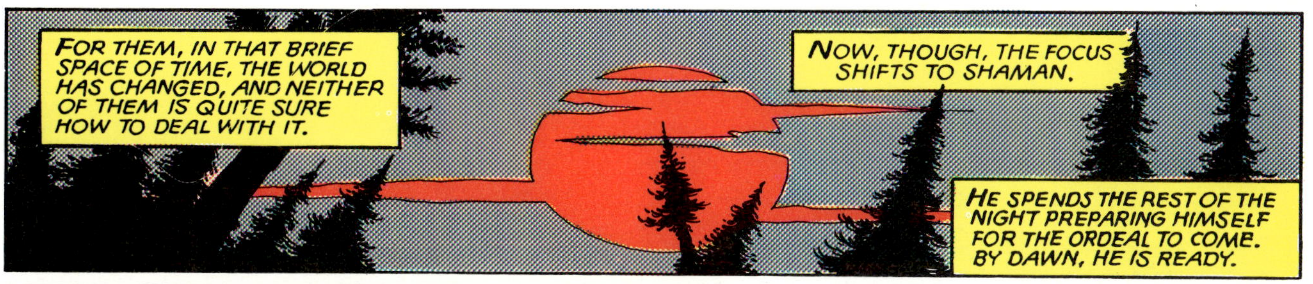
FOR THEM, IN THAT BRIEF SPACE OF TIME, THE WORLD HAS CHANGED, AND NEITHER OF THEM IS QUITE SURE HOW TO DEAL WITH IT.
NOW, THOUGH, THE FOCUS SHIFTS TO SHAMAN.
HE SPENDS THE REST OF THE NIGHT PREPARING HIMSELF FOR THE ORDEAL TO COME. BY DAWN, HE IS READY.

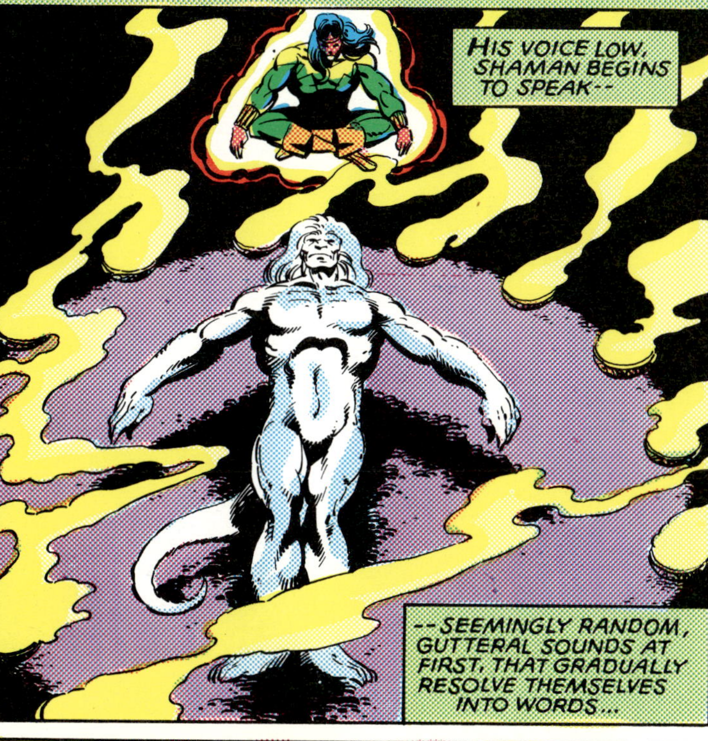
THE OTHERS STAND GUARD, ALERT SHOULD ANYTHING GO WRONG. AROUND THEM, THE FOREST HAS GONE DEATHLY STILL -- NO SOUND OF MAN OR BEAST, NOT EVEN A WAYWARD BREATH OF WIND, DISTURBS THE EERIE SILENCE.
HIS VOICE LOW, SHAMAN BEGINS TO SPEAK--
--SEEMINGLY RANDOM, GUTTERAL SOUNDS AT FIRST, THAT GRADUALLY RESOLVE THEMSELVES INTO WORDS...

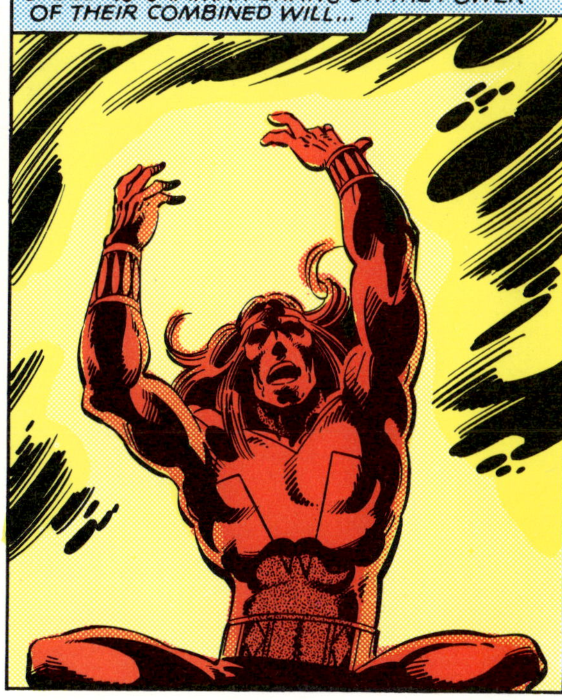
...THE WORDS INTO A SING-SONG RHYTHMIC CHANT. THE LANGUAGE IS OLDER THAN RECORDED HISTORY, AND BESIDES SHAMAN, ONLY SNOWBIRD KNOWS THE WORDS' MEANING. ALL, HOWEVER, RESPOND TO THE SPELL AS SHAMAN DRAWS ON THE POWER OF THEIR COMBINED WILL...

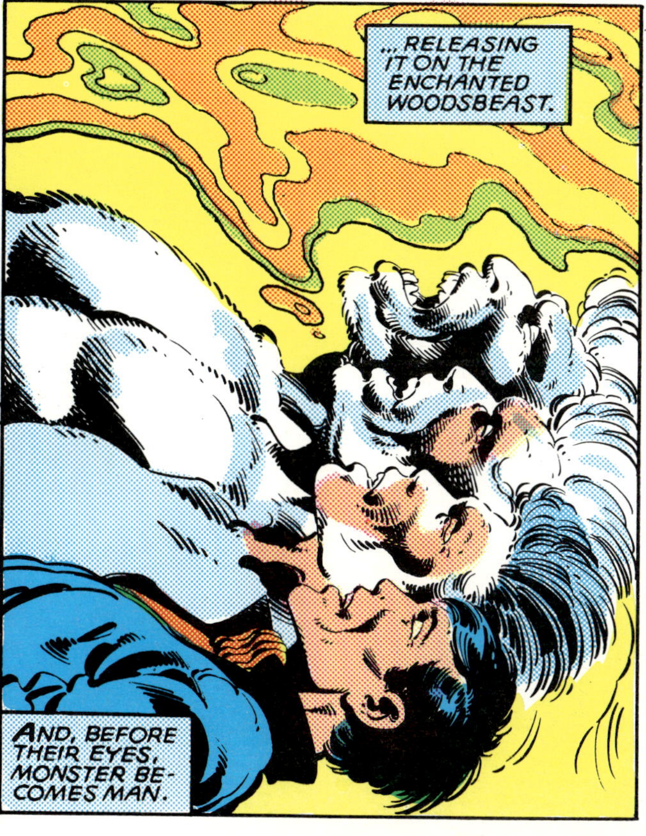
...RELEASING IT ON THE ENCHANTED WOODSBEAST.
AND, BEFORE THEIR EYES, MONSTER BECOMES MAN.

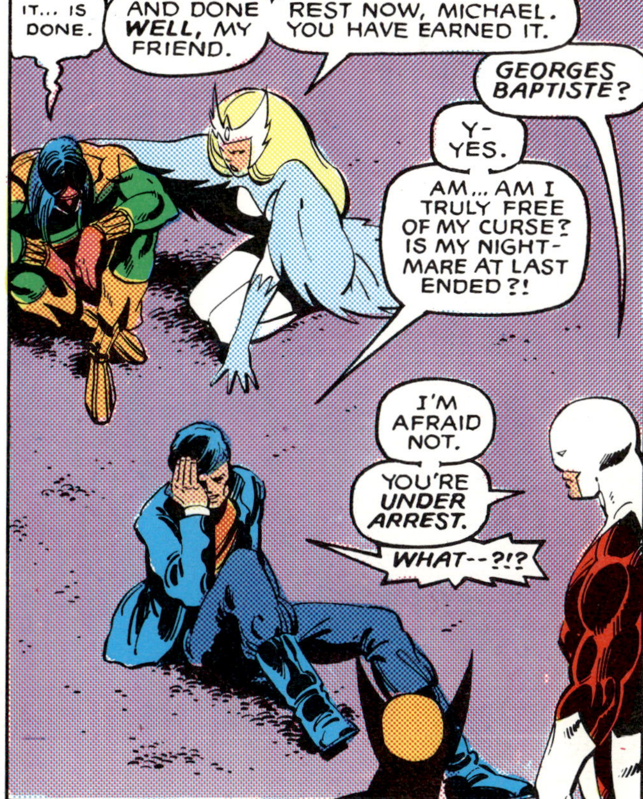
IT... IS DONE.
AND DONE WELL, MY FRIEND.
REST NOW, MICHAEL. YOU HAVE EARNED IT.
GEORGES BAPTISTE?
Y-YES.
AM... AM I TRULY FREE OF MY CURSE? IS MY NIGHTMARE AT LAST ENDED?!
I'M AFRAID NOT.
YOU'RE UNDER ARREST.
WHAT--?!?

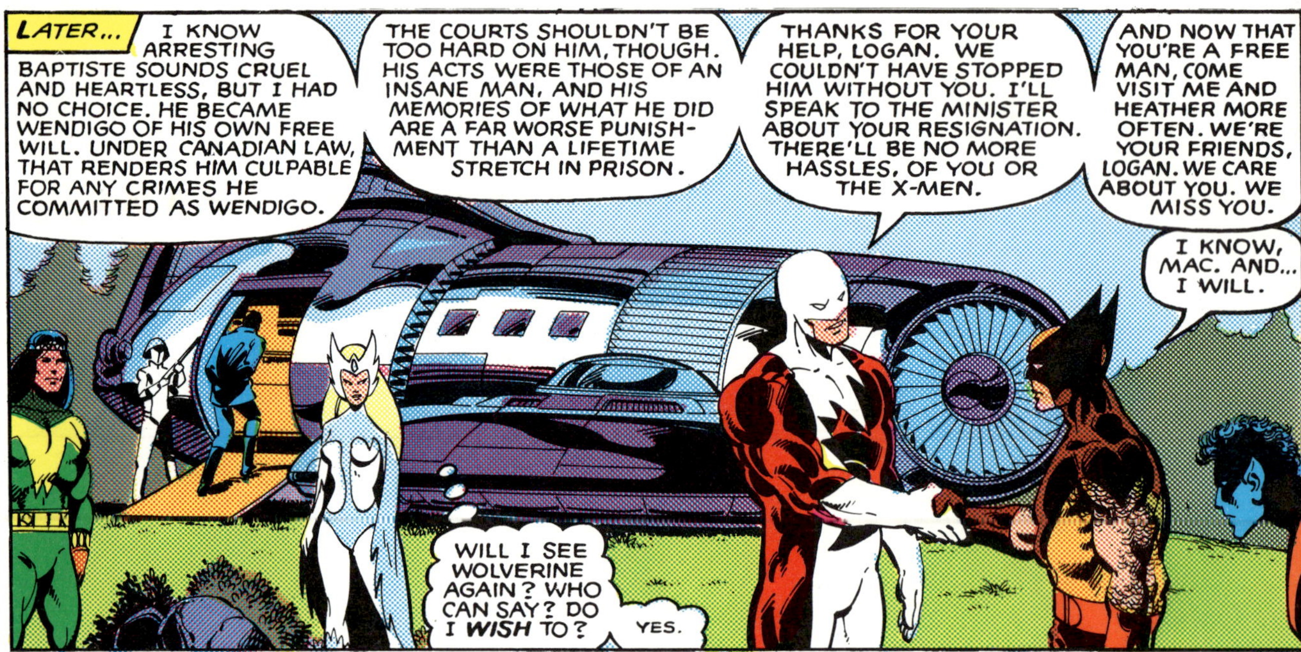

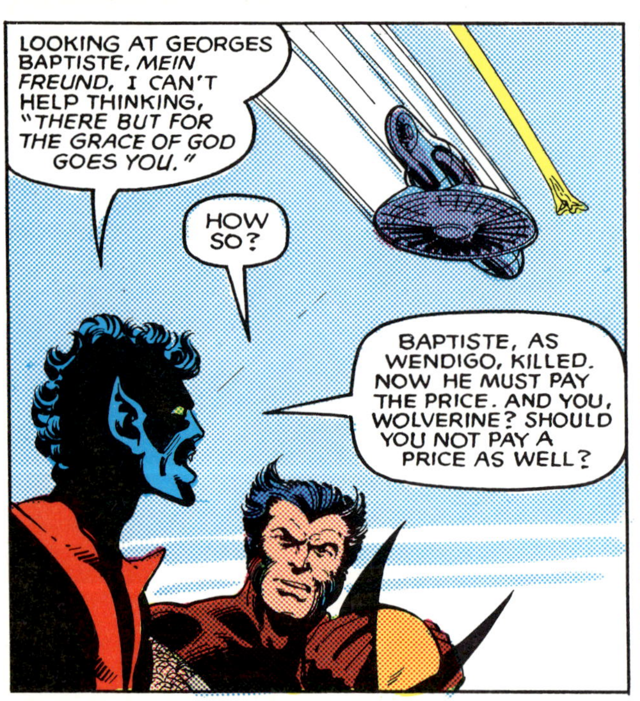

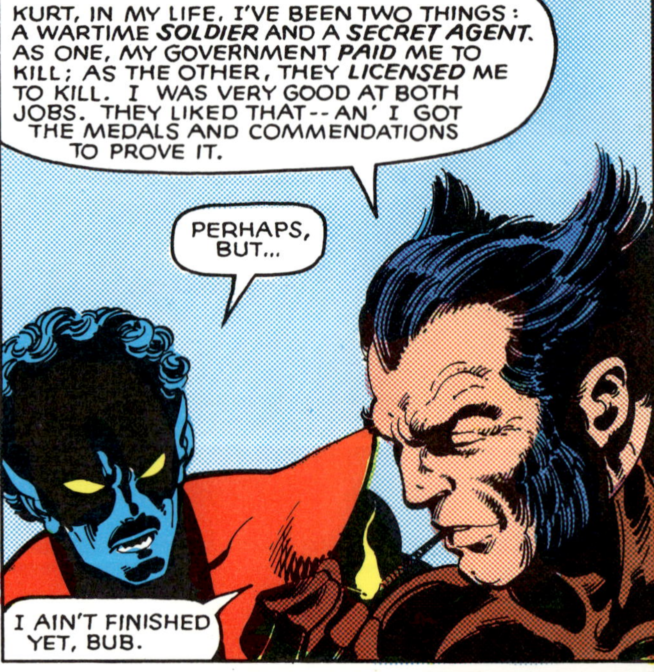

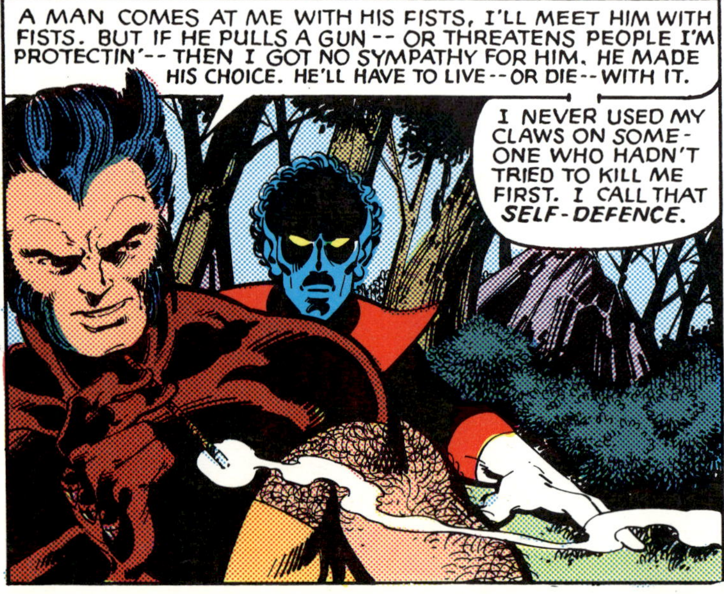

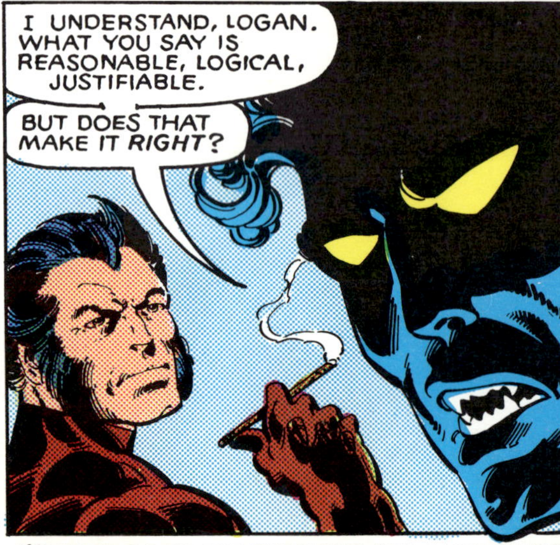

WOLVERINE DOES NOT REPLY AND, FOR A LONG WHILE, THERE IS SILENCE BETWEEN THE TWO MEN...

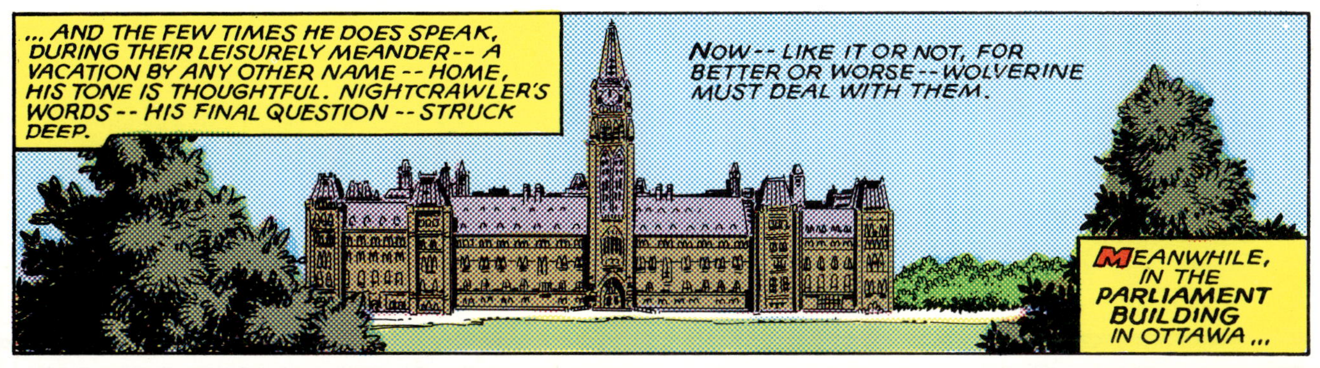
...AND THE FEW TIMES HE DOES SPEAK, DURING THEIR LEISURELY MEANDER-- A VACATION BY ANY OTHER NAME -- HOME, HIS TONE IS THOUGHTFUL. NIGHTCRAWLER'S WORDS -- HIS FINAL QUESTION -- STRUCK DEEP.
NOW -- LIKE IT OR NOT, FOR BETTER OR WORSE -- WOLVERINE MUST DEAL WITH THEM.
MEANWHILE, IN THE PARLIAMENT BUILDING IN OTTAWA...

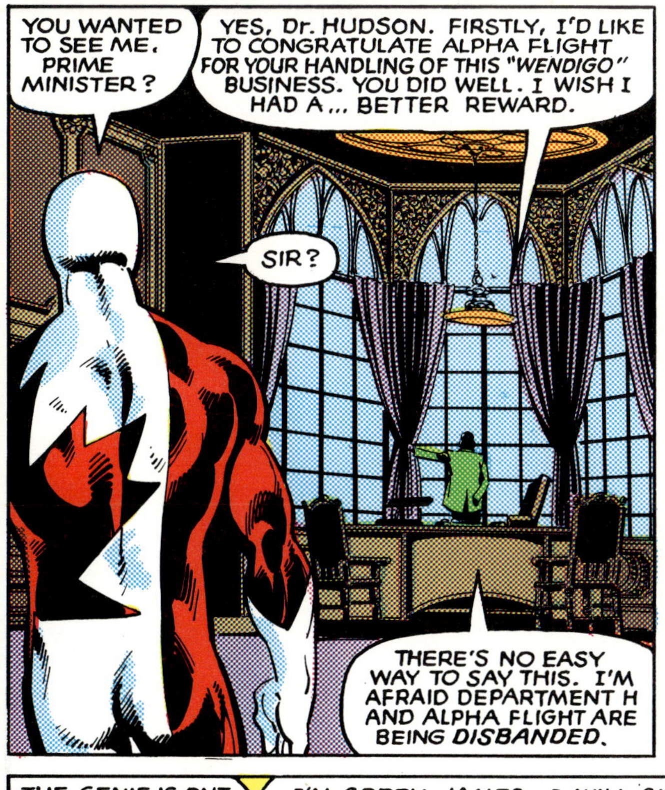
YOU WANTED TO SEE ME, PRIME MINISTER?
YES, Dr. HUDSON. FIRSTLY, I'D LIKE TO CONGRATULATE ALPHA FLIGHT FOR YOUR HANDLING OF THIS "WENDIGO" BUSINESS. YOU DID WELL. I WISH I HAD A... BETTER REWARD.
SIR?
THERE'S NO EASY WAY TO SAY THIS. I'M AFRAID DEPARTMENT H AND ALPHA FLIGHT ARE BEING DISBANDED.

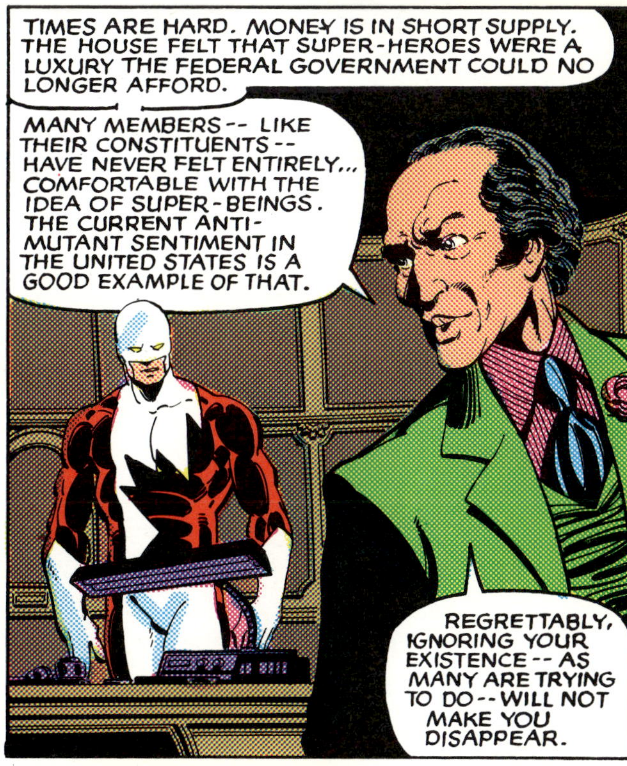
TIMES ARE HARD. MONEY IS IN SHORT SUPPLY. THE HOUSE FELT THAT SUPER-HEROES WERE A LUXURY THE FEDERAL GOVERNMENT COULD NO LONGER AFFORD.
MANY MEMBERS -- LIKE THEIR CONSTITUENTS -- HAVE NEVER FELT ENTIRELY... COMFORTABLE WITH THE IDEA OF SUPER-BEINGS. THE CURRENT ANTI-MUTANT SENTIMENT IN THE UNITED STATES IS A GOOD EXAMPLE OF THAT.
REGRETTABLY, IGNORING YOUR EXISTENCE -- AS MANY ARE TRYING TO DO -- WILL NOT MAKE YOU DISAPPEAR.

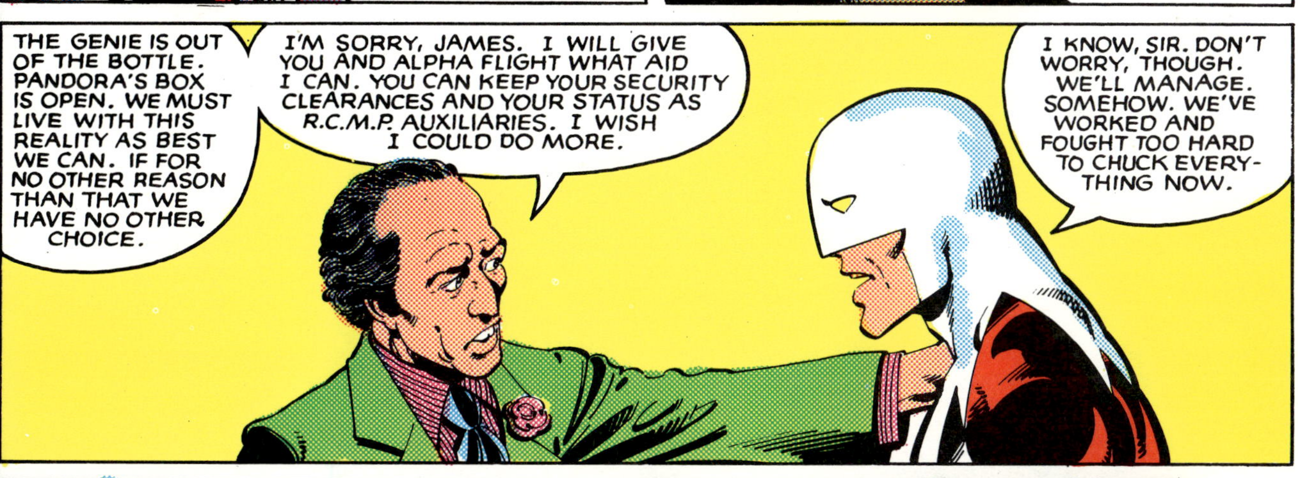
THE GENIE IS OUT OF THE BOTTLE. PANDORA'S BOX IS OPEN. WE MUST LIVE WITH THIS REALITY AS BEST WE CAN. IF FOR NO OTHER REASON THAN THAT WE HAVE NO OTHER CHOICE.
I'M SORRY, JAMES. I WILL GIVE YOU AND ALPHA FLIGHT WHAT AID I CAN. YOU CAN KEEP YOUR SECURITY CLEARANCES AND YOUR STATUS AS R.C.M.P. AUXILIARIES. I WISH I COULD DO MORE.
I KNOW, SIR. DON'T WORRY, THOUGH. WE'LL MANAGE. SOMEHOW. WE'VE WORKED AND FOUGHT TOO HARD TO CHUCK EVERYTHING NOW.

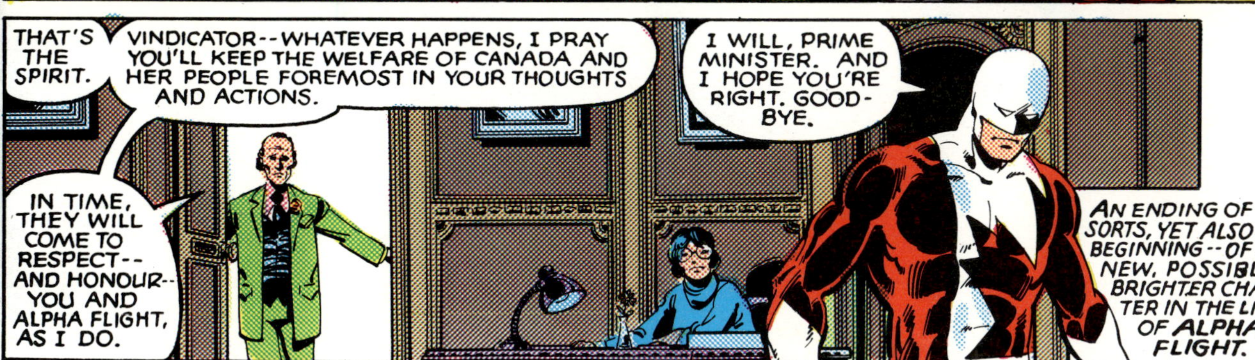
THAT'S THE SPIRIT.
VINDICATOR -- WHATEVER HAPPENS, I PRAY YOU'LL KEEP THE WELFARE OF CANADA AND HER PEOPLE FOREMOST IN YOUR THOUGHTS AND ACTIONS.
IN TIME, THEY WILL COME TO RESPECT -- AND HONOUR -- YOU AND ALPHA FLIGHT, AS I DO.
I WILL, PRIME MINISTER. AND I HOPE YOU'RE RIGHT. GOOD-BYE.
AN ENDING OF SORTS, YET ALSO A BEGINNING -- OF A NEW, POSSIBLY BRIGHTER CHAPTER IN THE LIFE OF ALPHA FLIGHT.

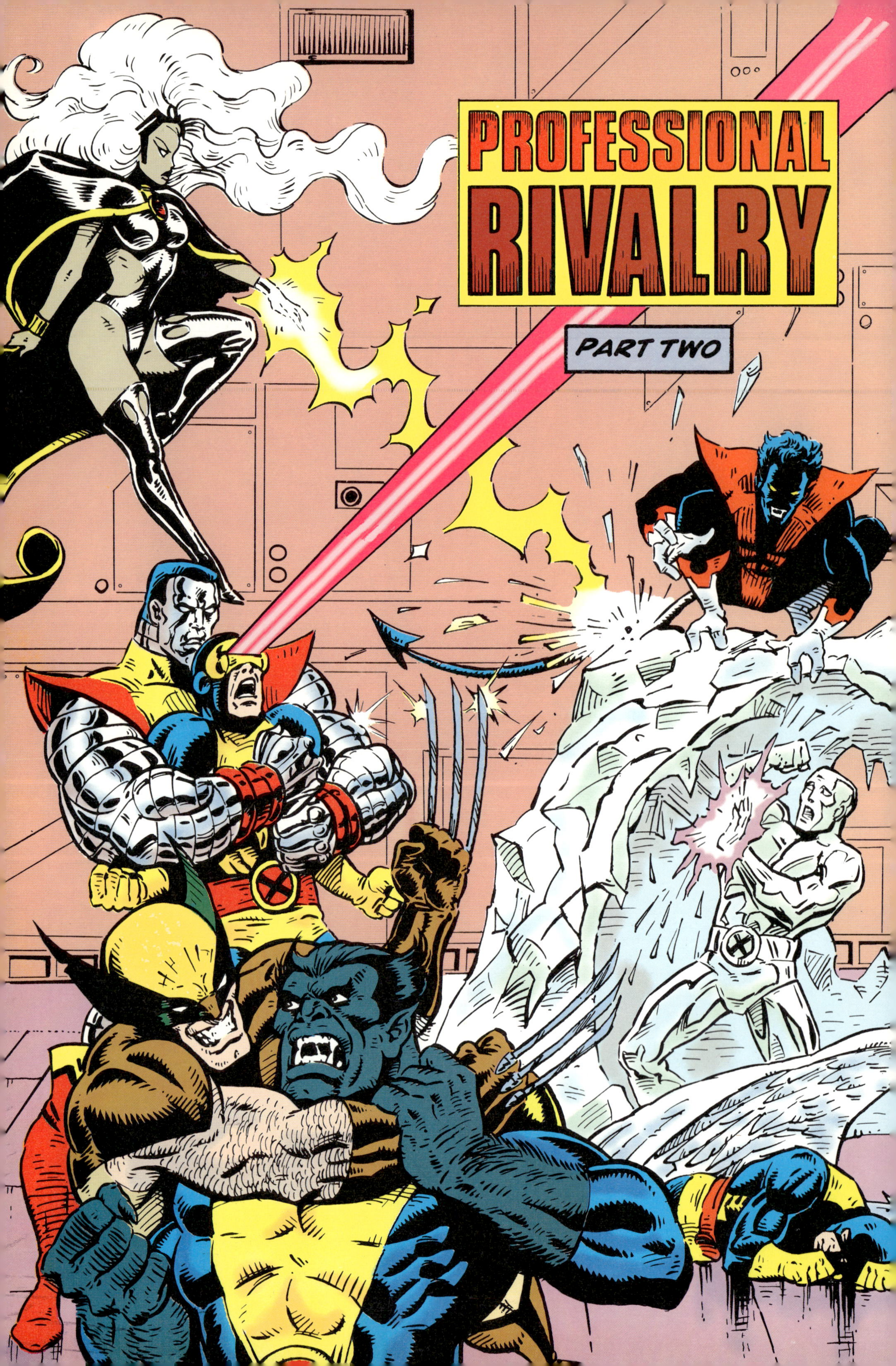
PROFESSIONAL RIVALRY
PART TWO

Nightcrawler was glad to return home to his friends – the X-Men. He had joined Wolverine on the Canadian mission to keep the feisty little berserker out of trouble. Instead he had wound up in more trouble than he cared to remember. At his side stood Wolverine, wearing civilian clothes and his cowboy hat, as they stepped from the aeroplane and into their waiting taxi. The taxi driver was clearly startled by Nightcrawler's appearance – built like a man but covered in blue velvety fur, sporting pointed ears, fangs and those eerie, glowing, yellow eyes. And, of course, Kurt's pointed tail didn't help matters. That was one of the reasons he enjoyed the X-Mens company so much. For the first time in his life he hadn't been treated as an outcast. These people had looked beneath Nightcrawler's demonic appearance and seen a man, a real man. For once he had been treated like a human being.

The short Canadian mutant known as Wolverine, or Logan to his few friends, also looked somewhat different. Not inhuman, but the lashing wings he gelled his hair into, with vicious points which seemed to exemplify his own animalistic nature, gained him as many sideway glances as his blue -skinned partner. Of course, nobody ever took a dislike to Wolverine, or, if they did they never admitted to it. For nature had given Logan the deadly animalistic urges of his namesake and technology had given him six adamantium claws which could slice through you as soon as look at you. Logan was not a man to be trifled with, not by a longshot, especially when one realised the short fuse temper and deadly rage the barely five foot mutant contained.

As the taxi pulled away from X-Men mansion, having dropped the two mutants off, the driver couldn't resist a final glance in his rearview mirror. What he saw would stay with him to the grave: the blue fuzzy elf disappeared in a puff of orange smoke and, perhaps more shocking was the shorter man's reaction – none at all.

Kurt Wagner reappeared in the grand hallway of the mansion and opened the heavy doors wide to allow his friend to enter.

"Forgot my key," he told Wolverine with a smile across his thin blue lips.

"Showoff," muttered Logan as he puffed on his cigar and pushed past to enter the mansion he had called home for longer than he could remember.

When you can teleport from point to point in the blink of an eye, as Kurt Wagner could, it only makes sense that you'd want to save your legs now and then!

Wolverine glared at him for a moment: "Who's that?" he asked his fuzzy friend, who looked confused. "I can smell a strange scent, 'Crawler – don't tell me Charlie's been having trouble while we've been away!"

"Trouble" was an understatement! Professor X sat by Cerebro deep in thought. He had let people whom he thought were old friends into the mansion with hardly a question. Now, he realised, these original X-Men were pretenders. They were not all they seemed and that scared him. Of course, he had wondered why he couldn't read their thought patterns when he first met them but had arrived at the obvious

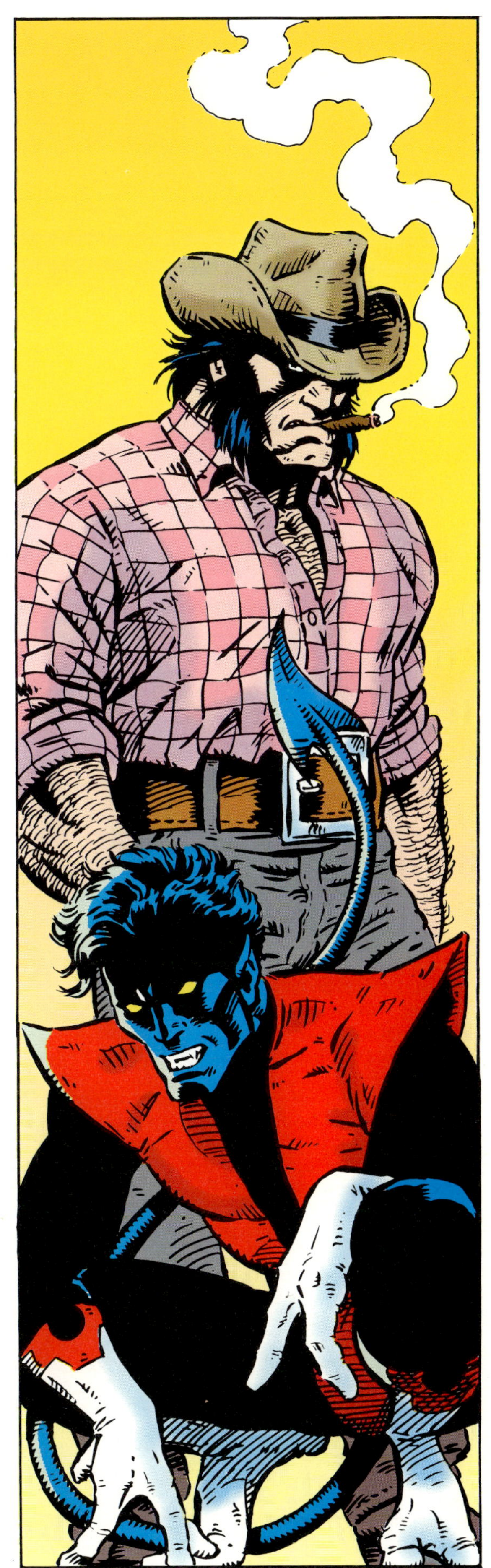

conclusion that they were simply employing their training to resist mind control. Training he had given them in days long passed. Xavier had been proud – of them for employing his teachings, and of himself for not looking for some illogical and ridiculous answer. Now, he wished he'd been his usual wary, scaremonger self. He looked at the words he had written whilst he'd observed Cyclops, the Beast, Iceman and the Angel in the Danger Room. Scribbled in pencil in his desk top journal were his thoughts as he'd tried to mindscan these newcomers: "Blasted privacy" was what he had written. Protecting their thoughts from his. It was as if they hadn't trusted him – thought he'd betray their innermost secrets. Now he realised that there was much more to it than that. These were not X-Men. In fact, they were not even men at all. No wonder they had been so eager to get the new X-Men out of the mansion. The new X-Men must have proven a threat to their mission, whatever that might be.

"Professor?" Scott (Cyclops) Summers had entered Xavier's study and was busily closing the door behind him. "We would appreciate your assistance in the Danger Room, Sir. . ."

Xavier felt a hundred-thousand emotions flow through his body. "Who. . . what are you?" Charles Xavier couldn't bear to look up at this mockery of his longtime friend.

"I'm sorry, sir?"

"I bet you are! But I know that you aren't Scott Summers . . . so who are you?"

Xavier didn't even feel the blow to the back of his head as he slipped into unconsciousness.

Storm had explained the situation to Wolverine and Nightcrawler in her calmest voice. The calmest she could manage under the circumstances.

"So, what yer sayin' is that we ain't X-Men no more!" Wolverine always had had a knack of stating the obvious.

"That's preposterous, mein friend," Kurt Wagner was clearly amazed at the news, "To say that we are not *good enough* to uphold Xavier's dream. I haven't heard so much rubbish in all my years."

"Calm down, elf," Logan placed his hand on Nightcrawler's shoulder, "I'm sure Ororo ain't gonna take this lyin' down!" He turned to Storm, still standing by her houseplants as she gazed out of her attic room's skylight.

"Of course not, Logan, but with Warren and the Professor on their side I can't really see that there's much we can do. We are, after all, only the replacement team."

"Yeah, but no-one said anything about us gettin' the push soon as Scotty returned!" Wolverine toyed with his mask's 'horns' to ease his own tension. "For a start off, it's dangerous to just send Pryde back to her family with such a small grasp on her powers . . . an' we got a responsibility to uphold the school for others like her."

"Yes," Kurt said, "they can do what they want with us but to throw young mutants like Kitty out is mindless . . . why, it could prove downright dangerous if their power were to fall into other people's hands."

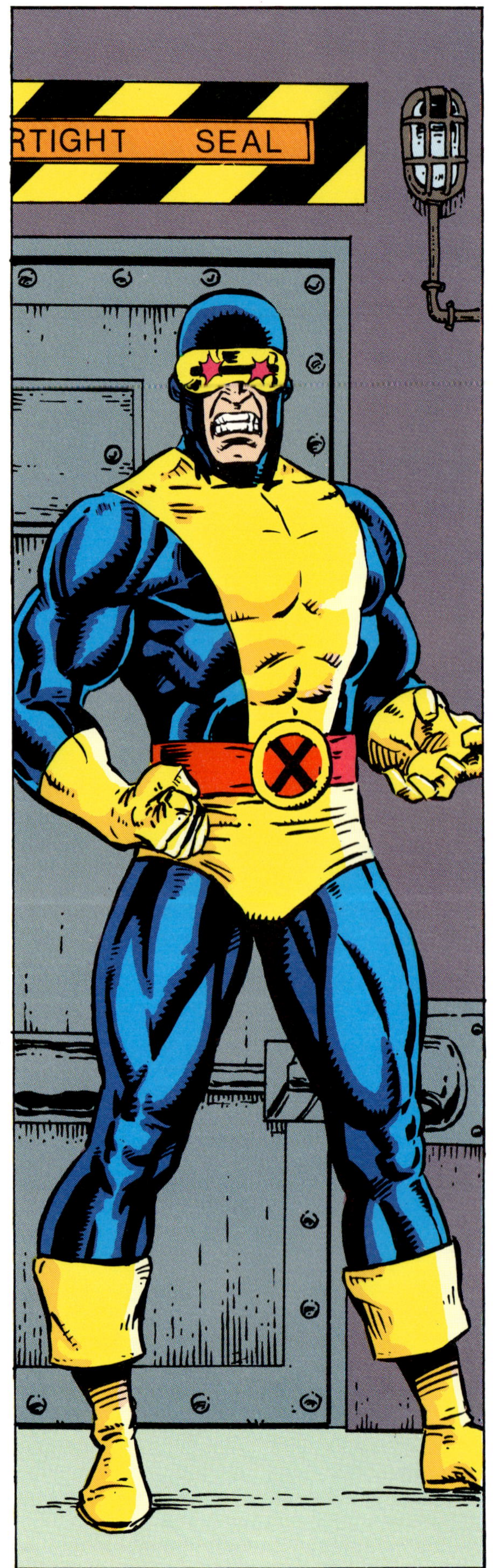

"But, as I said, the Profess . . ." Storm was cut short by Wolverine.

"Ferget 'em, bub – what is this? A blasted old boys' club or a superteam pledged to the protection of the human race?!"

"Well, when you put it like that . . ." Kurt began with a cunning smile on his face.

Colossus, Wolverine, Nightcrawler and the young mutant known as Sprite or Kitty, depending on whether she was *really* to be an X-Man or not, sat in the dining room as Storm stood at the head of the table discussing their plans for the future.

"As Wolverine has kindly pointed out," Storm began as the others sat with bated breath, "our responsibilities do *not* lie with the X-Men, as such, but rather we are pledged to the protection of the human race. Thus, it is my firm belief that we band together and . . . Logan – is there something wrong with your nose?"

"Either I've got a stinkin' cold or there's been someone in here who ain't an X-Man."

"But there's only been Cyclops an. . ." Kitty began.

"There's no hint of Scott in here, darlin'! There's three scents that ain't even human. I'm tellin' ya – whatever else these guys might be they sure as hell ain't the original X-Men!"

Nightcrawler added his own touch to the otherwise sombre atmosphere: "With his heightened senses Wolverine smells a rat?!"

"Laugh while ya can, bub – this is about to get nasty!" Wolverine popped his claws out of their sheathing in his forearms – possibly as an unconscious reaction to his anger, perhaps simply for effect. Whatever the reason, everyone in the room felt it captured the mood of the occasion.

Colossus and Nightcrawler stood outside the Danger Room as Storm entered. It had been left to Wolverine to talk to Xavier, since he was known for having a unique ability of making his point clear. Kitty had been told by the others to wait in her room and keep out of danger.

In the Danger Room the four original X-Men trained. It seemed they had been training ever since they had arrived. Storm hoped that they wouldn't put all that training into practice against her. There was a time delay lock on the room door to prevent people walking in mid-battle but eventually the session ended and Ororo confronted Cyclops with their decision.

"Don't be so ridiculous," he told her. "What makes you think you can protect the world when you can't even make the grade as an X-Man?!"

The Beast and Iceman backed Scott up with cheers and whoops. Angel stood in the background, hoping not to get involved in this professional rivalry.

Slowly, Storm leaned her head towards the three X-Men and, taking a deep breath, played her ace: "At least we're who we say we are!"

Scott was the first to react, feigning shock, "Whatever do you mean, woman? Stop talking in riddles!"

"You know exactly what I mean, 'Scott Summers' – if that's what you call yourself. You had us fooled for a while, made us believe that we were amateurs, even had some of us ready to pack up and go, but Wolverine's sniffed you out for the creeps you are.

"In the dining room Wolverine could tell from your lingering scents that you weren't the *real* X-Men. You're not even *human*. So now it's my turn to ask *you* to pack up and leave!"

Warren Worthington III looked at his fellow team mates: "Is this true? Aren't you real X-Men?"

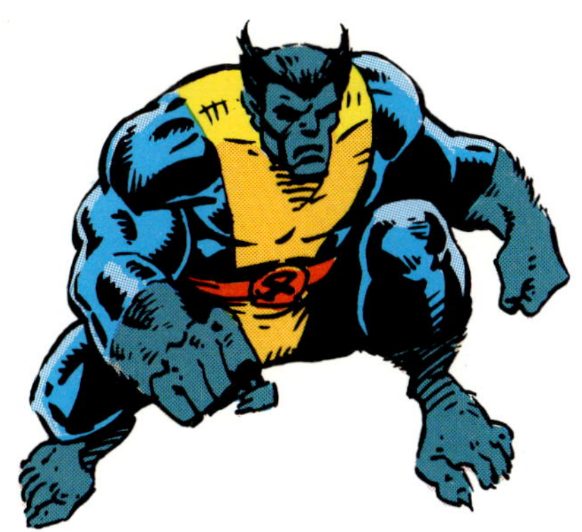

The Beast threw his massive furry form at Storm in a rage of blind fury. She slammed to the floor as he answered the Angel's question: "Of course we're your old buddies, Warren. *That* was simply a cheap shot by a jilted superhero."

"NO! That wasn't a cheap shot, Beast." Wolverine entered holding Professor Xavier's unconscious form across his muscular arms as Colossus and Nightcrawler followed, "knocking out Charlie 'coz he knew too much was a cheap shot. I take it he was onto your scam – ain't much you can hide from a telepath, bub – and so ya had to dispose of him as quickly as possible! But you bodged it up – the Professor is still alive and his notes reveal his findings quite clearly. He couldn't read your minds coz they were too alien for him."

Colossus added, "And that call from the Avengers was a dead giveaway, too. That's why I didn't leave this morning! When Captain America called I could see the other Avengers in the background as they passed the screen: People like the Vision, Iron Man, Thor and a certain blue furred Hank McCoy. . . better known as the *BEAST*!"

The Angel was really mad at all this. He screamed that these 'original' X-Men had ruined his chances of being trusted in the team as he slashed his heavy wings through the air and knocked the Iceman down. Cyclops shot a beam of energy to cut the Angel down in his tracks and the battle was begun.

Wolverine placed Xavier carefully outside the door with a silent "We'll be back" mouthed on his lips and then unleashed his claws as the door slammed shut behind him. He leapt through the air at the acrobatic Beast, flooring him in a second. The Beast fought back but Wolverine's berserker rage had already taken control. Knowing that these were not humans meant Logan could unleash his full fury on them. Something the others had more trouble doing as they fought enemies with the faces of their friends.

Storm sent a mighty rainshower at Iceman, followed by thunderbolts travelling the length of the Danger Room. Iceman retaliated by freezing the water into a protective dome around himself. Whilst he couldn't fight in this position he could plan his counter-attack in relative safety . . . or so he thought . . .

Kurt Wagner, the Nightcrawler, teleported inside the dome and kicked the fake Iceman full in the jaw, knocking him down for the count.

Colossus had Cyclops in a vice-like grip from behind, where Cyclops's energy beams couldn't hurt him as they had the Angel. Storm was glad that they were in the Danger Room where nothing could be damaged. She was also glad that the walls were made of a special material, designed by Xavier, which could deflect and contain violent surges of energy, such as Cyclops's force beams. She removed a panel from the wall and placed it in front of Cyclops from above, where she too was safe.

"Now," she told him, "if you fire you will only hurt yourself."

Wolverine had finished off the Beast using his own fighting prowess. A swift upper cut to the jaw and a knee to the stomach, closely followed up with Wolverine's claws aimed at the Beast's throat and the battle was over.

"Okay, bub," he said to the frightened Beast stand-in, "I think we all deserve an explanation . . . don't you?"

And so the seven mutants and the three fake X-Men sat down to hear the explanations. The fake Cyclops asked what would happen if they didn't tell the real X-Men what was going on and was met by the youthful Kitty Pryde's effervescent voice: "Wolverine'll unsheath his claws and kick your. . ."

"Thanks Kitty, but I really don't think so," replied Cyclops, his voice wavering a little as Wolverine shot him a glance.

"You yourself said how . . . unpredictable Wolverine was, my friend," said Storm in defence." do you really want to find out if you were right to judge him so?"

Logan popped his claws with a snikting noise of metal on flesh to reiterate the point.

"Okay then," Cyclops said eventually, still trapped in a helmet restraining his force beams, "we know when we're beaten."

At this his features began to deteriorate. His face, or, at least, the face of Scott Summers, dissolved to show the green lizard-like flesh and pointed ears of a Skrull. Iceman and the Beast followed suit. All three were Skrulls – members of the alien race of shapechangers. Warmongers with the ability to take on the appearance of anything they chose. The X-Men had met these creatures in their past under different circumstances – when they had been forced to fight the imperial Shi'ar army on the surface of the moon to save the life of Marvel Girl. The Skrulls had been important observers and members on the alien council of war then.

"We are powerful members of the Skrull army." The alien who had, moments before, been Cyclops began, "We came to Earth to fulfill the destiny of the Skrull race – *galactic domination*. By infiltrating the Earth's super-teams we thought we could further that destiny. The X-Men were the logical choice since we had

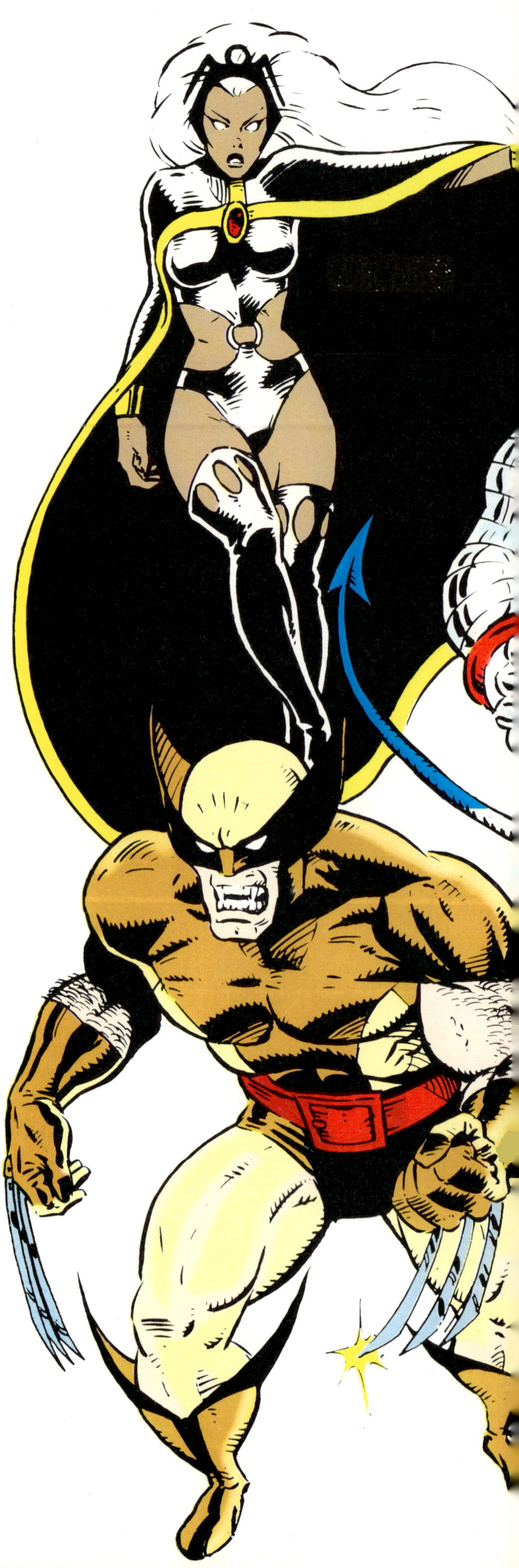

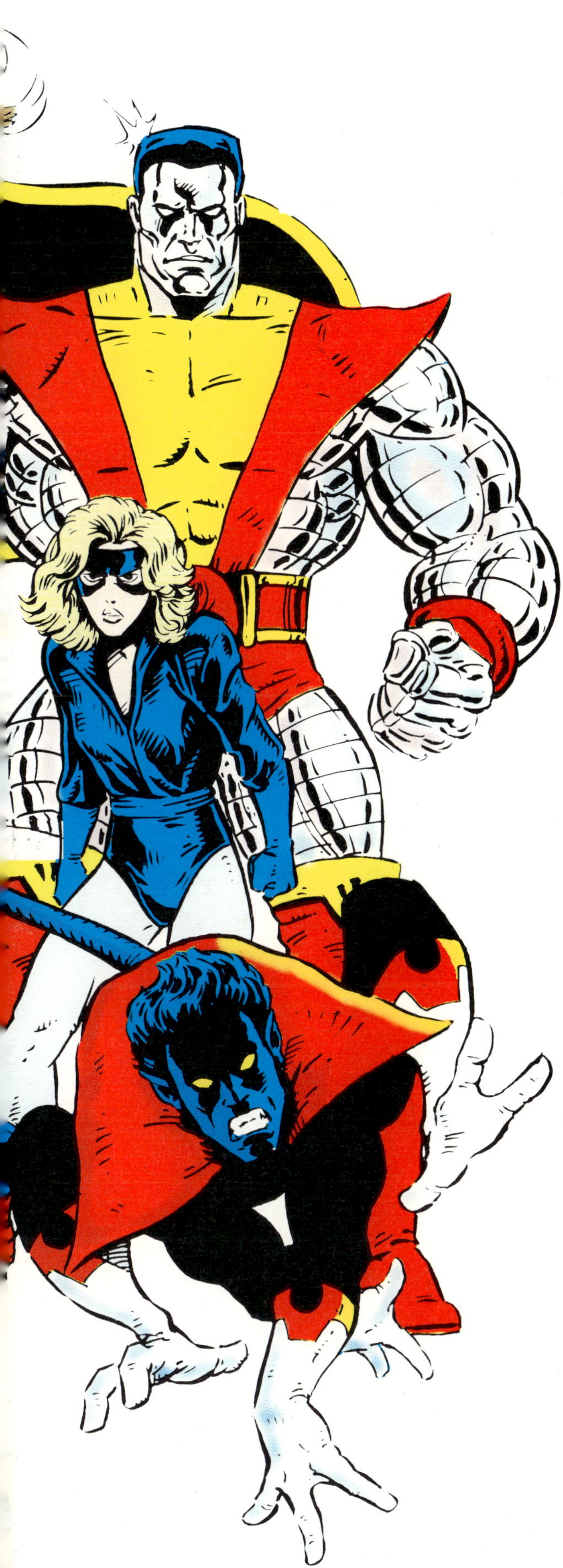

already witnessed you in battle on the moon against the Shi'ar. Your own power is quite limitless and you posed a major threat to our army. Thus, by breaking your wills we thought to take our first steps towards control of the Earth. And we almost succeeded!"

"But you didn't, bub," said Wolverine in a deep growl, "so now that you've admitted your failure why don't you just pack up your tents and get the heck off our planet?!"

The Skrulls began to laugh, as if this were the most ridiculous thing they had ever heard. In truth, mercy was a rather different concept for the aliens to grasp.

So Wolverine made it clearer to them, slamming his 12 inch claws into the wall behind 'Cyclops-Skrull's head, "'Fore we change our minds."

Quite where the Skrulls had left their spacecraft was never disclosed by Xavier or his mutants but they seemed happy that this portion of their lives was concluded at last.

"The Skrull race seemed a bit like Samurai to me," Wolverine told the others from his experiences of Japanese culture, "I reckon they'll be severely punished for this mess-up. Prob'ly choose death before loss of face. Or end up in the Skrull equivalent of the Siberian salt mines . . . sorry, Petey," He said to the Russian Colossus.

"Well then, my pupils," said Xavier from his wheelchair as they walked back through his estate. "It seems that that is the end of it."

"For the time being at least," Nightcrawler added. "People like the Skrulls never give up. No matter how many times they get their faces slapped."

Perhaps to lighten up the mood or perhaps just to speak from the heart, the Angel continued Kurt's thought. "And the X-Men will always be there to stop them in their tracks. I'm proud of you guys . . . you're everything the original X-Men ever were, perhaps more besides. I'm glad that I'm with you. . . even if I haven't shown it."

"You came through for us in the end, Warren – that's all that matters," said Storm, the team leader of the new X-Men. "We're glad to have you."

"Thank you," Worthington said with a tear in his eye, "I hope that I'm up to your standards."

"'Course you are, Angel," Colossus said placing his heavy arm across the Angel's shoulders.

"Welcome aboard, bub!"

"Weren't you paying attention, Wolverine?" said Kitty with a mischievous grin across her face, "It's welcome *back,* 'bub'!"

With that the X-Men returned to the mansion that they knew as home. They laughed and chatted as friends do. And their high spirits were well earned. They were the X-Men. Pledged to forward the dream of Charles Xavier and to continue the legacy that the original X-Men had left in their wake.

. . . And they were, most assuredly, up to that task.

THE END

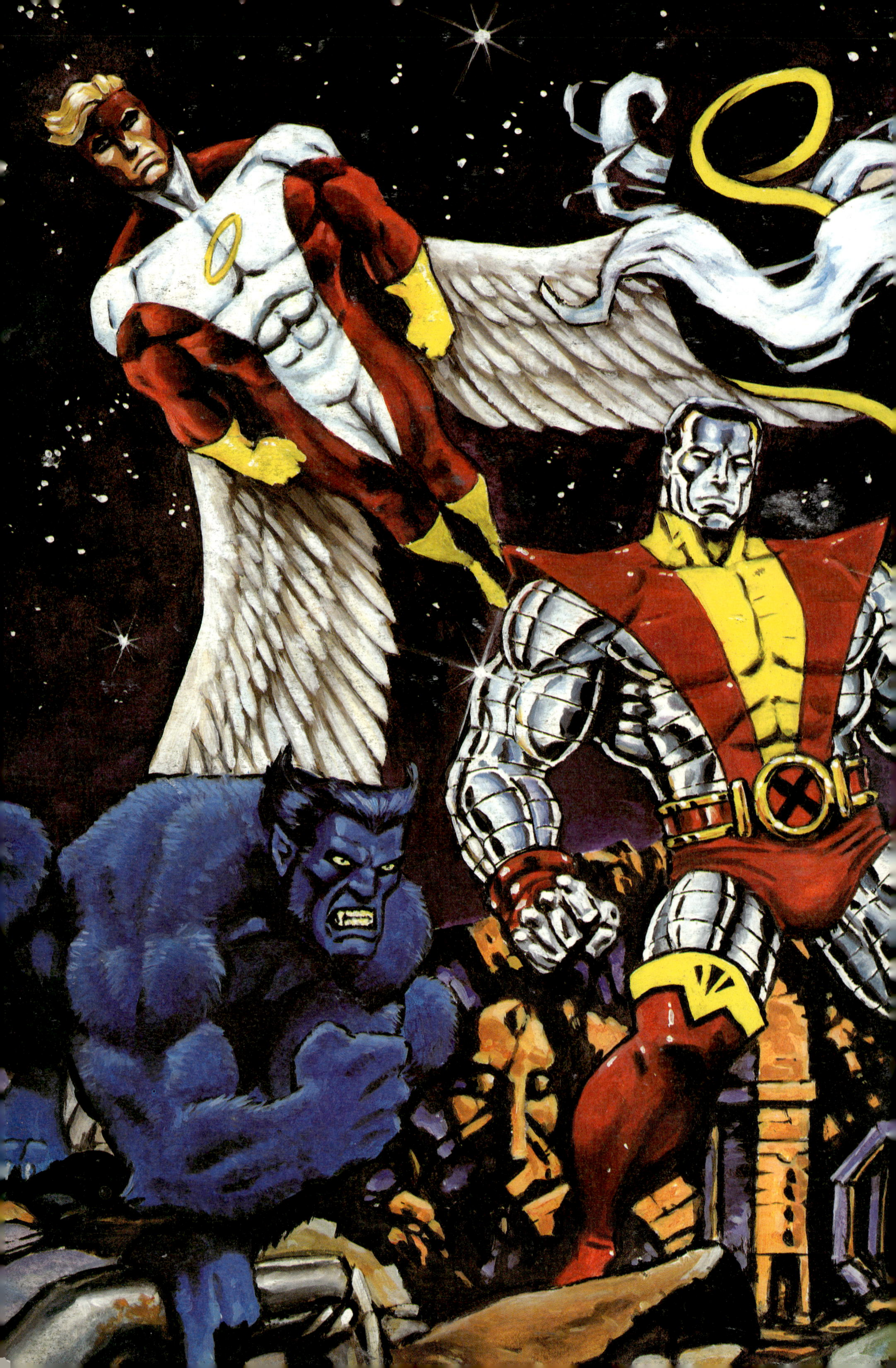